Two w
loan

ore the last

ate return.

THE ANGLICAN COMMUNION

THE ANGLICAN COMMUNION

A Brief Sketch

By

G. F. S. GRAY

LONDON

S·P·C·K

1958

First published in 1958
by S.P.C.K.
Holy Trinity Church, Marylebone Road, London, N.W.1
Made and printed in Great Britain by
William Clowes and Sons, Limited, London and Beccles
© *G. F. S. Gray, 1957*

To Peter, Patrick, Kathleen,
and their Mother

Contents

THE CHURCHES OF THE ANGLICAN COMMUNION   vii

PREFACE   viii

PART ONE

1. To 1814   1
   - I America   2
   - II Asia   9
   - III Australia   11
   - IV Africa   12

2. 1814–1836   14
   - I America   14
   - II Asia   16
   - III Australia and New Zealand   19
   - IV Africa   20

3. 1836–1867   23
   - I America   23
   - II Asia   26
   - III Australia and New Zealand   35
   - IV Africa   38

4. 1867–1888   45
   - I America   45
   - II Asia   46
   - III Australia and New Zealand   55
   - IV Africa   55

5. 1888–1920   60
   I America   60
   II Asia   61
   III Australia and New Zealand   69
   IV Africa   69

6. 1920–1956   75
   I America   75
   II Asia   77
   III Australia and New Zealand   92
   IV Africa   94

PART TWO

7. ANGLICANISM AND THE BIBLE   99

8. DOCTRINE   107

9. WORSHIP   121

10. ORDER AND ORGANIZATION   134

11. CHRISTIAN UNITY   146

12. CONCLUSION   163

BIBLIOGRAPHY   170

INDEX   171

The Churches of the Anglican Communion

The Church of England: Provinces of Canterbury and York (43 Dioceses); 18 Overseas and Missionary Dioceses: Gibraltar, North and Central Europe, Argentine and Eastern South America, Bermuda, Borneo, Central Tanganyika, Hong Kong, Korea, Madagascar, Masasi, Mauritius, Mombasa, North Africa, Singapore, South-West Tanganyika, Uganda, Upper Nile, Zanzibar.

The Church in Wales: 6 Dioceses.

The Episcopal Church in Scotland: 7 Dioceses.

The Church of Ireland: Provinces of Armagh and Dublin (14 Dioceses).

The Protestant Episcopal Church in the U.S.A.: Provinces of New England, New York and New Jersey, Washington, Sewanee, the Mid-West, the North-West, the South-West, the Pacific (96 Dioceses); 8 Foreign Dioceses: Europe, Central America, Central Brazil, Southern Brazil, South-West Brazil, Cuba, Liberia, Mexico.

The Anglican Church of Canada: Provinces of Canada, Ontario, Rupertsland, and British Columbia (28 Dioceses).

The Church of England in Australia and Tasmania: Provinces of New South Wales, Victoria, Queensland, and Western Australia (22 Dioceses); 3 Extra-Provincial Dioceses: Tasmania, Adelaide, Willochra.

The Province of New Zealand: 9 Dioceses.

The Province of the West Indies: 8 Dioceses.

The Church of India, Pakistan, Burma, and Ceylon: 16 Dioceses.

The Holy Catholic Church in China (Chung Hua Sheng Kung Hui): 13 Dioceses.

The Holy Catholic Church in Japan (Nippon Sei Ko Kwai): 9 Dioceses.

The Church of the Province of South Africa: 14 Dioceses.

The Province of West Africa: 9 Dioceses.

The Province of Central Africa: 4 Dioceses.

The Archbishopric of Jerusalem: 5 Dioceses.

Preface

THE original conception of this book goes back some years. The writer, when in China, taught theological students Church History and other subjects related to Anglicanism, and was impressed by the lack of any book which sets out to do for the Anglican Communion the sort of thing done by the late Bishop of Chichester's *A Brief Sketch of the Church of England*. In China, above all in the first years of the Communist régime, it was not enough to advance, as is so often done in books on the Church of England, as two great arguments for Anglicanism that it suits the English temperament, and is old; such facts indeed were enough to condemn it out of hand. The first draft of this book resulted, and, had circumstances permitted, it would have been translated into Chinese and published there. Since then much of the material has been used for lectures at St Augustine's College, Canterbury; parts have been expanded, other parts cut down, all has been rewritten as for English readers, and the result is a new book.

1

To 1814

THE expansion of Anglican Christianity and the growth of the Anglican Communion has been the work of many very different people. Partly it has been the result of the migration of Anglicans from the British Isles, who have settled in distant places, and, at first with help from the mother Churches in the British Isles, have gradually built up a self-governing Anglican Church. Partly it has come about through Anglicans spreading the Faith among non-Christians. This again has taken many forms. Sometimes the agency has been unofficial missionary societies; sometimes the older Church, acting in a corporate and official manner, has made itself responsible for the extension of Christianity. In part the Gospel has been spread either by the lives and example or by the conscious effort of ordinary lay people, engaged in ordinary occupations; in part it has been spread by the efforts of clergy and lay missionaries giving all their time to this task. And no small contribution has been made in countries without a long Christian tradition by many who received the Faith comparatively early and after that did much to spread it among their fellow-countrymen: Philip Kwaku, Samuel Adjai Crowther, Abdul Masih, and Y. K. Yen may be taken as representing a great number whose names are forgotten. While Anglicans, unlike most other Christian Communions, have usually scrupulously refrained from proselytizing other Christians, and consequently in some countries have remained comparatively very few in number, occasionally either individuals or groups of non-Anglicans have been so much attracted by the ethos of Anglicanism that they have insisted on coming over.

Anglicanism and Romanism as we know them to-day date from the sixteenth century, and here we cannot concern ourselves with the early extension of Christianity by Boniface or the English missionaries in Scandinavia. Compared with the sixteenth-century Jesuit missions in

China, Japan, and the Americas, it is only recently that Anglicans have been at all alive to their responsibility in propagating the Gospel. The year 1814, when the first Anglican bishop was consecrated for a country outside Europe and America, may be taken as marking the end of the first period in the growth of the world-wide Anglican Communion. This period saw the birth of three great Anglican missionary societies, all not unnaturally in England—S.P.C.K. (1698-9), S.P.G. (1701), and C.M.S. (1799).

The Church in Wales was from the twelfth century till 1920 part of the province of Canterbury; then, on its disestablishment, it became a self-governing Anglican Church, quite independent of the Church of England. Its diocese of Bangor claims to have the longest continuous history of any diocese in the Anglican Communion. The Irish Church accepted the Reformation under Elizabeth, but became very much anglicized, and most church people soon went over to Rome. From 1800 till its disestablishment in 1870, the Church of Ireland was united to the Church of England in "The United Church of England and Ireland"; in 1870 it became in the modern sense a self-governing Church of the Anglican Communion. Scotland hesitated long between episcopalianism and presbyterianism. The latter became finally established in 1689, when the bishops, feeling bound by their oaths of loyalty to James II, refused to swear allegiance to the new sovereigns, William and Mary; and as a result of persecution, the number of Episcopalians was reduced to very small proportions. The Scottish Episcopalians have never formed part of, or been united with, the Church of England. These three Churches have all played their part, side by side with the Church of England, in the expansion of the Anglican Communion.

On the whole, Anglicanism spread earlier to the overseas English-speaking nations—indeed, it was in at the birth of those nations—and rather later to other countries; and it came to the Americas earlier than to Asia and Africa. So we shall review first its extension to the west, and then its spread to the east and the south.

I. AMERICA

In the West Indies, the indigenous population has almost entirely died out, and though there are now numbers of (East) Indians, Chinese, and Europeans settled there, most of the inhabitants are of mixed race or descendants of Africans originally brought there as slaves. Barbados came under British rule in 1625, Jamaica in 1658, Trinidad in 1802. There were government chaplains from the start, not all equally faithful; and in 1712 the S.P.G. sent Joseph Holt to Barbados. After that, the S.P.G. sent clergy and schoolmasters there, though never very many at one time. General Codrington had, in 1703, left all his property in Barbados to the S.P.G., to be used to provide education for negro slaves; Codrington College was consequently founded, and for long was the chief centre of higher education in the West Indies. Church work was maintained through the S.P.G. in Honduras from 1767, and an Anglican chaplain first came to Trinidad in 1801; but till after 1814, Church life in the Caribbean area was at a low ebb. The Church was nominally under the jurisdiction of the Bishop of London; though in fact the clergy had virtually no supervision except that of the Governor of the colony, there was no Confirmation, nor were there any Church assemblies or synods.

Outside Europe, Anglicanism spread first of all to what is now the United States of America (till 1783, the British colonies in North America). The first Anglican or "Prayer Book" service in the U.S.A. was held in 1579 on the coast of Golden Gate Bay at San Francisco, when an expedition under Drake was exploring the North American coast, and the chaplain attached to the expedition conducted a service there. In 1587 the colony of Virginia was founded through Sir Walter Raleigh, who gave £100 to be used for the planting of Christianity in America; and in the same year the first American Indian was baptized there by Anglicans. Probably a priest had come there either with the settlers or the fleet.

While in New England, where the Pilgrim Fathers landed in 1620, the settlers were mostly Puritans (Congregationalists or Presbyterians), in Virginia most were adherents of the Church of England. The first permanent work in what is now the U.S.A. began in 1607, in Jamestown, Virginia; settlers came there with an (English) priest, Robert Hunt, and regular worship and Church activity was established. In Virginia, and a little later Maryland, Anglican Christianity came to be quite flourishing, though it was suppressed by the Puritans during the time of the Commonwealth in England.

In New York, Anglican services began in 1664, after it was ceded by the Dutch to the British. Trinity, the first Anglican parish there, was organized, and the church built, in 1697.

Such Anglicans as there were in New England were repressed by the

3

Puritans. Till 1735 in Massachusetts, and about the same time in other states, they had to pay taxes to support the Congregational Church, and the use of the Prayer Book and the observance of Christmas were long forbidden in Massachusetts. In Boston, Anglican worship began in 1686 (in King's Chapel) despite bitter opposition; and after 1692, some of the more liberal Puritans became Anglicans.

The parish of Christchurch, Philadelphia, was organized in 1695. Probably it had no priest at first, but was occasionally visited by a priest from Maryland. A local schoolmaster, Arrowsmith, was in charge; and he was probably, like most Church of England schoolmasters then, in deacon's orders. In Connecticut, where by 1783 Anglicanism was stronger than in any other State, it did not begin till 1706. It received great new strength in 1722, when Timothy Cutler, then President of Yale College, and several other leading non-episcopal ministers became Anglicans. They crossed to England soon afterwards and were ordained.

Unfortunately, for a long time there was no bishop in America, and the life and growth of the Church were consequently greatly hindered. The Church in America was in the jurisdiction of the Bishop of London, who sent commissaries to superintend the clergy and Church work, but these commissaries were not always successful. They sometimes held conventions of clergy; but the Church in America had as yet no constitution and hardly any organization; it was little more than an agglomeration of virtually independent parishes, and the commissaries had, of course, no power to ordain or confirm. In Virginia, Maryland, and some other colonies, the Church of England was more or less "established" and the Governor then sometimes appointed the clergy and exercised discipline over them. Any man who wished to be ordained had to go to England, and it is said that nearly a quarter of those who went lost their lives on the journey through shipwreck, capture by pirates, or disease; and some after ordination remained in England. Moreover, some of the clergy sent to America from England were not of very high character.

The founder of the S.P.G. had in 1696 been commissary for the Bishop of London in Maryland. During the eighteenth century this society sent many clergymen, of a better type both in devotion and ability than were some of the others, to care for the white settlers and evangelize the Indians in America. In 1702, the year after its foundation, it sent two clergymen (its first missionaries), G. Keith and J. Talbot, in the little ship "Centurion". The S.P.G. helped the Church in all the colonies where it was not established, but especially in New England. Among the clergy

4

whom it sent were John Wesley (who worked in Savannah, Georgia) and his brother Charles, but neither of them stayed long in America.

The non-episcopal religious bodies in this century had many revivals, which mostly involved an excessive and uncontrolled emotionalism and neglected Christian nurture and discipline. Not a few Protestants who disapproved of these features left their own Churches and became Episcopalians. Nevertheless, the Episcopal Church did not flourish, and many nominal Anglicans who migrated to America joined other Churches, chiefly because of the lack of bishops, and the consequent weakness, indeed almost total absence, of ordered Church life.

It was not mainly the fault of the Church of England that the American Church for so long had no bishops; in fact, continual efforts were made to secure the appointment of a bishop for America. In 1638, Archbishop Laud had a plan for a bishop in New England, and a priest appears to have been chosen about 1670 to be bishop in Virginia, but owing to political opposition he was never consecrated. The S.P.G. from its foundation urged the appointment of bishops, and early in the eighteenth century a plan to send out two bishops was almost successful. Later, the Bishop of London and the colonial churchmen themselves tried to get bishops appointed.

The fundamental difficulty was the opposition of some politicians and nonconformists. Bishops in England were in effect nominated by the government of the day, and were expected to support the government in Parliament; a bishop with purely spiritual, and no political, responsibility seemed inconceivable. English nonconformists then were more inclined to hinder than aid the extension of Anglicanism. Many colonists had gone to America to escape from the Church of England, and in some colonies for a long time they even prohibited Anglican worship. The nonconformists in America were all unwilling that there should be bishops there, fearing lest their own freedom should be limited. Politicians and business interests, indifferent to religion, regarded episcopacy as a matter of religious controversy which might disturb peace and trade. Some regarded the S.P.G. and its missionaries as High Church, and for this reason wished to hinder, not aid, its work.

By the outbreak of the American Revolution (1776) there were Anglican parishes in all parts of the present U.S.A. which had been settled by that time—principally, that is, the east and south-east. The Episcopal Church was strongest in the coastal towns. There were besides chaplains about eighty missionaries, mostly sent by the S.P.G.

Anglicans in 1754 established King's College, or the Church College for Higher Education, in New York, for which the S.P.G. raised a large sum of money in England, and Trinity Church, New York, gave a great deal of land. A missionary of the S.P.G., Samuel Johnson, was its first President. This college has since grown into Columbia University. The S.P.C.K. also gave great help in the early days to the building up of the Church in America.

Anglicans were not so much concerned as were Roman Catholics and Moravians to spread the Gospel among the Indians; but nevertheless a number of churchmen, mostly S.P.G. missionaries, worked among them, and the S.P.G. emphasized the duty of spreading the Gospel, whenever possible, among the negroes and Indians. The College of William and Mary was founded by Anglicans in Virginia about 1693, to provide higher education for Indians as well as whites, and there were Indian students there in its early days.

During the war of American Independence (1776–1783) Anglicanism inevitably suffered very much. George Washington and many other leaders of the rebelling colonists were Anglicans; William White, rector of Christchurch, Philadelphia, was chaplain to Washington's army, and many of the clergy in the south also supported the Revolution. But most of the Anglican clergy and church people were loyalists, and desired to retain the connection with England. They supported England in the war, and when the American colonies became independent many of them migrated to Canada to keep the connection.

Besides Washington, such leaders as Alexander Hamilton and Thomas Jefferson were Anglicans, and so were a majority both of those who signed the Declaration of Independence and of those who framed the American Constitution. Nevertheless, after the war the Episcopal Church had in effect to be refounded. Hitherto it had been known simply as the Church of England, and had in fact been part of the English Church, but a Maryland convention in 1780 proposed the name Protestant (in the sense then normal of non-Roman Catholic) Episcopal Church, and this title was eventually adopted.

When America became independent, Anglicans there could clearly no longer remain in the jurisdiction of the Bishop of London. The Church in Connecticut therefore in 1783 elected Samuel Seabury as its bishop, and he went to England to obtain consecration. For several reasons the Archbishop of Canterbury felt unable to consecrate him: the Connecticut government had not given permission for a bishop there, there

6

was no provision for his financial support, and Seabury could not take the oaths of allegiance to the King then required at the consecration of an Anglican bishop. So Seabury went to Scotland, and on 14 November 1784 three Scottish bishops consecrated him at Aberdeen as the first bishop of America.[1]

In October 1784 a conference was held in New York of clerical and lay delegates from eight of the thirteen states, to plan a constitution for the American Episcopal Church. They decided that there should be a General Convention of clerical and lay deputies, and that the doctrines, and as much as possible of the Prayer Book, of the Church of England should be maintained. Next year the first General Convention met at Philadelphia. Massachusetts was not represented on account of distance, nor Connecticut, because the principles laid down at New York did not provide for the presidency at General Convention of a bishop. This Convention approved of the Church's constitution, and requested the English bishops to consecrate such men as the State conventions might choose. A committee was appointed to revise the Prayer Book to suit American conditions (for example, omitting prayers for the King).

The revision of the Prayer Book was mainly the work of William White and William Smith. They proposed to omit both the Nicene and the Athanasian creeds, the "descent into hell" from the Apostles' Creed, and all expressions implying baptismal regeneration, and to allow the omission of the sign of the Cross at baptism. The General Convention, however, in 1786, through the influence of the English archbishops, voted to restore the Nicene Creed, and the "descent into hell" in the Apostles' creed, but not the Athanasian creed.

The English archbishops persuaded Parliament to change the law, so that American bishops could be consecrated, and in 1787 they consecrated White, who had been elected Bishop of Pennsylvania, and S. Provoost, who had been elected by New York. Some doubted the validity of Seabury's consecration, but the General Convention of 1789 recognized its validity. Connecticut and the New England states in consequence joined the Convention, and American Anglicans were united in one Church. This Convention ratified the revised Prayer Book.

English bishops in 1790 consecrated James Madison, whom Virginia had chosen as its bishop; but John Claggett was consecrated in 1792 for

[1] The service was in a chapel at the top of the house of one of the bishops, since the Scottish Episcopal Church was proscribed till 1792. There was, it may be noted, no Roman Catholic bishop in the U.S.A. till some years later.

Maryland by American bishops, and after this all American bishops were consecrated in America.

The American Episcopal Church for a long time had no endowments, and each bishop was also in charge of a parish, which provided his salary. A bishop's powers were considerably limited; American Episcopalians were determined that their bishops should not be autocratic, as English bishops (owing to the suppression of the Convocations) then tended to be. Because at first many church people were suspicious of them, the bishops for some time were rather inactive. For twenty years after the Revolution, the Episcopal Church was at a low ebb, partly because so many of its clergy and people had been loyalists. As a result of the war it had lost most of its church buildings and other property, and the help from the S.P.G. in regard to both clergy and finance had to cease. In colonies where it had been established, the Church was disestablished. Attempts to prevent the American Methodists from leaving the Episcopal Church were unsuccessful, and when William White came to England in 1787, with a letter of introduction to John Wesley from an American Methodist, Wesley declined to see him.

The American clergy were not very active either, and the Church spread only slowly. When white men settled in the central and western parts of America, the Methodists and Baptists, who used laymen more, were much more active on "the frontier" than the Episcopal Church; so they became, except for the Roman Catholics, the largest religious bodies in America, and in those areas the Episcopal Church is still weak.

A new period of expansion began in 1811: this will be dealt with in the next chapter.

In Canada Anglicanism began, at least on any appreciable scale, considerably later than in the United States. Until the thirteen American colonies broke away from England, the great majority of the white settlers in what is now Canada, where the indigenous population was extremely small, were French and Roman Catholics.

Frobisher in his voyage of exploration in 1578 had with him a chaplain, Wolfall, who probably took the first Anglican service in what is now Canada. Regular Anglican services were first held, beginning in 1710, at Annapolis Royal, Nova Scotia, where J. Harrison was the chaplain. From 1728 the S.P.G. sent some clergymen and schoolmasters, at first on a very small scale. The Church of England was legally established in Nova Scotia in 1758. Next year the first Canadian parish, St Paul's, Halifax was regularly organized, with Breynton as its rector; in

8

the same year the first Anglican service was held in Upper Canada (now Ontario) by a chaplain named Ogilvie; and in 1760, after the British had captured Canada from the French, the first Anglican service was held at Montreal. About this time, Thomas Wood worked among the Indians in what is now Canada, the first Anglican priest to do so, and learnt one of their languages.

Many people in the Thirteen Colonies wished to retain the connection with England, and in 1783 forty thousand of them, at the cost of great loss and hardship, left their homes and migrated to Canada, many of them settling in Ontario. A large proportion of them were staunchly Anglican, and a number of the clergy came with them, including Charles Inglis, who had been a S.P.G. missionary and rector of Trinity Church, New York.

This loyalist migration marks the beginning of Anglicanism in Canada on a considerable scale. Inglis was in 1787 consecrated in England as Bishop for "Nova Scotia and its dependencies", in effect, for such Anglicans as there might be anywhere in what is now Canada. Apart from the three American bishops consecrated very shortly before, he was the first Anglican bishop outside the British Isles. Next year, Inglis opened an Academy at Windsor, now King's College School, and King's College.

The first Anglican church in the province of Quebec was built in 1785, and a diocese of Quebec was formed in 1793, with Jacob Mountain as bishop: there were now only four Anglican clergymen in Lower Canada, and three in Upper Canada. Except for St Paul's in London, Quebec cathedral, consecrated in 1804, was the first Anglican cathedral to be built since the Reformation.

II. ASIA

Before 1814, the expansion of the Anglican Communion was on a very restricted scale. With one exception, it had not yet reached western Asia. All that can be recorded is that the great Henry Martyn had been in Iran. He came there from India, already a sick man, to revise his translation of the New Testament and Psalms into Persian. He was in Shiraz from June 1811 to May 1812, occupied with this, and also studying Islam, and conversing and debating with Muslim scholars. He then left Shiraz, hoping to present a copy of his work to the Shah, but was unsuccessful in this, and died on his way home to England.

In India the first beginnings of Anglicanism go back to the early years of the seventeenth century. British trade with India had begun, and the British East India Company in 1614 appointed five chaplains to the British community in India. In 1616, one of them brought a Bengali boy to London where he was baptized, but otherwise the chaplains do not seem to have regarded it as part of their responsibility to spread the Faith among Indians. The first Anglican church in India, or indeed Asia, was consecrated in 1680, St Mary's, Madras.

Even after the founding of the S.P.C.K. and the S.P.G., there were very few in the Church of England concerned to spread the Gospel overseas. For almost the whole of the eighteenth century, therefore, the S.P.C.K. financed German and Danish Lutheran missionaries, who worked in the Danish Lutheran mission begun in South India in 1706. Meanwhile the work of the English chaplains continued in the important centres of trade in India, being appointed by, and under the direction of, the East India Company; till the nineteenth century there was no episcopal supervision, nor was there even a commissary from the Bishop of London.

The S.P.C.K. in 1789 sent a priest, A. T. Clarke, for mission work in Calcutta; but after a year or two he became a chaplain. At the end of the century, however, several chaplains, such as David Brown and Claudius Buchanan, who had been influenced by the Evangelical Revival, were able to do some mission work, and urged the Church of England to send missionaries to spread the Faith among Indians: and eventually this call was answered.

However, before any Anglican missionaries reached India, much was done in a short time by Henry Martyn, who reached India in 1806 and worked in Patna and Cawnpore as a chaplain. At Cambridge he had won distinction as a mathematician. But he had also great linguistic gifts: he not only learnt Urdu quickly, but by 1810 had translated the New Testament into that language; he also worked on a Persian translation of the New Testament, and the next year, already a sick man, went to Iran to get help in perfecting it. He won to the Faith directly only one Indian, Abdul Masih, a Muslim.

A great step forward was taken in 1813 when, after a historic night of debate in Parliament, and largely through the influence of William Wilberforce, it was decided that a bishopric of Calcutta should be established. This was the first Anglican see in Asia. Next year, T. F. Middleton was consecrated quietly in Lambeth Palace chapel, lest Hindus should take alarm and commerce should in consequence suffer.

It was not till after 1814 that Anglican Christianity reached eastern Asia. The C.M.S., it is true, very soon after its foundation considered undertaking work in China, and publishing a Chinese translation of part of the New Testament, made presumably by a Roman Catholic, which Sir Hans Sloane had brought to England in 1738. However, it was decided that this was financially impracticable.

III. AUSTRALIA

Captain James Cook had in 1769 taken possession for England of the region round Botany Bay, and called it New South Wales. But it was twenty years before English settlement and the work of the Church of England began in Australia. When the American colonies became independent, Australia, then inhabited only by a very small number of primitive blacks, was suggested as a place of refuge for the loyalists who wished to remain under the British flag. However, they went instead to Canada. But convicts could no longer be sent to America, and in 1788 seven hundred and fifty of them, under guard of two hundred soldiers, were sent to Botany Bay. A few free settlers went with them, and also a chaplain, Richard Johnson.

Johnson, like other early chaplains in Australia, received his salary from the government, but was given, at least at first, very little support or sympathy from the authorities. The first church, of wattle and daub, was completed in Sydney in 1793, at his expense, only to be burnt down after five years. Johnson also started some educational work for the families of the soldiers, but returned to England in 1800.

Samuel Marsden went to Australia in 1794 as chaplain. He was a man of considerable practical ability, who himself engaged in sheep-farming, and indeed did much to start the Australian wool-trade. Through it he became wealthy, and he was criticized for neglect of his strictly ecclesiastical duties. He also acted as a magistrate, and persuaded the government to take much better care of the convicts and their families, in both material and spiritual matters. He continued till his death in 1838 as a chaplain in New South Wales, largely at Paramatta. The first whites settled in Tasmania in 1803, and the first chaplain went there next year.

The earliest extension of the Anglican Communion outside Europe and America was to West Africa in the middle of the eighteenth century. Thomas Thompson, who had been Fellow and Dean of Christ's College, Cambridge, and then worked for several years in North America, reached Cape Coast on the Gold Coast in 1752. He went under the auspices of the S.P.G., and was chaplain to the British residents, as well as seeking to spread the Faith among Africans. He was able to baptize some adult negroes, and then in 1754 sent three boys from Cape Coast to England for education; but in 1756 his health broke down, and he had to leave Africa permanently.

The three African boys were sent to school in Islington; one after some years died of consumption, the other two were baptized in 1759. One of these soon lost his reason and died, but the third, Philip Kwaku, survived, and was eventually ordained, the first native of Africa to receive Anglican orders. He was sent by the S.P.G. in 1765 as both missionary schoolmaster and catechist to the negroes on the Gold Coast, and also as chaplain to the British residents at Cape Coast Castle. He worked in different parts of the Gold Coast till his death in 1816, with little apparent result. He seems to have engaged in trade, to the detriment of his Church work; but, lonely as he was, it is not surprising if his devotion faltered somewhat. More than one English clergyman was sent to succeed Kwaku, but most quickly died of fever, and Anglican work here was given up in 1824.

There were churches for British residents in Sierra Leone during the last few years of the eighteenth century, but as yet there was no attempt to take the Gospel to Africans there. Sierra Leone was colonized in 1787 as a philanthropic experiment under Church auspices, partly as an asylum for negro slaves emancipated through the ruling of Chief Justice Mansfield in 1772, that slaves who set foot on English soil automatically became free. Negroes who had fought in the American War of Independence to maintain the British connection also took refuge here, and after Britain abolished the slave trade in 1807, British warships deposited here many cargoes of slaves from captured slave-ships.

In the year of its founding (1799), the C.M.S. resolved to attempt a mission to Sierra Leone. Rather curiously, however, its first missionaries, two German Lutherans, were sent in 1804, not to the colony but to the Rio Pongas, which had been a principal centre of the slave trade, some distance to the north. In 1806, three more Germans were sent. It was actually not till 1808 that work on the Rio Pongas could be begun, and then it was limited to the opening of schools for children; and the local chiefs soon forced the schools to close.

The British at Cape Town in South Africa first had a chaplain in 1811, and those at Simonstown in 1813. But the beginning of the Church of the Province of South Africa did not really come till after this period.

2

1814–1836

THE second period in the story of the growth of the Anglican Communion takes us up to 1836, when the original one Anglican diocese in Asia was divided into three (or even four), and the first Anglican see south of the equator was established. Anglican Christianity was planted during these years in a number of other countries: while in countries where the seed had already been sown, it extended not a little and took deeper root.

I. AMERICA

The Church in the West Indies till 1824 had no bishop, and was nominally responsible to the Bishop of London. In that year, W. H. Coleridge was appointed Bishop of Barbados and the Leeward Islands; and this diocese for some time included also Guiana, Antigua, and Trinidad. C. Lipscomb was in the same year consecrated Bishop of Jamaica, and in his diocese the Bahama Islands and Honduras were for the time included. Here we see the beginnings of what has become the Province of the West Indies.

In the U.S.A., two bishops had been consecrated in 1811 who did much to extend and awaken and strengthen the Church. Griswold was bishop till 1843 of the so-called Eastern diocese, which included the states of Massachusetts, Rhode Island, New Hampshire, and Vermont, an area which now contains many dioceses. The Church grew rapidly here at this time owing to the breakdown of Puritanism. Griswold inclined to the more Evangelical Anglican position. Hobart was Bishop of New York till he died, prematurely worn out, in 1830, and was rector, while Bishop, of Trinity Church, New York. He inclined to the more strongly Catholic position, and opposed co-operation with nonconformists in Bible societies; but he founded many organizations to promote different kinds of Church work, and organized many new parishes. The training of the clergy was much improved when in 1819 the General Theological Seminary, New York, was founded, the first Anglican theological college in any country. Its aim has always been to train ordinands for all the American dioceses. In 1824 Virginia Seminary was opened, and the Episcopal Church also established many schools, chiefly secondary. To promote the extension of the Church both in the newer areas of the United States and overseas, the General Convention in 1820 organized the Domestic and Foreign Missionary Society. Soon after it was founded, this society received a gift of £200 from the English C.M.S. It was reorganized in 1835. Every member of the Episcopal Church was regarded as automatically a member of the society, which was thus not merely to be the responsibility of a few individuals.

Philander Chase went in 1817 as a missionary to Ohio, then a newly-opened area, and the next year, he and the other clergy and lay representatives organized a diocese, for which he was chosen bishop. Chase secured some help from England and did much to build up the Church in Ohio, founded Kenyon College; but he was somewhat autocratic, and in 1831 resigned, because of opposition to his absolutism. However, in 1835 he was chosen Bishop of Illinois.

Western Canada began to be settled during this period, and with or soon after the settlers went the Church. Before there were clergy in the west, Prayer Book Mattins were regularly read by the agents of the Hudson's Bay Company, and this company also appointed chaplains to some of its trading-posts. For a hundred years, also, the English C.M.S. gave much help to the building up of the Church in western Canada, as the S.P.G. did in eastern Canada. The first Anglican priest in the west was John West, who was both a chaplain to the Hudson's Bay Company and a C.M.S. missionary, and reached the Red River settlement, or what is now Winnipeg, in 1820. West worked among whites and Eskimos and Indians, and established schools for the Indians, but only stayed three years. Later, W. Cochran, sometimes called the Apostle of the Red River, worked there.

When Jacob Mountain, Bishop of Quebec, died in 1826, the clergy in his diocese numbered sixty-one, of whom forty-eight were S.P.G. missionaries, compared with seven when the diocese was formed in 1793.

To the east, also, Anglicanism was extending at this time, and in fact it now first took root in the Near East. Since the Eastern Orthodox Church in Palestine was rather weak and inactive, Anglicans (through the London Society for Promoting Christianity among the Jews, the predecessor of the present Church Missions to Jews) in about 1820 began Christian work among Jews in Jerusalem. The well-known traveller Joseph Wolff for a time shared in this. They began in 1826 much-needed medical work in Jerusalem and, in addition to the hospital, soon established a school there. In the eighteen-thirties Joseph Wolff also travelled in Iran, visiting and trying to evangelize the colonies of Jews.

Even after a bishop was appointed for India, the Church's progress was slow. Three archdeacons were appointed, for Bengal, Madras, and Bombay, but their concern was almost solely chaplaincy work among Europeans. Middleton's position was obscure, partly because the Church in England was established. His salary came from the East India Company; and the Company insisted that it, not the bishop, should decide where each chaplain was to be stationed. Middleton conceived his chief duty to be to superintend the chaplains, of whom there were then thirty-two, and felt unable to license, still less ordain, anyone born in India.

One of his great achievements was the foundation in 1820 of Bishop's College, Calcutta. The S.P.G., C.M.S., and S.P.C.K. each contributed £5,000 to this, and a King's Letter, read in all English parish churches, produced £45,000 for it. Middleton's idea was that it should become a great Christian university, to rival Oxford and Cambridge, but it was never adequately equipped or staffed. However, it became and remained the chief centre of Anglican theological training in India.

Claudius Buchanan had in 1806 visited the old Syrian Church in South India, which was then greatly in need of reform, and helped to provide funds needed to translate its liturgy and Bible from the old Syriac into the vernacular Malayalam. At the request of its Metran[1], the C.M.S. in 1814 appointed missionaries to help, for example, with producing literature and vernacular translations, with a college just established at Kottayam to train Syrian clergy, and with establishing schools.

This co-operation continued for about twenty years. The C.M.S. tried to help the Syrian Church to be true to its own ancient worship and discipline, and in the area covered by the Syrian Church no independent

[1] i.e. Metropolitan or Archbishop.

Anglican work was done. During this time, much was done to revive the Syrian Church, to promote the education of both clergy and laity, and to deepen the spirit of devotion. Then there came to be friction: perhaps the missionaries showed excessive zeal and lack of prudence, but possibly the Metran was the more to blame. Bishop Wilson of Calcutta paid a visit to the area, but his suggestions for a settlement of the points at issue were all rejected, and in 1836 the Syrian Metran forbade his people to associate with the C.M.S. group.

The C.M.S. was active in Bengal from about 1816, in Bombay from 1820. From 1813 it financed Abdul Masih, at first as a reader or catechist, who worked mostly in Agra, and in 1820 it undertook the care of about three thousand Christians in South India who had been won to the Gospel through the work of C. F. Schwartz and other Lutherans supported by the S.P.C.K. Not a few of the early C.M.S. missionaries to India were actually Lutherans, though some of them eventually received Anglican orders. The S.P.G. assisted Bishop's College, Calcutta, with staff and finance from about 1820.

Middleton died, worn out, in 1822, and was succeeded as bishop by R. Heber, the well-known hymn writer. Australia was now added to his jurisdiction, which already included Ceylon and Malaya as well as the Indian sub-continent. Heber, unlike Middleton, felt himself authorized both to license the missionary clergy, and to ordain men born in India; and he ordained the first Indian clergymen, Christian David in 1824 for work in Ceylon, and Abdul Masih in 1826. Unlike Middleton, Heber expected the Lutheran pastors who worked in an Anglican mission to receive Anglican orders.

The S.P.G. became responsible in 1825 for the care of several thousand Christians won by the Lutherans in South India, and for a time, owing to lack of Anglican staff, used Lutheran workers. In 1833 it undertook work in Cawnpore.

Bishop Heber died in 1826. Neither of his two successors lived long, but in 1832 Daniel Wilson was appointed and continued till 1858. It had become clear that a single bishop could not possibly oversee adequately such a huge area, and also that the attempt to do so wore out a man quite prematurely. Accordingly, new dioceses were constituted, of Madras in 1835, with Daniel Corrie as its first bishop, and Bombay in 1837, with Thomas Carr as bishop, while Daniel Wilson became metropolitan. The creation of the diocese of Australia in 1836 also relieved him of part of his responsibility.

Daniel Wilson was a strong Evangelical, but there was some friction between him and the C.M.S., and he would not let the C.M.S. withdraw its work from his episcopal supervision. He was much more definitely opposed to the observance of caste than most, including Heber, had been before him; he regarded it as completely non-Christian, whereas some had tolerated it in a modified form as an Indian social custom. No little controversy was caused by his attitude, and numbers of *sudras*, or middle-caste people, in consequence left the Church.

During these years, Anglican Christianity first reached Ceylon, where Rome had been active since early in the sixteenth century, and Reformed Christianity under Dutch rule from the seventeenth century. The first Anglican clergymen were chaplains who arrived soon after the beginning of British rule. They did not have much time or opportunity to extend Christianity among the Ceylonese, though laymen attempted this under their guidance.

The early propagation of the Faith here by Anglicans was mainly the work of the C.M.S., which in 1817, sent out four clergymen, who were welcomed by the governor, himself an active Churchman. At his suggestion they began evangelistic work at Kandy, but progress was slow. Christian David, an Indian who received Anglican orders in 1824, worked many years at Jaffna.

After 1819, when Raffles by a treaty with a local Sultan brought Singapore, then an almost uninhabited island, under British rule, Anglican chaplains went with British residents to Singapore, Penang, and elsewhere in Malaya. The Church here was in the jurisdiction of the Bishop of Calcutta, and Bishop Middleton visited Penang in 1819. Raffles was a devout Churchman, and helped to establish more than one branch of the S.P.C.K.; but for long no organized attempt was made in Malaya by Anglicans to win the local inhabitants to the Church.

Elsewhere in Eastern Asia, it was still later that the Anglican Communion was planted. In the early nineteenth century, there was a small British trading settlement in Canton, which after 1819 had an Anglican chaplain from time to time, but there is no record of any chaplain attempting to spread Christianity among the Chinese. With the partial exception of Canton, foreigners were in effect completely excluded from China, though the C.M.S. was able to give some financial help to a German Protestant missionary, Gutzlaff, who managed to make several evangelistic trips along the China coast.

The first Anglican missionaries to reach China were two American clergymen, Lockwood and Hanson, who reached Canton in 1835. However, the Chinese government of that time forbade on pain of death any Chinese to teach a foreigner the Chinese language, and public feeling was so hostile to foreigners that no Chinese dared to associate closely with them. So the two Americans soon moved to Singapore, and a few months later to Batavia, where there were many Chinese and they could learn the Chinese language and customs, and might be able to influence some Chinese to Christianity.

III. AUSTRALIA AND NEW ZEALAND

There was more progress at this time in Australia, which in 1823 was constituted an archdeaconry in the diocese of Calcutta. In Western Australia the first settlement was at Albany in 1825, and in Queensland at Moreton Bay and the site of the present Brisbane in 1824. Here there was no clergyman for twenty years, but in general the Church followed very soon after the first settlers, and by 1825 there were eleven government chaplains in the settled areas. In Tasmania, the first permanent church was built in 1817.

The first archdeacon, T. H. Scott, was succeeded in 1829 by W. G. Broughton, who is deservedly regarded as the Father of the Church in Australia. He obtained much help from the S.P.G. and the S.P.C.K., and the numbers of the clergy were therefore considerably increased, and the scattered settlers (who now numbered about thirty-six thousand) could be better shepherded. In what is now New South Wales, there were then eight churches and twelve clergymen. Australia was constituted a diocese in 1836, with W. G. Broughton as bishop, and after this the Church there grew rapidly.

At this period European settlement had not yet begun in New Zealand, nor had this come under British rule. But Christianity was now taken to the Maoris by Anglican missionaries.

Samuel Marsden, whom we have met as a chaplain in New South Wales, was much impressed with the character and ability of Maoris whom he met in Sydney, and conceived a project of taking the Gospel to their home land; and, though he never lived permanently in New Zealand, he was mainly responsible for the foundation of the Church there. He suggested to the C.M.S. in London in 1807 that an industrial mission should be begun there, but it was not till the end of 1814 that, getting four months' leave of absence from Paramatta, he was able himself to lead an expedition to New Zealand.

Marsden took with him a schoolmaster, Kendall, a carpenter, Hall, and a shoemaker, King, with their wives and children; and also horses and cattle, sheep and pigs, goats and poultry. The way had been prepared by a Maori chief whom Marsden had got to know in Sydney, and his nephew Ruatara who welcomed the mission party, and allowed them to settle on the Bay of Islands, in the north of the North Island. They held the first Christian service in New Zealand on Christmas Day, 1814.

The mission began in a quiet and unspectacular way. Marsden himself had soon to return to Australia, but the lay missioners sowed the first grain sown in New Zealand, and started the great New Zealand pastoral industry. They also learned the Maori language, for which Kendall devised a form of writing, and taught the Christian Faith to those who would learn it. Marsden paid them occasional visits.

The mission group was joined in 1823 by Henry Williams, a priest who before ordination had been a naval officer, and who brought to the mission leadership and power which hitherto had been lacking. A new beginning was in fact now made. Three years later, Henry Williams' brother William, also ordained, arrived, and several other clergymen soon afterwards; and the mission was greatly strengthened. The plan of starting with an agricultural and technical settlement does not seem on the whole to have been a success. Henry Williams set up schools, which came to have more influence, and the first Maori was baptized in 1825. After 1830 the mission began to extend, and established some new stations, though its work was still limited to the northern part of the North Island.

IV. AFRICA

In West Africa, Anglican Christianity, which had just begun before this period, now made several steps forward. We have seen that on the Gold Coast Kwaku died in 1816. More than one English clergyman was sent to succeed him; but most died quickly of fever, and Anglican work was given up here in 1824, not to be resumed until eighty years later.

The real beginning of the Church in Sierra Leone dates from 1816, when Edward Bickersteth, who had been sent on a tour of inspection, summoned the C.M.S. to evangelism among the freed slaves, of whom there were by then over ten thousand in the colony. This call was accepted, and in 1817 the government divided the colony into twelve parishes, each of which was to have a minister and a schoolmaster. The C.M.S. was to provide the staff, while the funds were largely to come from the government. The C.M.S. in the years between 1817 and 1822 actually sent seventeen men; but there were never enough suitable men willing to go, and the climate and disease took a very heavy toll of those who did. In one year (1823) seven schoolmasters and five wives went; six of them died in the same year, and within eighteen months ten were dead; and in twenty-five years a hundred and nine C.M.S. missionaries were carried off by fever, most of them after a very short spell of work.

Because the climate was so bad for Europeans, the C.M.S. was anxious that as soon as possible the Sierra Leone Church should be provided with an African clergy, and Fourah Bay College was founded in 1827, partly to train Africans for the ministry. When it opened it had but six students; it was the first institution of higher education in Africa, except for El Azhar university in Cairo.

In Nigeria the Church was not to start till after this period; but in Liberia, the old "Pepper Coast", where from about 1822 freed negroes were brought from America, some Anglicans among them organized a parish at Monrovia in 1834, and next year the American Church sent a missionary there, a negro layman, James M. Thomson, primarily to act as schoolmaster.

Anglicanism first reached South Africa in the wake of the early British settlers who went there at the beginning of the nineteenth century. The first clergymen there were chaplains with the British troops; a little later, some came as chaplains to the settlers, and some chaplains took services at the Cape on their way to or from India. But virtually nothing was done till after 1819.

William Wright, who reached the Cape in 1821, and was on the S.P.G. list, not only acted as chaplain, but also established schools for Africans, and was the first Anglican to seek to extend the Faith in South Africa. His concern for justice to the Africans made him unpopular with the authorities, and after some years he returned to England. Other clergymen came as chaplains, appointed and paid by the government, but practically nothing was done to spread the Gospel, though the C.M.S. made an unsuccessful attempt to start work in Zululand in 1835–8. Bishops on their way to or from India conducted confirmations from time to time, but of regular episcopal supervision there was none. Not surprisingly, when Bishop Daniel Wilson visited Cape Town in 1832 on his way to Calcutta, he was struck by the lack of discipline in the Church there—everyone did what was right in his own eyes. There were in 1825 six Anglican clergymen at the Cape.

Mauritius and the Seychelles, which had been occupied for some time by the French, came under British rule in 1814, and Anglicanism then began to have a foothold there. The British government promised to preserve the privileges of the Roman Church, and heavily subsidized it, and the majority of the population are Roman Catholics. The present inhabitants are none of them native to the islands: two-thirds of them are by birth or descent East Indians, and there are also Europeans, Chinese, Africans, and not a few of mixed race. An Anglican chaplain was appointed by the government in Mauritius in 1821, and a second one in 1833; the first Anglican church was built in 1828. After 1833 the S.P.G. financed a number of schools for freed negroes.

In Ethiopia, where two-thirds of the population belong to the Coptic Church, Anglicans have in consequence never attempted any large-scale mission. The C.M.S. sent two missionaries in 1830, but one soon died and the other retired through ill-health.

The C.M.S. sent five men, all of them Germans or Swiss from Basel, to Egypt in 1825; one of them, Lieder, worked there over thirty years. The Muslim law of apostasy was still in force, and the conversion of Muslims was therefore in effect impossible, so their primary aim was to revive the somewhat somnolent and decayed Coptic Church. They itinerated from Cairo both in the Delta and into the Northern Sudan; but in the Sudan at least there was no visible result. The distribution of Christian literature engaged much of their attention, and they also started some schools, including a boys' boarding-school in Cairo.

3

1836–1867

THE middle years of the nineteenth century were a time of unparalleled expansion and growth for the Anglican Communion, in America, Asia, and Africa alike. They fittingly culminated in the meeting of Anglican bishops from all over the world at the first Lambeth Conference in 1867.

I. AMERICA

After the Emancipation Act (1834), a great Negro Instruction Fund was raised through the S.P.G., one half of which was used to provide churches and clergy, mainly in the West Indies, the other half for schools and schoolmasters.

As the Church grew in the West Indies, more dioceses were established: Antigua and Guiana were cut off from Barbados and constituted a diocese in 1842, while from the diocese of Jamaica, the diocese of Nassau (the Bahamas) was cut off in 1861.

In the United States, the Church spread with the extension of settlement to the west. Jackson Kemper became in 1835 Bishop of Missouri and Indiana, and later also of Wisconsin and Iowa, and worked untiringly over a very large area in the North-West, in which several dioceses were eventually established. Kemper at his death in 1876 was Bishop of Wisconsin only, where he founded Racine College and the Nashotah Mission, later Nashotah House, a theological College.

During the first half of its existence the main concern of the missionary society of the American Church was to build up the Church in the newly settled areas of the U.S.A.; but it gave increasing help to missions in Liberia, China, Japan, and elsewhere. For a time in the middle of the century Evangelicals distrusted the society and in 1851 they organized

23

a society of their own which in 1859 became the American Church Missionary Society; later, however, this was included in the original society again.

The American Episcopal Church was affected by the Oxford Movement in very much the same way as the Church of England. At times, the result was much controversy in the Church; but all church people came to be influenced by it in varying degrees.

During the Civil War (1861-5), the Southern dioceses organized themselves into a union covering the Confederate (or Southern) States, and in effect set up a separate branch of the Anglican Communion. The General Convention of 1862, however, which was held in the North, left seats for representatives of the Southern dioceses. After the defeat of the South, the separated Southern Church as such automatically came to an end; some of the Southern dioceses were represented in the General Convention of 1865, and all of them in 1868. Most other Communions, on the other hand, such as Presbyterians, Methodists, and Baptists, have continued till our own time to be divided between North and South.

In Canada also during these years the Church was gradually spreading towards the west, and in 1839 a third diocese, that of Toronto, was established, with John Strachan as its first bishop. Strachan was a little unsympathetic to other Christian Communions, but was perhaps the ablest of the early bishops in Canada, and did much to promote education.

The expansion of the Church during this period is demonstrated by the formation of the dioceses of Newfoundland, including Bermuda, in 1839; Rupertsland, with Winnipeg as its centre, and David Anderson as its bishop, in 1849; and Montreal in 1850. In the latter year, the first American Indian, Henry Budd, was ordained by Anglicans in Canada.

For a considerable time the Church of England in Canada was regarded as "established"; and the government set apart land, called "Clergy Reserves", from the proceeds of which many of the clergy were supported. Bishop Strachan strongly supported the rights and responsibilities of the Church of England, but in 1854 the Canadian legislature passed an act secularizing the Clergy Reserves, and declaring that there should be no connection between Church and State. Strachan had founded a college in Toronto, but in 1848 all connection between this and the Church was abolished; and Strachan therefore established Trinity College, Toronto, which continues to this day as a Church college.

The Church of England in Canada for a long time had little organization. The bishops had considerable autocratic power, which was not in accordance with the practice of the ancient Church, and was specially unsuitable in Canada, where the Church had no endowments and had to be financially self-supporting. The great difficulty was that, according to laws passed in the time of Henry VIII and Elizabeth I, the Church of England might not hold synods or pass canons without royal licence. The tendency of the time was to withdraw official recognition from religion, and therefore no royal licence could be obtained for the setting up of new synods. Anglicans in Canada (and elsewhere) were very anxious to remain as an integral part of the Church of England; yet by 1850 they were, partly under the influence of the example of the General Convention in the U.S.A., coming more and more to feel that synods and constitutional Church government were necessary.

Strachan, who was in close touch with Church leaders in the U.S.A., and partly influenced by them, in May 1851 held a diocesan conference in Toronto, including the clergy and lay representatives; and this resolved that a regular Diocesan Synod should be formed. In September of the same year five of the seven bishops in British North America met in conference at Quebec (the Bishop of Rupertsland could not be present because the notice of the meeting took too long in reaching him, nor could the Bishop of Nova Scotia who had only just reached his diocese from England). This meeting prepared a plan for both diocesan synods and a provincial synod, for which it sought the approval of the Archbishop; and also decided to ask the Archbishop's help in removing the legal obstacles to forming such synods, and in obtaining the Crown's sanction for the appointment of a Metropolitan for Canada.

There was a similar movement at this time in Australia; and after a meeting in London of bishops from Canada, Australia, and England, the "Colonial Church Regulation Bill", to allow such synods, was moved in August 1853 by the Archbishop of Canterbury in the House of Lords, and by Mr Gladstone in the House of Commons. This was passed by the Lords, but rejected by the Commons—partly from lack of time, partly from fear of sacerdotalism and of infringing the royal prerogative, and partly from sheer conservatism.

Mr Gladstone then advised the overseas churches to organize themselves on the basis of "voluntary consensual compact", that is, by the agreement of their members without obtaining specific Parliamentary approval. The Toronto Diocesan Conference met again in October 1853, and resolved that it constituted itself a Diocesan Synod on the plan already agreed. In 1857 a Diocesan Synod was established in Quebec.

However, the consciences of some churchmen were still not at ease, and at their desire the Canadian legislature requested the British Parliament to abolish, so far as Canada was concerned, the legal obstacle to the Church holding synods and passing canons. The British Government's law officers decided that this could not be done without affecting the relations of Church and State elsewhere overseas also. Accordingly, in 1857 and 1858 the Canadian legislature itself passed two short acts to this effect. In 1861 Church organization was completed for the time being by the formation of a Provincial Synod consisting of the bishops and clerical and lay representatives from the Canadian dioceses (except for Newfoundland and Rupertsland, which were left out owing to the difficulties of distance). The Bishop of Montreal, F. Fulford, was, on the petition of the Canadian bishops, appointed by the Queen as Metropolitan (it was for some time not realized that the Church in Canada now had freedom to choose its bishops without reference to the British Crown).

Meanwhile, the far west of Canada and the Pacific coast were being settled, and the Church followed. The first Anglican clergyman, Staines, reached Victoria, B.C., in 1849, as a chaplain for the Hudson's Bay Company. The first church in British Columbia was completed in 1856, and three years later a diocese of British Columbia was established, with G. Hills as the first bishop.

It was a resolution passed at a Canadian synod in 1865, requesting the Archbishop of Canterbury to summon a meeting of Anglican bishops from all over the world, which led to the first meeting of the Lambeth Conference in 1867.

Since the great majority of the population of Latin America (Central and South America) are at least nominally Roman Catholic, the Anglican Communion has for the most part attempted no work there. But in 1844 a mission was begun among the primitive and pagan aborigines in Patagonia, in the extreme south.

II. ASIA

This period was at least as important for the extension of Anglicanism in the Eastern hemisphere, as it was for America.

We have seen that by 1836 Anglican mission work had been begun among the Jews of Palestine. After a while, a need was naturally felt for an Anglican bishop there, but up to this time no one could be consecrated a bishop in connection with the Church of England without oaths of allegiance to the British sovereign, and recognizing the latter's supremacy. There could therefore be no Anglican bishop in Palestine, which was then under Turkish rule. In 1841 an Act of Parliament, colloquially known as the Jerusalem Bishopric Act, empowered the Archbishop of Canterbury to consecrate clergy who were not British subjects without their taking these oaths. This cleared the way for a curious scheme for an Anglican bishopric of Jerusalem whose occupant should be chosen alternately by the rulers of England and Prussia. The king of Prussia, Frederick William IV, seems to have wished to introduce episcopacy into his kingdom, in the hope that it might unite his Lutheran and Calvinist subjects, and regarded this scheme as a step towards that.

The first bishop, chosen by England, was M. S. Alexander; by origin a Polish Jew, he was baptized at Plymouth in 1825 at the age of twenty-six, and had worked with the C.M.J. He confirmed some Hebrew Christians, and ordained two Hebrew clergymen, but died in 1845.

As Alexander's successor, the king of Prussia chose Samuel Gobat, a German-speaking Swiss who had earlier worked in connection with the C.M.S. in Abyssinia. He was bishop for over thirty years (1846–79), but not surprisingly found it a hard task to satisfy both English Anglicans and German Lutherans and Calvinists. A number of schools were established and some church people gathered, some of them previously Orthodox Christians, others Jews and Muslims.

At the invitation of Bishop Gobat, the C.M.S. began work in Palestine in 1851, but so hostile to Christianity was public feeling that efforts had to be confined to medical and educational work. The C.M.S. worked chiefly in Jerusalem and Nazareth. There were few schools other than Church schools, and those of the Greek and Latin Churches were mainly for their own people. Christian witness to Islam was largely left to Anglicans and Anglican schools.

In Iran there was very little activity during this period. The American Anglicans became interested in Iran in the eighteen-thirties. A priest, Horatio Southgate, was sent there to investigate in 1835, and worked there for some years, and in 1844 he was actually consecrated in America as bishop for Iran; but he resigned after a short while, and this enterprise lapsed. About this time, the Nestorians round Urmia received some help from the work of an English priest, G. P. Badger, at Mosul. The London Society for Promoting Christianity among the Jews initiated work in Iran which continued for most of the century.

In India, on the other hand, great advances were made during the thirty years in the middle of the nineteenth century. In what is now Pakistan chaplaincy work continued; and Anglican mission work, begun about the middle of the century, came to be on a considerable scale. This was mainly the responsibility of the C.M.S., which began work at Karachi in 1850, at Multan in 1856, at Peshawur about 1858, and at Dera Ismail Khan about 1862.

From 1835, work in Tinnevelly was strongly staffed by both the S.P.G. and the C.M.S., and much more was done than had been done by the Lutherans to develop an Indian ministry.

When the mission of help to the Syrian Church ceased in 1836, the C.M.S. started to evangelize non-Christians in the Malabar area. A number of Syrian Christians begged to be admitted to the Anglican Communion, but this was allowed only after repeated petitions; gradually a considerable number of Syrians left the Jacobite Church for Anglicanism. In 1841 the C.M.S. began work in the Telugu area at Masulipatam on the east coast, and this was the beginning of what was later the Dornakal diocese.

By 1850 there were over forty thousand Indian Anglican church people, the majority of them in Tinnevelly, and there were over a hundred chaplains and about a hundred and thirty other clergymen, most of the work being financed by missionary societies.

After the middle of the century, Anglicanism expanded greatly in India. Mission work was begun in Delhi in 1851, and went forward, despite tragic losses in 1857 at the time of the Mutiny.

Whereas previously caste people had been those chiefly influenced, after 1850 great numbers of outcastes came into the Church in mass movements. One such mass movement, in what was later called the Dornakal diocese, began in 1859 with the baptism of Venkayya. This man was an outcaste and robber chief, but came to feel drawn to God; he made contact with a C.M.S. missionary named Darling, who had been working over eight years among caste people and was in desperation over his complete lack of success. Venkayya was duly instructed and, with his family, was baptized, and became an ardent Christian evangelist. The outcastes, who had been much despised and oppressed, were very impressed when they found that the Church did not despise them, but wanted to help them and improve their miserable conditions, and lead them to worship a God of love.

Daniel Wilson died in 1858, and was succeeded as bishop of Calcutta and Metropolitan by G. E. L. Cotton, who did much to promote education, and not least schools for Anglo-Indians. He was drowned when touring his diocese in 1866.

Ceylon was for some years an archdeaconry in the diocese of Madras, but in 1845 a diocese of Colombo, conterminous with the island, was established with James Chapman as the first bishop.

Help from the S.P.G. began in Ceylon in 1840, when it financed a priest named Mooyart, in Colombo; others were sent soon after. A few years later, at the bishop's request, it established a mission centre in Kandy. Both the S.P.G. and the C.M.S. from the first attached much importance to educational work; and eventually they became responsible, in addition to maintaining many lesser schools, for two of the island's chief secondary schools, St Thomas' College, Colombo, which was founded in 1851, and Trinity College, Kandy, whose first beginnings were in 1857.

The complete Prayer Book was first published in the Sinhalese language in the sixties.

These years saw the real beginning of Anglican Christianity in Burma. There had indeed been some Anglican chaplains to the East India Company in Burma in the eighteenth century. But it was only after 1853, when Lower Burma came under British rule and there were Anglican chaplains and English residents there, that some of these became concerned to extend the Faith among the Burmese, as a result of which in 1859 the S.P.G. sent two men who began mission work at Moulmein. They opened a school, and next year a young layman, J. E. Marks, was sent to take charge of this. The school came to have great influence, and caused the Burmese king at Mandalay to look favourably on the Church, and provide funds for both another Church school and a church; the school was moved to Rangoon in 1864, and grew into St John's College. Marks became the chief figure in the early Anglican mission in Burma, and through the various schools which he founded had a wide influence.

In Malaya, Anglican chaplains held services for English residents, but till 1856 there was apparently no organized attempt by Anglicans to win Malays or local Chinese to the Faith. Local Anglicans then began this, and two catechists, a Tamil and a Chinese, worked under the supervision of the chaplain, so that by 1859 about sixty Tamils and Chinese had been won to Christianity. In answer to local requests the S.P.G. sent out a mission priest in 1861, but he died in 1866 before there had been much visible result from his work.

There was more progress during this period in Borneo. An Englishman, James Brooke, had in 1842 become rajah of the independent state of Sarawak, and he appealed to the Church of England to establish a mission there. Since neither the S.P.G. nor the C.M.S. had the means to undertake this, some of Brooke's friends in 1846 organized the Borneo Church Mission Fund (to which the S.P.G. gave some help).

F. T. McDougall, who before ordination had been trained as a surgeon, and another priest (who resigned next year), with their wives reached Kuching, the chief town of Sarawak, in 1848. McDougall started both educational and medical work, making progress not least among the immigrant Chinese, and in 1851 a church was consecrated by Bishop Wilson of Calcutta, in whose jurisdiction Borneo then was. By June 1852 about fifty persons had been baptized.

It was felt that Borneo should be cut off from Calcutta and constituted a diocese. Some in England still doubted the propriety of establishing an Anglican bishopric outside British territory: so the see took its name from the island of Labuan, which was British; and Brooke, to guard against any intrusion on his rights, added Sarawak to McDougall's title and jurisdiction. McDougall, consecrated in Calcutta, was the first English overseas bishop consecrated outside England (1855).

The mission in Sarawak, which was prospering, suffered a big check in 1857, for, as a result of an attack on Kuching by Chinese gold miners from across the border, which nearly wiped out the whole community, most of the Chinese, good and bad, were driven out of the country by the Malays and Dyaks, and the old custom of head-taking revived. There was another check two years later, when there was a Muslim plot to kill all Europeans, root out Christianity, and proclaim the rule of Islam. However, progress was seen in 1864 when the first Diocesan Synod was held, and in the following year, when a Chinese was ordained deacon. Evangelism of the Muslim Malays in Sarawak was prohibited.

It was only at this time that Anglican Christianity could be planted in China. William Jones Boone was, at least so far as the American Church was concerned, the chief founder of what was to become the Chung Hua Sheng Kung Huei. He had originally been trained as a lawyer, and had then studied theology and been ordained; after that, with a view to mission work in China, he trained and qualified as a doctor. Since Westerners were still in effect excluded from China, he and his wife were sent to Batavia, which they reached in October 1837, to prepare for work in China. His spirit was shown by his remark, when someone mentioned the obstacles to Christianity in China, that he was glad to go if the result of his whole life's work there would only be to oil the hinges of the door for the next missionary to enter. A few months after his arrival in Batavia, Lockwood and Hanson had to return to America.

Both English and American church people deplored the first war (1839–42) between China and Britain, and regretted that the door should be opened only as the result of war. However, it would have been the height of folly if the Church had not taken the opportunity that offered of starting work in Hongkong (a barren rock ceded to Britain) and the five ports opened to foreign residence.

In 1842 Boone spent some months on the island of Kulangsu, but had to return to America early in 1843. Next year the American Church resolved to appoint a bishop and several clergymen and women missionaries to work in China, and Boone was consecrated bishop. He found it practicable to settle in Shanghai, which he thought would be the best centre, though Ningpo, Hangchow, and Soochow then had larger populations and were regarded as more important. Roman Catholics and Congregationalists were already active in Shanghai.

The C.M.S. sent George Smith and McClatchie to investigate the five ports now open, and they actually reached Shanghai in June 1845 some weeks before Boone. McClatchie stayed there, while Smith visited the other ports; on his recommendation the C.M.S. opened work in Shanghai and Ningpo.

Before 1860, the foundations were laid of four dioceses, all in the south and east of the country, to which the open ports were restricted, Hongkong and South China, Fukien, Chekiang, and Shanghai. An institution, later St Paul's College, was established in Hongkong to train Chinese catechists and Christian teachers. George Smith was in 1849 consecrated Bishop in charge of English Anglican work in Hongkong and all parts of China, with his see in Hongkong. As several other Communions were active in Canton, the Anglicans for long did no mission work there.

Boone's early work in Amoy was not followed up, and the beginning of the Fukien diocese was made in 1850, when two clergy sent by the C.M.S., W. Welton, who was also a doctor, and R. D. Jackson, reached Foochow. There was much opposition, and, as so often, it was only with difficulty that they could rent living quarters; but Welton's dispensary won popular sympathy. In 1859, as no one in Foochow had shown any interest in the Gospel, the London committee of the C.M.S. proposed to abandon work in Foochow and concentrate on Chekiang. However, the committee was persuaded to wait another year, and in 1860 W. H. Collins, who was both priest and doctor, came on a visit from Shanghai and opened a temporary dispensary, as a result of which three men began to study Christianity.

The beginnings of the Chekiang diocese also were due to the C.M.S. Two clergymen, R. H. Cobbold and W. A. Russell, reached Ningpo in 1848. The first baptisms in Chekiang were in 1851, so the Faith spread more quickly there than in Fukien, where both early and late there was more bitter opposition to the Church. Nevertheless, eventually the Church spread much less extensively in Chekiang than in Fukien. J. S. Burdon was able in January 1859 to visit Hangchow and begin Church work there; although this was not one of the five cities where alone foreigners were explicitly allowed to live, the local authorities raised no objection to his presence, and he was soon joined by another English priest and two Chinese catechists.

For several decades the English contribution to the Church in Shanghai was very considerable. A church (the first Holy Trinity) was opened for foreign Anglican residents there in June 1848; another (represented to-day by St Paul's) was opened in January 1850 as the centre of the C.M.S. work; next year the English mission had its first baptisms, three blind men. The C.M.S. concentrated much less than did the American Anglicans on educational work, and more on direct evangelism. Its staff visited as many towns and villages as they could, away from Shanghai, and proclaimed the Gospel; often they went by boat, and perhaps left quickly after midnight and returned just before the following midnight.

Hwong Kwong-ts'ai, a lad whom Boone had taken with him to America from Amoy, and who had come to admire Boone greatly, asked for instruction and was baptized on Easter Day, 12 April 1846. The service was in English (the baptismal office had not yet been translated into Chinese), but Boone gave some explanation in Chinese for others who were present at the service. Six years earlier some Chinese had been baptized by Anglicans in Bombay, but Hwong was the first Chinese baptized by Anglicans in China; later he was to be the first Chinese Anglican deacon (1851) and priest (1863).

The American Anglican plan from the first was to stress educational work, with a view to training Chinese who should be the chief agents in spreading Christianity over China. So as early as February 1846 Boone opened a boarding-school for boys (at first only twelve boys). About six years later a small girls' boarding-school was started, which was one of the earliest girls' schools in China.

Boone did some direct evangelistic work, but also spent much time, with Chinese help, in translating parts of the Prayer Book and preparing a catechism, and in revising with others the Chinese New Testament. In June 1849 he celebrated the Eucharist in Chinese, the first Anglican to do so. During the fifties work in and around Shanghai suffered a good deal as a result of the T'aip'ing rebellion. The Americans were able to visit the important cities of Soochow and Wusih, proclaim the Gospel, and distribute tracts; but, in comparison with other missions, their work was intensive rather than extensive, always aiming at producing Chinese clergy and evangelists.

Till 1860 missionaries, like all foreigners, were restricted by the Chinese government to the south-east coast. After this they were allowed to travel to all parts of China, and eventually to reside anywhere, and the Faith could be spread more widely; though there continued to be great opposition to the Church, partly for political reasons, partly because Christianity conflicted with many old Chinese customs and beliefs.

In Fukien the first two men were baptized by English Anglicans in March 1861, and two more in July; but three of them afterwards fell away from the Church. In the following years, Church centres were opened in a number of places, chiefly in the north of the province. Much of the work started by the Americans in Shanghai had to be suspended for a time, since for three years no funds were received from America on account of the Civil War. A Chinese working in the English mission in Shanghai was made deacon in 1862, the first ordination of a Chinese connected with English Anglicans.

J. S. Burdon, a member of the C.M.S., in 1862 was the first Anglican missionary to settle in Peking. At first he was only allowed there as chaplain to the British legation. Later that year S. J. J. Schereshevsky, an American priest, obtained admission as interpreter and Chinese secretary to the American Minister. Next year missionaries as such were allowed to settle in Peking. The S.P.G. in 1863 sent to Peking its first two missionaries to China, but they only stayed one year.

Boone died in 1864; his chief characteristics were his single-minded persistence, his intense devotion, and good judgement. No Westerner contributed more than he did to laying the foundations of the C.H.S.K.H. In his place, as American bishop in China, C. M. Williams was chosen;

33

he had at first to supervise American Anglican work in both China and Japan. George Smith was in this year succeeded as Bishop of Hongkong by C. R. Alford. Burdon and Schereshevsky in Peking had by this time completed the translation of the chief parts of the Prayer Book into Mandarin (the national language, spoken in most of China except along the south-east coast). They also co-operated with non-Anglicans in translating the Bible into Mandarin. Schereshevsky, by origin a Lithuanian Jew, who had migrated to America as a boy and there become a Christian, and a very good Hebrew scholar, was mainly responsible for the translation of the Old Testament.

By the time, therefore, of the first Lambeth Conference, Anglican Christianity had done little more than reach China and make a first beginning.

Much the same was the case in Japan. Roman Catholic missions had been active there in the sixteenth and seventeenth centuries, but Anglican Christianity did not reach Japan till after 1854, when the American admiral Perry persuaded the Japanese government, after a long period of exclusion of all foreign influence, to open two ports to foreign residents.

The first American consul to Japan, Townsend Harris, was a loyal Anglican, and often read Morning Prayer at his residence in Tokyo for such Anglicans as were there. The Japanese were still, as they had long been, prohibited on pain of death from becoming Christians; but naturally missionaries no less than traders came to the open ports. Two American Anglican clergymen, J. Liggins and (soon after) C. M. Williams, were the first missionaries to arrive now (in 1859); they settled in Nagasaki. The atmosphere was still very anti-Christian—the anti-Christian proclamations were not withdrawn till 1873—and for some time little mission activity was possible apart from selling Christian books. Christianity was criticized for undermining the traditional autocratic power of the Emperor and the father of the family, and for minimizing the distinction between upper and lower classes of society.

The first Anglican church in Japan was built in 1863, in Yokohama, largely for foreign residents, and services were taken there by the chaplain of the British Legation. In 1866 Williams baptized the first Japanese won to the Faith by Anglicans, Shiomura, and in the same year was consecrated bishop with oversight of American Anglican work in both Japan and, as we have seen, China.

In the growth of the Australian Church, important stages are marked by the beginning of settlement in 1836 both in what is now Victoria, at Port Philip, from which Melbourne has grown, and in South Australia, near the present Adelaide. The population increased rapidly, especially after the discovery of gold at Ballarat and elsewhere in the fifties, and in Western Australia in the nineties.

A diocese of Tasmania was formed in 1842, with F. R. Nixon as its first bishop. But even the Australian mainland was an impossibly large area for one bishop to supervise, and in 1847 the three dioceses of Newcastle (in Northern N.S.W.), Melbourne, and Adelaide were founded, with William Tyrrell, Charles Perry, and Augustus Short as their bishops. Broughton became Metropolitan of Australia, and was given jurisdiction over the Bishops of Tasmania and New Zealand. When he died in 1854, the Anglican clergy in Australasia numbered a hundred and fifty.

On the initiative of Broughton and G. A. Selwyn, Bishop of New Zealand, a historic meeting was held at Sydney in 1850. All the bishops of Australasia were present—New Zealand, Tasmania, Newcastle, Melbourne, and Adelaide, besides the Metropolitan himself. This meeting recommended, among other things, that provincial and diocesan synods of clergy and bishops should be established, and also provincial and diocesan conventions of laity; questions affecting the Church's temporalities should not be decided without the concurrence of these conventions. This was not done at once; as elsewhere, many church people feared that to hold synods, without an explicit summons from the Crown, would be contrary to the old English laws and would result in a break with the Church of England. But eventually this was done in all dioceses; in some, as in New South Wales and Victoria, Enabling Acts were passed through the local legislatures explicitly permitting the organization of synods. In others, as for example in Adelaide, Perth, and Queensland, the advice of W. E. Gladstone was followed, to the effect that in self-governing colonies the Church of England had the same freedom as any other religious body, and could organize itself on the basis of voluntary consensual compact without the authorization of any Parliamentary Act. Sometimes there was much lay opposition to such government by synods as showing sacerdotalist and hierarchical pretensions. After 1866, no more bishops were appointed, as the earlier ones had been, by the Crown under Letters Patent; they were instead elected by ecclesiastical synods.

Soon after this, government grants for chaplains and other church purposes ceased. The S.P.G. and the S.P.C.K., and to a lesser degree the C.M.S., then gave much help to the young Australian Church. At first, as a result of government grants, almost all schools in Australia were Church of England schools; but the Church was not vigorous enough to make full use of her opportunity, and eventually nearly all schools were taken over by the State. In some States instruction in consequence became wholly secular, in others the clergy were admitted to give denominational instruction.

The Church in Western Australia was under the jurisdiction of the Bishop of Adelaide till 1857, when the diocese of Perth was founded, organizing itself by consensual compact without legislative enactment. In what is now Queensland, the Church had been in the diocese of Newcastle; and in this same year, in which the colony of Queensland was separated from New South Wales, the diocese of Brisbane was founded.

It was only in 1839 that European settlement began in New Zealand on a substantial scale, with the New Zealand Company established by E. G. Wakefield. Many of the settlers imagined that the world was made for the Englishman, and if the Maori was in the way, so much the worse for him; and they were inclined to ignore the Maoris' rights to the land. English church people therefore prevented the grant of government recognition to the New Zealand Company, and relations between settlers and mission in New Zealand were for some time strained; moreover, while the latter was so far working only in the very north, the settlers were mostly at what is now Wellington. The S.P.G. had sent a chaplain with the first settlers to Wellington, but he received so little support that after nine months he moved to Auckland.

W. G. Broughton, Bishop of Australia, paid a brief visit to the New Zealand Church in 1838, though he had no formal jurisdiction over it. But clearly the islands needed a bishop of their own, and in 1841 a diocese of New Zealand was founded, with George Augustus Selwyn as bishop. Selwyn, an outstanding ecclesiastical statesman, was in a real sense the second founder of the New Zealand Church, and created it as we know it to-day. He made first Waimate, in the Bay of Islands, and then Auckland, his centre, rather than Wellington, as some wished, and gradually overcame the tension between the C.M.S. clergy in the north and the settlers in the south. Anyhow, as the settlers quickly came greatly to outnumber the Maoris, the Maori mission came to form but a small part of the Church's work in the islands. In 1853 Selwyn was able to ordain the first Maori deacon.

Settlement of the South Island began on a considerable scale with the coming of the Canterbury Pilgrims. The aim of this scheme was to found a definitely Anglican settlement; in this it was only partially successful, but it resulted in 1856 in the foundation of the second diocese in New Zealand, that of Christchurch, of which H. J. C. Harper was the first bishop. Selwyn opened a theological college at Waimate, which was the germ of the later St John's College, Auckland. He insisted that teachers and students in it should share in manual labour such as ploughing and printing, and set an example of hard work and austere living. The college, however, had more than once to close for a considerable period.

Statesman as he was, Selwyn realized that the Church needed proper organization and rules. To this end he summoned synods of his clergy in 1844 and 1847, which both made canons and helped to create a sense of unity in the Church. But the English Convocations had been suppressed for so long that any attempt to revive synods was regarded as an act of priestly assumption and an affront to the Royal Supremacy. Selwyn's synods, in particular, threw the London committee of the C.M.S. into transports of alarm.

Sir George Grey, the Governor of New Zealand, in 1850 drew up a scheme for a Church convention in which there would be lay as well as clerical representatives, as in the U.S.A. Selwyn took a leading part in the meeting of bishops at Sydney in the same year which greatly encouraged the movement to establish synods; and in 1856 the legal authorities in England decreed that any colonial Church might make whatever rules it liked for its own government, provided that these were to apply only to those willing to be bound by them.

Finally, in 1857, a representative meeting was held at Auckland, to devise a Constitution and General Synod for the Church in New Zealand. Sir George Grey and the meeting of bishops at Sydney had insisted that no convention or synod should have the power to alter the doctrine or ritual of the Church of England or the Authorized Version of the Bible. The Canterbury churchmen, under the influence of their lay leader, J. R. Godley, had at first opposed this, and insisted that even the infant Church of New Zealand should have the right to deal, if necessary, with questions of doctrine and ritual and the translation of the Bible. However, when Godley left, the Canterbury churchmen swung over to the conservative view; and the C.M.S. London committee, which had previously forbidden its missionaries to attend the proposed meeting, then allowed them to do so.

A main topic of discussion was whether the ecclesiastical franchise should be limited to communicants, or should be given to all baptized persons unless they declared themselves dissenters. Selwyn and the Canterbury churchmen favoured the former alternative, but the latter view was strongly maintained by the Auckland laymen, and prevailed. The first meeting of the General Synod was held in 1859. In strong contrast to Australia, the diocesan synods in New Zealand are very definitely subordinate to the Provincial Synod.

Two new dioceses were established in 1858, that of Wellington, with C. J. Abraham as its first bishop, and that of Nelson, in the South Island, with E. Hobhouse as bishop. Next year, a fifth diocese was founded, that of Waiapu in the North Island, with the veteran missionary, William Williams, as its bishop.

The years 1860 to 1862 were a sad time for the New Zealand Church. It could not but suffer much from the war, started, apparently from fear of a possible rebellion, by the government against the Maoris in 1860. On behalf of the Church, Bishop Selwyn and Archdeacon Hadfield sent protests and petitions to the government and the Queen, but they were told not to interfere.

Selwyn had visited some of the Melanesian islands as early as 1849, and next year mission work was begun there, and some Melanesian boys were brought to New Zealand for education. In 1861 work had advanced so far that it was possible to establish a missionary diocese of Melanesia, with J. C. Patteson as its bishop.

IV. AFRICA

The middle decades of the nineteenth century saw the Church make big advances in West Africa, as in so many other parts of the world.

In 1836 the American Church sent Savage, who was both priest and physician, to Cape Palmas in Liberia, both to shepherd the Christian immigrants and to take the Gospel to the non-Christians. J. Payne, who came a few months later, was in 1851 consecrated bishop (of West Africa —later the bishop's sphere was defined as Liberia), and was the first Anglican bishop in West Africa.

The main early stronghold of the Church in West Africa, however, was Sierra Leone. Here in 1840 the C.M.S. reported fifteen hundred communicants, with a regular attendance at public worship of over five thousand others. By 1846, fifty thousand slaves freed by the British had been landed in the colony. They spoke, it is said, no fewer than a hundred and seventeen different languages and dialects; accordingly, English was adopted as the language of the colony, and most of the population who live near the coast speak no other language to-day.

For over twenty years, from 1840, the Principal of Fourah Bay College was a negro priest of the American Church. The C.M.S. in 1845 started a grammar school in Freetown; this was for many years the only second-ary school in West Africa, and as such drew pupils not only from all over West Africa, but from places as far distant as Zanzibar and Cape Town.

A diocese of Sierra Leone was established in 1852, and for a time included all English Anglican work in West Africa (the American mission worked quite separately). The first three bishops, Vidal, Weeks, and Bowen, all died at their post within ten years. Because of the very high missionary death-rate the C.M.S. relatively early reduced its help both in personnel and finance; and the Sierra Leone Church seems to have been left alone rather too early to exist and evangelize on its own resources.

In what was later to be Nigeria, the Church began in 1841. The freed slaves in Sierra Leone came from many districts of West Africa; some of them came from Nigeria, among them a boy who was to be Samuel Adjai Crowther, who reached Freetown in 1822 when he was about sixteen years old, after being rescued by a British warship. Crowther was one of six young men with whom Fourah Bay College opened. He was one of two persons appointed by the C.M.S. to accompany the unlucky expedition which explored the Niger river in 1841. After this he was invited to England, and was ordained in London in 1843. About this time, several hundred ex-slaves, some of them Anglicans, returned to their homes in and around the city of Abeokuta, in Western Nigeria, north of Lagos. The Church followed them. H. Townsend first visited Abeokuta, and in 1844 he, another missionary, and Crowther established a mission there. Crowther now met his mother and sister for the first time since he had been captured by slave-traders as a boy, over twenty years before. His mother was soon afterwards baptized. Crowther visited England in 1851, and was received by Queen Victoria and Prince Albert, and also by Lord Palmerston, who was then Foreign Secretary. He also, six years before Livingstone's appeal in the Senate House appealed to Cambridge undergraduates to go and help the infant Church in Africa. In 1852 the Church began work in Lagos, and beginning in 1857, mission centres were established up the river Niger itself. The founding of the Church here was mainly Crowther's own achievement.

Because the West African climate was then so deadly to Europeans, it was planned that the Nigerian mission should be the responsibility of Africans, and accordingly Crowther was consecrated bishop of the Niger on St Peter's Day, 1864, in Canterbury Cathedral. He was the first bishop from tropical Africa of any Communion, except for a Roman Catholic from the Congo consecrated about 1700, and was the first Anglican bishop of non-European stock. He produced a Yoruba grammar and a Yoruba–English dictionary, and translated many books of the Bible into Yoruba, and on the strength of these was given a D.D. by Oxford.

On the Rio Pongas, where a C.M.S. effort in the early years of the century had come to nothing, Anglicanism made a new beginning in 1855, when Anglicans from the West Indies began an enterprise. Leacock, from Barbados but of European stock, came with a negro colleague; Leacock died next year, but the mission continued, though it did not have great results.

In South Africa, at the beginning of this period there were, scattered over a wide area, only thirteen Anglican clergymen and eleven churches. There was no episcopal supervision, and no common church life except in the individual congregations, and each cleric and congregation did as they pleased. Church life as a whole was at a desperately low ebb. There was no attempt to spread the Gospel among the Bantu. The main church in Cape Town, which later became the cathedral, was owned by a joint-stock company, in which some of the proprietors were Jews or atheists, who are even said to have received the collections as their dividends.

In response to an appeal for a bishop from church people at the Cape, and as a result of the influence of the Oxford Movement, Robert Gray was appointed in 1847. He was consecrated in Westminster Abbey on St Peter's Day, together with bishops for three new Australian dioceses.

Gray had been influenced by the Oxford Movement, and was completely devoted to the Faith and Order of the Church; he was perhaps too direct of mind to be conciliatory or diplomatic, and certainly was no lover of compromise or appeasement. He described the Church in South Africa when he came, as "on one dead level of inefficiency, incompetency, and neglect", with hardly a vestige of Church order or doctrine or seemliness. This was gradually changed.

Within two years of his arrival, the numbers of the clergy had been increased, by securing new men from England, to forty-two, and twenty new churches were being built. Gray travelled indefatigably, in a waggon drawn by eight horses, over all of South Africa where English people had settled, and in 1849 visited St Helena, which, as well as the whole of South Africa, was in his jurisdiction.

Gray also initiated mission work among the Bantu, and saw to its vigorous prosecution, both around Cape Town and to the east. He founded Christian settlements or villages for the Christian Bantu. He started schools and also training for ordination. In all this, he was greatly helped both by the S.P.G. and by N. J. Merriman, a rugged pioneer.

It was clearly necessary to divide Gray's huge diocese, and in 1853 the dioceses of Grahamstown and Natal were cut off, with John Armstrong and J. W. Colenso respectively as their bishops. Armstrong in his diocese found sixteen clergymen at work but only six churches. He vigorously extended the Church, and initiated much new work among the Africans. However, he died in 1856, and was succeeded by Henry Cotterill. By 1853 Anglican work was being carried on in Natal at such places as Durban and Pietermaritzburg, though so late as 1850 there was no church there. Gray himself in 1853 received new Letters Patent as Metropolitan.

With his strong sense of the Church, Gray was convinced that it should be self-governing, and he therefore in 1857 convened a synod, including lay representatives. The holding of synods was at that time an innovation and was regarded by not a few of the laity as papistical and a sign of sacerdotal arrogance. Another synod was held in 1861. A small minority of clergy and laity were so much opposed that they refused to attend the synods. When Gray brought pressure to bear on the Reverend W. Long, who had refused to obey his citation to attend, Long carried it to the Privy Council. This body in 1863 ruled that the Letters Patent issued to Gray in 1853 were invalid, since South Africa had become self-governing in 1850. The only thing therefore was for the Church to organize itself, with its own constitution and canons, on the basis of voluntary consensual compact; and this was soon done.

Meanwhile, Bishop Colenso was arousing much controversy. His views and attitude were unusual, and, the most serious point, he appealed against the authority of the Church to that of the State. His commentary on the Epistle to the Romans seemed to attack the whole sacramental system; he attached very little importance to the Eucharist, and was more lenient regarding the baptism of polygamists than was then approved. In addition, he held views on the authorship of the Pentateuch which were then not yet generally accepted. But it was probably not so much his opinions themselves, as his mainly negative and destructive attitude, and his scorn for those who differed from him, which caused opposition. His zeal in spreading the Gospel among Africans, and his sympathy for them, was not denied. But his Dean and Archdeacon "presented" him for heresy to Gray as Metropolitan. Gray first obtained advice from the Archbishop of Canterbury and other English bishops, who almost unanimously recommended that Colenso should be inhibited. Colenso refused to appear for trial, and was therefore in 1864 deposed from office, as a destroyer of the Faith, and later excommunicated. The secular courts, however, and the Privy Council, to which Colenso appealed, upheld him on the ground that Gray's Letters Patent were, as we have seen, invalid, and that he had therefore no jurisdiction over Colenso.

The controversy over Colenso was one of the reasons for the summoning of the first Lambeth Conference. A number of the English bishops were unsympathetic to Gray's Tractarian and anti-Erastian standpoint, but fifty-six out of seventy-six bishops present at the conference finally upheld him.

In Natal the Church was inevitably hampered by this unfortunate controversy, but elsewhere it made steady progress. In 1859 it was possible to establish a diocese of St Helena (hitherto under the Bishop of Cape Town), with the islands of Ascension and Tristan da Cunha included in it. St Helena had a population of only a few thousands, but almost all of them were Anglicans; Tristan da Cunha (which was first visited by an Anglican clergyman in 1835) first had a resident chaplain in 1851.

Gray had got Church work started in Bloemfontein, and a deacon was stationed there in 1850. A diocese of the Orange River (later renamed Bloemfontein) was set up in 1863, but for some time consisted of little but a bishop, E. Twells, who next year visited Pretoria, and two years later stationed a deacon there; the latter was the only English clergyman in the Transvaal till 1870.

East Africa was hardly touched in this period. The first non-Roman mission work here was Anglican, but as in South India the first C.M.S. missionaries were Germans. J. L. Krapf, who had previously done pioneer mission work in Ethiopia, settled at Mombasa in 1844, and with local help, started to translate the Bible into Swahili. He dreamed of a chain of mission stations across Africa, of a colony for freed slaves similar to that in Sierra Leone, and of an African bishop and clergy. Two years later he was joined by John Rebmann, also a German, but trained and ordained in the Church of England. The two of them did much to explore East and Central Africa, and to make this known in Europe, and so prepared the way for those who came later, though their discovery of the snow-clad Mount Kilimanjaro almost on the Equator was received with scepticism by many scientific journals. They also established a mission station some miles inland. Krapf went to England in 1853, broken down in health and did not return to East Africa; Rebmann, however, remained till 1874, and reduced three languages to writing, preparing a dictionary in each. But of extension of the Church there was little sign.

But it is mainly to the C.M.S. and the Universities' Mission to Central Africa that the Anglican Communion owes its beginning in East Africa. The U.M.C.A. began in 1858 as a response to the appeal made in 1857 by David Livingstone in the Senate House at Cambridge, reinforced by Robert Gray of Cape Town; it was supported by members of the universities first of Oxford and Cambridge, then of Dublin and Durham also. On 1 January 1861, C. F. Mackenzie, archdeacon of Natal, was consecrated at Cape Town as missionary bishop "to the tribes on the Zambezi": he promised canonical obedience to the Bishop of Cape Town. The plan was that Mackenzie and his party should take the Faith to the region near Lake Nyasa and the Shiré river. But the mission met disaster after disaster. Mackenzie died of a fever after twelve months, and other lives also were lost. Next year, W. G. Tozer was consecrated with the title "Bishop of Central Africa".

The Shiré river district proved so unhealthy that in 1864 the mission headquarters were moved to Zanzibar, which was then perhaps the most important centre on the coast of East Africa.

A priest was sent to the Seychelles by the S.P.G. in 1843. Bishop Chapman of Colombo visited Mauritius in 1850, and confirmed a considerable number. He found only five Anglican priests, compared with fourteen Roman Catholics, all of whom were financed by the government. Chapman reported on the need for a bishop, and in 1854 a diocese of Mauritius was constituted, with V. Ryan as bishop; the S.P.G. contributed to its endowment and continued to support it with men and money. The C.M.S. started work among the Indian labourers there in 1856, and was for some time more active than the S.P.G.; a considerable number of Indians were won to the Faith. The numbers of the clergy increased, and the Church went forward, though in 1867 a fever swept away many of the mission staff, as well as one-tenth of the whole population.

Congregationalism reached Madagascar nearly fifty years before Anglicans first began mission work there, and the Roman Catholics also began somewhat earlier than the Anglicans. The Queen of Madagascar (which came under French rule in 1896) from 1835 till her death in 1861 proscribed Christianity. But the King who succeeded her was well disposed to Christianity and granted religious liberty. Bishop Ryan of Mauritius visited the capital, Anantanarivo, and in 1864 the S.P.G. and the C.M.S. each sent two men to the island. The Anglicans at first did not work at the capital or among the Hova tribe, since the London Mission was already active in that area; the two S.P.G. deacons settled on the east coast, at Tamatave, the chief port, and the C.M.S. men settled at Vohimare in the north. Some Malagasy who had become Christians in Mauritius helped as interpreters and catechists, and eighty-one persons were baptized in the first year.

In Egypt, the C.M.S. attempt to influence and help the Coptic Church continued, and in 1842 a theological college for Coptic clergy was started; but the old Church was as yet not affected very deeply. A church for British residents was built in Alexandria in 1840. The C.M.S. ceased its work for the time being in 1865 when Lieder died. The Church Mission to Jews worked among Jews in Ethiopia for some years from 1855.

44

4

1867–1888

IN the period between the first and third Lambeth Conferences, Anglicanism continued to extend greatly. In some areas of the world these years saw primarily the growth of an already founded and well-established Church; such was the case with the English-speaking countries outside Europe, but even here church people were to be found over a much arger area, as the settled districts expanded. Elsewhere it was still a question of founding the Church in new areas, or at least in areas in which at the time of the first Lambeth Conference it had barely taken root.

I. AMERICA

In the West Indies the Church of England was at first, and for some time, regarded as "established", and the Government, moreover, paid the salaries of many of the clergy. About 1870, however, the State ceased in most dioceses, except Barbados, either to recognize the Church or to pay the salaries of the clergy. Diocesan synods were usually established soon after the Church was disestablished.

As the Church grew, more dioceses were formed. Trinidad was cut off from Barbados and constituted a diocese in 1872; a diocese of the Windward Islands was formed in 1879, though this continued for long to be administered by the Bishop of Barbados; and a diocese of Honduras was cut off from Jamaica in 1880. In this same year, an ecclesiastical Province of the West Indies, comprising eight dioceses, was formed; and canons were drawn up in 1883.

The Episcopal Church in the U.S.A. was by this time well established, though it was still extending to the west, following, if not as quickly as many other Communions, the tide of settlement. It made in this period one of its first great contributions to world-wide Anglicanism. W. R. Huntington, rector of Grace Church, New York, proposed (in 1870) that the Anglican Communion should set out four points as a basis for Christian unity; these were—

the Holy Scriptures as the Word of God,
the Apostles' and Nicene creeds as the rule of Faith,
the two sacraments of Baptism and Holy Communion,
and the Episcopate as the keystone of governmental unity.

Huntington's proposal was accepted in substance by the House of Bishops in 1886, at a meeting of the General Convention in Chicago, and then by the Lambeth Conference in 1888, and the four points are now known as the Chicago–Lambeth Quadrilateral.

In Canada, the Church at this time grew rapidly, especially in western Canada under Machray, whose diocese became the mother of several other dioceses. So in 1875 an ecclesiastical Province of Rupertsland was created, with Machray as Metropolitan; and a Domestic and Foreign Missionary Society was founded in 1883, to set forward the Church's extension both in the new areas of Canada and in non-Christian countries.

Anglicans of the South American Missionary Society were now at work among the aborigines of Patagonia. Charles Darwin was so much amazed at the Church's achievements in helping these very backward people that he subscribed regularly to this mission work. Later (in 1890) the Church of England also began work among the primitive tribes of the Gran Chaco in the centre of South America. There were also Anglicans ministering to British residents in several big towns in South America; and in 1869 a bishop of the Falkland Isles was appointed to supervise such Anglican work as there was in any part of South America. Anglicans from the U.S.A. had a mission in southern Brazil.

II. ASIA

The hybrid Jerusalem diocese did not prove a success in practice. It was not liked by the German Evangelicals because it was a bishopric; and it was the centre of much controversy in England. The more strongly Catholic element deplored it as an intrusion into the sphere of the Orthodox and as leading to the proselytizing of Orthodox Christians, and criticized the close co-operation with Protestants which was involved.

Bishop Gobat died in 1879, and his successor two years later. The bishopric was vacant for some years, and finally lapsed in 1886, when the German government withdrew. The scheme had in practice worked mainly for the benefit of the Anglicans.

Next year, however, the Orthodox Patriarch of Jerusalem declared that an Anglican bishop should be appointed in Jerusalem, to promote good relations between Anglicans and Orthodox, and to strengthen them in face of the great opposition which they faced from Muslims. In consequence, a purely Anglican bishopric (not "of" but "in" Jerusalem) was established, to which G. F. P. Blyth was appointed. The bishopric was to have three objects: oversight of British church people in Palestine, Syria, Egypt, and Turkey; supervision of Anglican missions to Jews and Muslims in that area; and promotion of good relations with the Orthodox. The Jerusalem and the East Mission was founded in London to aid the new diocese. It was understood that no attempt would be made to win the Orthodox over to Anglicanism.

It was not till this period that what was to be the main Anglican enterprise in Iran was initiated. By this time there were there, besides the remnants of the old Persian or Assyrian Church (the so-called Nestorians), Roman Catholic and American Presbyterian missions. Bruce, an English priest connected with the C.M.S. in India, in 1869 began relief work in a very bad famine which was then raging in Isfahan, giving a practical demonstration of Christianity. His stay in Iran had not been intended to be more than temporary, but in 1871, as he was preparing to return to India, nine Muslims asked to be prepared for baptism. Bruce consequently stayed and followed up this opening. He then urged the C.M.S. to undertake responsibility for this work, and in 1875 it at length agreed to do so; additional missionaries were sent and centres of work were established, chiefly in south Persia.

At first the Church met bitter opposition; the Muslim law of apostasy was still effective, and not a few early Christians were martyred. Little direct evangelism could be attempted; and the C.M.S. group concerned themselves mainly with the Armenians, feeling that if this old Church could be revived and strengthened, it would eventually influence Muslims to Christianity.

The Nestorians had again appealed to the Church of England for help, and as a result the Archbishop of Canterbury's mission to the Assyrian Christians was established in about 1884. The main centre of this work was at Urmia, in the far north of Persia; its aim was to strengthen, mainly by education, the old "Church of the East" (as the Assyrian Church is officially called), and help it to reform itself; all proselytizing was completely repudiated.

In India, Anglican Christianity at this time was spreading fairly rapidly and was also becoming more firmly rooted. In what is now Pakistan, the Church advanced, as seems normally to be the case in a Muslim country, much more slowly. The bishops, only three in number at the time of the first Lambeth conference, met occasionally to take counsel, and in 1873 there took place what may be regarded as the first formal meeting of the bishops, and from these meetings, which were purely consultative and without binding power, there eventually grew the Episcopal Synod. The meeting in 1877 recommended the establishment of diocesan synods. In 1883 the bishops issued a notable pastoral letter, in which they declared that the Truth and Order for which they stood were not to be purchased only by conformity to English ways. They did not aim at imposing on an Indian Church anything distinctively English or even European; the Word, the sacraments, and the episcopal ministry are, they pointed out, unchangeable and belong to no age or country. Constitutionally and legally, however, Anglicanism in India was at this time tied to the Church of England in all points, and had no power, for example, to vary the Prayer Book in any respect—it was just the Church of England in India.

Some new Anglican groups now began to help the spread of the Gospel in India. From 1874 the Society of St John the Evangelist (the Cowley Fathers), whose founder, R. M. Benson, had wished to do mission work in India, undertook work in Bombay and Poona. They were followed by the Community of St Mary the Virgin (the Wantage Sisters). The Cambridge Mission to Delhi was founded in 1877, largely as a result of T. V. French's talks at Cambridge with B. F. Westcott, with the aim in particular of influencing the Indian intelligentsia; and with this was connected the Cambridge Brotherhood. The Cambridge Mission assumed responsibility for work begun in Delhi by the S.P.G. in 1854, and, among many undertakings, built up St Stephen's College there. The similar Oxford Mission to Calcutta, with the Brotherhood of the Epiphany, was founded in 1880, and had much influence through hostels for students, schools, and its widely circulated paper *The Epiphany*. The Church of England Zenana Missionary Society was also founded in 1880, primarily to promote Christian evangelism among Indian women in their secluded Zenanas which men might not enter. This society worked closely with the C.M.S., which did not then appoint single women as missionaries.

In what is now Pakistan, T. V. French in 1867 began a Divinity school in Lahore.

During a great famine in South and Central India in 1876-7, relief was given without distinction to Christian and non-Christian; and on principle, so that no one should become a Christian merely to get help, the Anglicans baptized none of those who suffered from the famine till it was over. As a result, in about 1880 great numbers wished to come into the Church; but there was not sufficient staff to instruct and shepherd them all, and so many soon lapsed.

Cotton was succeeded as Metropolitan by R. Milman (1867-1876), but there were still only three dioceses in the whole of what is now India and Pakistan and Burma, and Milman is said to have been killed by the labours of his journeys. There were parliamentary obstacles to the creation of the obviously needed new dioceses; but at length, in 1877, two new dioceses, of Rangoon and Lahore, were established. The latter was almost entirely in what is now Pakistan. T. V. French, the founder of St John's College, Agra, was appointed its bishop and was the first mission priest in India to become an Anglican bishop.

The Church grew much more rapidly in southern India than in the north, and in the Tinnevelly area in particular great numbers had by 1880 become Christian and the Indian clergy there already numbered ninety. That area, and indeed the whole of south India, was in 1877 still in the diocese of Madras; and in that year two assistant bishops were appointed, to shepherd church people won to the Gospel there through the S.P.G. and the C.M.S. respectively. This plan was not at all liked by Church leaders in India, as tending to accentuate party distinctions within the Church. Anglican work in Travancore and Cochin was cut off two years later from the diocese of Madras and a new diocese formed. This caused distress to many Jacobite Christians in that area, who regarded it as an intrusion into the jurisdiction of their bishops, and as a slight on them; but the presence of many Anglican church people, and the absence of Intercommunion between the two Communions, made it inevitable.

Not a few notable Indians of this period became Christians through Anglican missions. Imad-ud-Din was a Punjabi Muslim, who in 1866 became a Christian partly as a result of a public debate which T. V. French and another C.M.S. missionary, a German named Pfander, held with Muslim representatives. He lived mostly in Amritsar, was ordained priest in 1872, and become a great literary champion of Christianity; he was the first Indian to receive the Lambeth D.D. Nehemiah Goreh was a Brahmin of Benares who sacrificed much when he became a Christian. He was ordained priest in 1870, and became the first Indian member of the Cowley Fathers; he was a scholarly man, and wrote much in defence of Christianity, and through him some other highly educated Indians became Christians.

When R. S. Copleston became Bishop of Colombo in 1875, there was at first some friction between him and the C.M.S. missionaries in the diocese, who had hitherto been largely independent of the bishop, and valued their independence. Copleston desired that they should become a more integral part of the diocese, but unwisely suggested assigning to the C.M.S. clergy the status of assistant curates to the chaplains.

Till the eighties, the Church of England in Ceylon was established, and the government made grants towards the salaries of chaplains and the upkeep of churches for the European residents, and nominated the bishop. In 1886, however, it was disestablished, and all such grants ceased. Under Copleston's able guidance, a constitution was framed and a diocesan synod, including lay representatives, established; and the bishop was henceforth elected by the diocesan synod.

The Anglican mission in Burma, which was the responsibility of the S.P.G., was till 1877 under the jurisdiction of the Bishop of Calcutta. In that year, with much help from the diocese of Winchester, a diocese of Rangoon was established with J. H. Titcomb as bishop. Titcomb was succeeded by J. M. Strachan (1882–1902).

Most of the inhabitants of Burma, the Burmese proper, are staunch Buddhists and have never been open to the Gospel. The great majority of Anglicans there, like other Christians in Burma, came from the Karen and other aboriginal hill-tribes, who were not Buddhists but animists, and were much despised and oppressed by the Buddhist Burmans. The S.P.G. started a mission among the Karens in and around Toungwoo, up the river from Rangoon, in 1873, and two years later a large group of dissident Baptist Karens were admitted into the Anglican community; they had wanted this for some years, but the bishop refused to admit them till it was clear that the only alternative was that they would relapse into heathenism.

The first Asians in the Rangoon diocese were ordained deacons in

1878; they were a Tamil and four Karens. Next year a Karen translation of the Prayer Book was published.

Anglicans in the Straits Settlements (as British Malaya was then called) were transferred in 1869 from the jurisdiction of the Bishop of Calcutta to that of the Bishop of Labuan and Sarawak. During the next few years, the S.P.G. began mission work in Penang, Province Wellesley, Selangor, and Perak. The first Anglican church in the strongly Muslim native states of the Malay peninsula was consecrated in 1887 at Kuala Lumpur, the chief town of the State of Selangor.

W. Chambers succeeded F. T. McDougall as Bishop of Labuan and Sarawak in 1869, when, as we have seen, the Straits Settlements were added to this diocese. The language of the Sea Dyaks was reduced to writing by the Anglican Mission. After a time the Church extended north from Sarawak, into the British North Borneo territory, and Sandakan, the capital, first had a resident Anglican priest in 1888.

In China, where at the time of the first Lambeth Conferences only a beginning had been made, the next twenty years saw great advances, and by the time of the third Lambeth Conference there were Anglican missions in most, though not all, of the eighteen provinces of China proper.

In the early years, there was more progress in Chekiang than in most areas; and here, at Ningpo, a school was started in 1868, which later developed into Trinity College, a great nursery of clergy, teachers, and evangelists. Three years later, the first Anglican church was opened in Hangchow. Anglicans had begun here about ten years before, and were the first non-Roman mission to arrive, a somewhat unusual event.

It was only about now that missions were first allowed in the interior of China. Augustus Höhing, an American priest, and Y. K. Yen, one of the outstanding early leaders of the Chinese Church, who had just been ordained, reached Wuchang in June 1868 and began what grew into the Hankow diocese. They had the usual difficulty in renting premises in which to live and work, but they managed to start a small school for ten boys. Next year they began evangelistic work and a small school across the Yangtze in Hankow, and the first persons were baptized in this year in both Wuchang and Hankow. Two years later, in Wuchang, a boys' boarding-school, named after Bishop Boone, was started. Progress was considerably more rapid in Wuchang than it had been at first in Shanghai, partly because the mission now had Chinese workers, partly because it included medical work.

J. S. Burdon became Bishop of Hongkong in 1872, and under him a number of evangelistic centres in the area round Canton were first established. Till now, all English Anglican mission work in China had been under the Bishop of Hongkong; but in this year W. A. Russell was appointed Bishop of what was called North China, with his centre at Ningpo, to be responsible for English Anglican mission work north of the twenty-eighth parallel of latitude. In Fukien direct evangelism was stressed and hardly any schools were started; here more than elsewhere there were anti-Christian riots from time to time. In 1875 entrance could at last be got to Kienning, and next year to Funing.

Bishop C. M. Williams in 1874 resigned his responsibility for Church work in China. S. J. J. Schereshevsky twice declined election as his successor, wishing to continue his literary work in Peking; but in 1877, on his third election, he could only accept. He had exceptional intellectual gifts and wide learning, especially in the field of linguistics, and on becoming bishop, he determined to establish a college and an institution for training clergy. His original plan was to start a college in Peking; but eventually a school, which absorbed existing and less ambitious schools, was started in Jessfield, Shanghai, which later developed into St John's University, under F. L. Hawks-Pott. A theological college was also started. In the summer of 1881, Schereshevsky had a sunstroke which permanently paralysed him, and when recovery was seen to be impossible he resigned his jurisdiction. After this, till his death in 1906, he gave himself entirely to literary work, using a typewriter with one finger. Among much else, he translated, with help from Chinese, the whole Bible into literary Chinese (Wenli).

The observance in England in 1872 for the first time of St Andrew's Day as a time of intercession for the Church overseas led some church people to think of China; and the result was that the S.P.G. in 1874 sent two clergymen, C. P. Scott and M. Greenwood, to Chefoo. In the spring of 1878 they visited T'aian, where no non-Roman mission was at work. Not till 1887 was it possible to rent a house here, and undertake settled work. This marks the beginning of what was later the Shantung diocese.

When Bishop Russell died, G. E. Moule was in 1880 consecrated as "Bishop of Mid-China", with responsibility for English Anglican mission work in Chekiang, Kiangsu, and to the west. A new diocese of North China was constituted, with C. P. Scott as its bishop. Scott continued to live at Chefoo till 1883, when he moved to Peking, which thus became the see-city of the North China diocese. The C.M.S. and the American Church Mission had been active in Peking twenty years before; but the American interest had ceased when Schereshevsky went to Shanghai and the C.M.S. now withdrew, so that the S.P.G. was left alone to help the Church in North China. The first Chinese in North China was made deacon in 1888.

The beginnings of the Anking diocese were made at Wuhu in 1886 and at Anking in 1894. In the eighteen-eighties a number of new centres were opened up the Yangtze from Wuhan and elsewhere in Hupeh, and the first ordination in Central China was in 1888, when five deacons, all the products of Boone school, were ordained at Hankow.

By this time, also, Anglican Christianity was spreading to West China. W. W. Cassels and other Anglicans in the interdenominational China Inland Mission settled in East Szech'uan at Paoning in 1887.

In Korea, Anglicanism has always been on a small scale compared with the big American Protestant missions. It was only in 1882 that this long closed country opened itself to external influences. Shortly before, in anticipation of this event, a Japanese catechist had been sent to China by the Anglicans in Japan to study the Korean language; but nothing had come of it. A C.M.S. missionary in China visited Korea in 1885, and on his return gave an enthusiastic account of the opportunity there; and as a result, Anglicans in Fukien sent two Chinese catechists, who settled at Fusan, on the south-east coast, and began evangelism. This was the sum total of Anglican activity in Korea by the time of the third Lambeth Conference.

Japan set out on a new course of modernization and westernizing in 1868, when the Shogunate (or regency) and the feudal system were abolished, and the rule of the Mikado restored. One consequence of this was that in 1873 the proclamations forbidding Japanese on pain of death to embrace Christianity were taken down, after which there was for the most part toleration of Christianity in practice, and open and public evangelism first became possible. From 1878 missionaries were allowed to travel freely and could proclaim the Faith in the interior.

George Ensor of the C.M.S. reached Japan in 1869 and settled in Nagasaki; he was the first English missionary of any Communion to work in Japan. The S.P.G. first sent two missionaries in 1873 who settled in Tokyo. Three years later, the S.P.G. began work in Kobe.

In 1874 Bishop Williams was relieved of his responsibilities in China, and could give all his time to Japan. The A.C.M. now opened St Paul's

School in Tokyo (at first with only five boys), which was in 1887 to develop into St Paul's College and then St Paul's University. The C.M.S. in this year began work in Hakodate in Hokkaido in North Japan, and the next year it erected a church in Nagasaki.

The three Anglican missions in 1878 held a conference in Tokyo, which agreed that there should be a common Japanese translation of the Prayer Book; translations already made of Morning and Evening Prayer and the Litany were adopted, and a committee chosen to translate the remainder.

The A.C.M., which hitherto had worked in Osaka and Tokyo, began work in Yokohama in 1881. Soon after this, Batchelor of the C.M.S. started a mission among the Ainu aboriginals in Hokkaido.

The English Anglican missionaries and their flocks were till 1883 in the charge of the Bishop of Victoria, Hongkong; in this year J. Poole was consecrated as Bishop for the English missions in Japan, but after only a few months he was forced by ill-health to leave Japan, and died in England in 1885.

Edward Bickersteth succeeded Poole as bishop in 1886. From the first he emphasized more than was then usual that the Church in Japan, while remaining faithful to historic Christianity, must be really Japanese. Through his vision, and that of Williams, it was agreed to unite the work of the three Anglican missions in Japan, and in February 1887 there met the first General Synod of Anglicans in Japan. The name Nippon Sei Ko Kwai ("Holy Catholic Church of Japan") was adopted, and also a constitution and canons, based on the Bible, the Nicene Creed, the two sacraments, and the threefold ministry. The Japanese clergy now numbered only two deacons, but the Synod looked forward to the time when there should be Japanese bishops, and in the General Synod the Japanese already outnumbered the foreigners. The N.S.K.K. had at this time about fifteen hundred adherents. That it was organized at so early a stage was due to the fact that the Church in Japan was mainly urban rather than rural, and attracted rather the more educated section of society. It quickly organized a Board of Missions, which undertook work among Japanese settlers in T'aiwan (Formosa). A common Prayer Book, following in some points the English, in some the American, usage, had already been composed.

In Australia this period was marked by important developments in the life of the Church. A meeting of seven bishops at Sydney in 1868 recommended that a General Synod of the Church of England in Australia should be set up, and this was done in 1872. The authority entrusted to the General Synod was, however, very limited, and no resolution passed by it was binding on any diocese until and unless accepted by that diocese. Nevertheless, the General Synod has not been ineffective; an Appeal Tribunal was established, and about 1880 a Board of Missions, such as the bishops had urged in 1850, was set up to extend the Faith among the islands of the West Pacific. Since 1886 its main work has been among the Papuans in New Guinea.

G. A. Selwyn, who had done so much for the young New Zealand Church, was in 1868 appointed Bishop of Lichfield, and returned to England; he was succeeded as Primate of New Zealand by Bishop Harper of Christchurch. The destruction of the Maori war of 1860–62 left the Church too weak to do very much to mould the young nation's life, and very few priests at this time came from England, while New Zealand was not yet producing many herself. A new diocese of Dunedin was established in the extreme south of the South Island in 1871, but after 1877 virtually all primary schools were under government auspices, and no religious teaching was allowed in them during school hours. About 1876, work (the seed from which came later the diocese of Polynesia) was begun in Fiji. J. C. Patteson, Bishop of Melanesia, was killed by islanders in 1871, together with a missionary and a Melanesian teacher, apparently in reprisal for the abduction of islanders as labourers by white traders. The Church in Melanesia lost much ground after this, and it was long before this was recovered, especially in the Solomon Islands. J. R. Selwyn, son of G. A. Selwyn, after a long interregnum succeeded Patteson in 1877.

IV. AFRICA

Samuel Adjai Crowther's episcopate included the whole of this period. He made Lagos his headquarters, but travelled widely. Under his leadership, Christianity spread extensively in Nigeria, and he ordained a number of African clergy. No one has ever doubted Crowther's devotion and genuine humility, but he seems to have lacked administrative ability, and during his declining years discipline and moral standards among his clergy and lay people became distinctly lax.

The West Indian Church was not always able to give the Rio Pongas mission all the support it needed. The Bishop of Sierra Leone gave it episcopal supervision, and it received some help also from England and the S.P.G.

The Church in Sierra Leone received government grants for some of its work till 1875, but after this it received such grants only for schools. In 1876, Fourah Bay College became affiliated to Durham University, and the African students there worked for Durham degrees.

In South Africa, in spite of the adverse judgement of the first Lambeth Conference, Colenso and his relatively few adherents, on the ground of the Privy Council's decision, retained the revenues and churches of the diocese of Natal till his death in 1883. Gray, as metropolitan, took charge of the diocese. The S.P.G., true to its principles, expressed no judgement on the controversy, but accepted that of the Church given through its proper authorities; its support now was invaluable to Gray. W. K. Macorie was consecrated at Cape Town in 1869 as Bishop of Maritzburg (in Natal); the Colenso party protested, but with little effect. A dissident remnant calling itself "Church of England in South Africa" continued even after Colenso's death, and tried unsuccessfully to get a successor to him consecrated. Several of his clergy were in time reconciled to the Church.

A Provincial Synod first met in 1870 at Cape Town, and ratified a Constitution and Canons for "the Church of the Province of South Africa", a self-governing province of the Anglican Communion. This came to include a considerably greater area than the political Union of South Africa formed in 1910. In the same year, a diocese of Zululand, where mission work had been begun under Colenso in 1859, was founded, with T. E. Wilkinson as its first bishop. But for some years the extension of the Faith here was greatly hampered by the Zulu wars.

Robert Gray died in 1872. He had laid the foundations of the Church of the Province, and was in the early days far and away the outstanding figure in the South African Church. Because of his defence of the Church's spiritual liberties against the State's Erastian dominance of it, he has been called "the Athanasius of the South". When he reached South Africa, there was no organized Anglican Church there; when he died, there were five dioceses with a ministry numbering a hundred and twenty-seven.

Gray was followed by William West Jones, who was Metropolitan from 1874 to 1908, and continued to build on the foundations laid by Gray. On his invitation, the Cowley Fathers in 1883 started a branch house in Cape Town, which has done much with the Bantu people.

In the north-east part of the Cape Colony, a diocese (which Gray had planned) of St John's, Kaffaria, was established in 1873, with H. Callaway as its bishop. This diocese was at first staffed and largely financed by Scottish Episcopalians; its church people were mostly African rather than European. The Church had started work in this area in 1855, though Gray had visited it seven years earlier, and it was here in 1877 that the first African in South Africa was ordained to the priesthood. Callaway was succeeded as bishop by Key, one of the greatest Anglican missionaries in South Africa. A mission farm was started here in 1870 and named Clydesdale: it became also a well-known industrial training centre. The bishop's see was at Umtata.

The Church of the Province began work in the Protectorate of Basutoland in 1875, when a priest came both to minister to the British administrators and to spread the Gospel among the Basuto.

At the beginning of this period, the Transvaal was in the jurisdiction of the Bishop of Bloemfontein, but it had only one Anglican clergyman. At the request of the Bishop, whose hands were full, it was visited by the Bishop of Zululand, who laid foundations for the future, and a diocese of Pretoria was set up in 1878, with H. B. Bousfield as bishop. After gold was found on the Witwatersrand (in 1886) large numbers of settlers, some Boers but many British, began to pour in to develop the mines. In the same year, Bousfield held the first Anglican service, indeed the first Christian service of any kind, at Johannesburg, and the Church grew rapidly there.

It was only at this time that Anglicanism really began in East Africa. The U.M.C.A. work was from 1870 recognized as wholly independent of the distant see of Cape Town and the Province of South Africa. Bishop Tozer resigned in 1873, and in that same year, part of the site of the slave-market in Zanzibar was bought, and on it was laid the foundation of the Cathedral. Next year, E. Steere was appointed bishop, and during the following eight years the mission expanded rapidly, especially on the mainland. A centre was established at Masasi in 1876, with a nucleus of Christian freed slaves; and in 1881, a beginning was made near Lake Nyasa, among the tribes who had been the original objective of the mission, by W. P. Johnson. The first East African was made deacon in Zanzibar in 1883 by C. A. Smythies.

By this time, Anglicanism was making a start in another part of East Africa, where, after early tragic losses, it was to have successes hardly paralleled anywhere else. *The Daily Telegraph* in November 1875 published a letter from the traveller H. M. Stanley, who had found Mtesa, the king of Uganda, willing to listen to the Christian Gospel, and urged the sending of a mission to Uganda. Within a week the C.M.S. resolved to send a mission, and this reached Uganda in 1877. Two years later, however, two of the group of eight had been massacred, two had died of disease, and two had been invalided home. One of the remaining two, Alexander Mackay, a layman, may perhaps be regarded as the real founder of the Church in Uganda. The king vacillated in his reception of the mission, and finally relapsed completely into paganism. When he died in 1884 there were thirty-eight Baganda Christians.

Next year his successor Mwanga tried by persecution to blot out the Church, perhaps because he feared that Christians were but the precursors of annexation. Six Christian boys were at once seized and, when they refused to renounce Christ, burnt to death. Other Christians were also done to death, though Mackay, who lived quietly and with calm faith in the capital, was untouched. A few months later, Hannington, who had been consecrated Bishop of Eastern Equatorial Africa, was killed on his way from the coast; he was going, perhaps unwisely, by a route not before used by Europeans. At least two hundred Baganda Christians (some of them Roman Catholics, but most Anglicans) were now put to death, while many more were banished or mutilated.

In 1875 the C.M.S. established near Mombasa a colony of freed slaves, named Frere Town, like the similar settlement in Sierra Leone, but the Church here did not make much advance till later.

The S.P.G. had by now sent more men to Madagascar, and in 1868 the Anglicans began work also in the capital, in the centre of the island. A bishop was becoming necessary, if only to ordain Malagasy clergy. But under the Jerusalem Bishopric Act a licence from the British Foreign Secretary was necessary before the Archbishop could consecrate a bishop for territory not under British rule: and the Foreign Secretary, under Congregationalist influence, refused this. Eventually, at the request of the English bishops, the Scottish bishops in 1874 consecrated R. Kestell Cornish as Bishop of Madagascar. The C.M.S. did not approve of this plan, and therefore discontinued its work in Madagascar. None of the friction which had been feared between the bishop and non-Anglicans resulted; there was and is virtually no overlapping of non-Roman missions in Madagascar. Next year the first two Malagasy were made deacons, and the Malagasy Prayer Book was published in 1878.

C.M.S. work in Egypt, which had ceased in 1865, was resumed in 1882, the year of the British occupation. The mission's desire still was in part to help and strengthen the Coptic Church, but it was now rather less impossible than it had been before to influence the Muslims. The Rev. F. A. Klein, who had worked in Palestine, was sent in 1882 to Cairo, which was now being much westernized.

5

1888–1920

THE thirty years between the third and the sixth Lambeth Conferences mark the transition, as from the nineteenth to the twentieth century, so also from the early or formative period of the Anglican Communion to its modern or recent stage. When this period was over, the prestige of the West had in most parts of the world vanished except in regard to technology. If the Church's extension was thereby deprived of an adventitious, and largely undesired, aid, it was also true that Asia and Africa were coming to be much less attached to their old ways; and the day was not far off when those who had previously opposed Christianity as too revolutionary would dismiss it as hopelessly archaic.

I. AMERICA

The Churches of the English-speaking countries outside Europe were coming more and more to be independent of the Church in the British Isles as regards both staff and finance.

In the U.S.A., indeed, the Episcopal Church had slowly and gradually built itself up without help from outside, in either staff, or money, ever since American Independence (1783). It was at this time that the noted and widely-admired American Anglican preacher, Phillips Brooks, became Bishop of Massachusetts (1892), and it was another American Anglican bishop, C. H. Brent, who proposed (in 1910) that all Christian Communions should hold a world conference on Faith and Order, and thus initiated what came to be the Faith and Order Movement.

The organization of the Church of England in Canada was completed in 1893 when a General Synod was formed, to bring together the two ecclesiastical provinces then existing, Canada and Rupertsland, and

Machray became the first primate of all Canada. When Machray died in 1904, his one diocese of Rupertsland had grown into a province with nine dioceses, and a new province of Ontario was formed in 1912, and a province of British Columbia in 1915.

Canadian Anglicans were now coming to take a considerable share in the spreading of the Gospel in Asia. Evangelicals in 1894 established the Canadian C.M.S., but in 1902–4 the Missionary Society of the Church in Canada was formed, which included both the C.M.S. and the older Domestic and Foreign Missionary Society. Through it, Canadian Anglicans, who previously had helped Anglican missions elsewhere, undertook responsibility for supporting the diocese of Honan in China in 1909, and the diocese of Mid-Japan in 1912.

In Latin America, where the diocese of the Falkland Islands had been founded by the Church of England, the mission of the American Church in southern Brazil was now constituted a diocese, in 1899, and a second diocese connected with the Church of England was formed in 1910, that of Argentine and Eastern South America, comprising English Anglican chaplaincies and missions east of the Andes.

II. ASIA

The new diocese of Jerusalem made steady progress during this period; it included at this time Anglican mission and chaplaincy work in Egypt. In 1899 Bishop Blyth, at the request of Christian and Muslim leaders, founded St George's School, Jerusalem, to be run on the lines of an English Public School.

In Iran, C.M.S. work developed steadily in such centres as Kerman, Yezd, Shiraz, and Isfahan, though insecurity on the roads, difficulties of transport, and the fanaticism of the population for long restricted mission work to these towns. However, by 1894 it had become less impossible to approach the Muslims. Although the Anglican mission was for many years not allowed within the town of Isfahan and had to establish its centre in the suburb of Julfa which was mainly inhabited by Armenians, by about 1901 Muslim hostility had sufficiently abated for the C.M.S. school and hospital to move into the town of Isfahan itself. Two years later the headquarters of the Archbishop's Mission to the Assyrians was moved from Urmia to Van, on the Turkish side of the frontier.

By 1912, the mission had developed enough for a diocese of Iran, with C. Stileman as its first bishop, to be established.

61

In India, the Church at this time continued to expand, as is shown by the increase in the number of dioceses. After 1860, a great number of Lutherans in the Ranchi area had begged to be received into the Anglican Church, owing to dissension in their own. Bishop Milman for some time refused this, and only admitted them in 1869, when it was clearly impossible to reconcile them to the Lutheran Church. The S.P.G. became responsible for work here. A diocese of Chota Nagpur was established in 1890, with J. C. Whitley as the first bishop and Ranchi as the see-city. During the next few years, the Church here expanded rapidly, chiefly among the Indian people. A Dublin University Mission, which was started in 1892 in loose connection, like the Oxford and Cambridge missions, with the S.P.G., made Hazaribagh in this diocese its chief centre.

A diocese of Lucknow was formed in 1893. Besides Lucknow itself, where the C.M.S. had started a centre in 1858, this included Agra, where the C.M.S. had been active much earlier, and Cawnpore, where the S.P.G. had begun work in 1833. A Cawnpore Brotherhood was formed in 1895.

In Central India, a diocese of Nagpur was set up in 1902. In the south, another diocese, Dornakal, was cut off from Madras in 1912. This marks an epoch in that V. S. Azariah was chosen as its bishop; he was the first, and for a long time remained the only, Indian to be a diocesan bishop.

The Church in Ceylon after 1889 received help not only from the S.P.G. and the C.M.S. but also, in regard to women's work, from the C.E.Z.M.S. According to the 1901 census, there were thirty-two thousand Anglicans out of a total of three hundred and forty-nine thousand Christians (this was about one-tenth of the population, a considerably higher proportion than in any of the bigger countries of Asia; nine-tenths of the Christians were and are Roman Catholics).

Bishop Jermyn wrote in 1873 that with an increase in staff and financial resources, all the Buddhists in Ceylon could be won to Christianity within a generation; the Hindu Tamils he found more difficult to influence. But, since the end of the nineteenth century, there has been a great revival of Buddhism in Ceylon, partly under the influence of nationalist feeling; and Buddhists have begun to imitate Christian methods, for example, in starting Buddhist Sunday Schools and in establishing Ananda College. As a result, though the numerical strength of Anglicanism, and of Christians in general, has increased, the Church has grown lately only in proportion to the growth of the population as a whole.

In Burma the Church during this period went ahead quietly, almost entirely among the Karens; there was little response from the Buddhist Burmans. In 1914, Anglicans began to help some of the many blind people, and from 1917 to 1931 a blind English priest, W. H. Jackson, was in charge of what grew into a remarkable Blind School.

The C.E.Z.M.S. began at this time to help the Church in Malaya, and in 1900 it became responsible for a school for Chinese girls which had been maintained in Singapore since 1843 by the Society for Promoting Female Education in the East. A diocese of Singapore was constituted in 1909, comprising Malaya and such Anglican work as there might be in Thailand and Indonesia. There was a chaplain in Bangkok from 1893, and at times efforts were made, though never on a large scale, to spread the Gospel among the Thai; one or two schools were started, and parts of the Prayer Book, including the Holy Communion, were translated into the Thai language.

In Borneo these years were uneventful. Shortage of mission staff was a very limiting factor, and it was long before the diocese produced Asian clergy in any numbers.

It was not till after the U.S.A. had turned out the Spaniards and occupied the Philippine Islands in 1898 that any non-Roman could do anything to extend the Faith there. The Anglican clergymen who first went there to shepherd Anglicans among the American forces of occupation and the American officials were responsible to the Bishop of Shanghai. In 1901, however, Charles Henry Brent was appointed bishop, and quickly extended Anglican activities. Unlike the Free Churchmen, he did not work among the at least nominally Christian lowland people, but among the non-Christians, and partly among the well-established Chinese business community in Manila. For this work, priests were brought from China, and an important girls' school was founded. By degrees also, centres of work were established among the Igorots, wild head-hunting pagan tribes in the mountains on the island of Luzon. Here, at Sagada, Bontoc, and other places churches, schools, and a hospital were built. A mission was also established among the Moros (Muslims), pearl-divers, fishermen, and pirates on the coasts of Mindanao in the south; a hospital was established at Zamboanga, and some schools; and some people were won to the Faith. But, as is always the case among Muslims, progress was very slow. In 1914, there were twelve hundred

Anglican communicants, and considerably more baptized, in the Islands.

In China, these were very eventful years: the public attitude both to Christianity and to the West in general after a while changed very much for the better. While the numbers of church people in China, as in Japan, have always remained very small compared with those in India and Africa, the Church did now grow greatly.

During the last decade of the nineteenth century, the Church was still extending into many new areas. In Fukien, work was first begun in the important city of Kienyang in 1891. The opposition which the Church met in Fukien is illustrated by the killing in 1895 near Kucheng of nine missionaries and two of their children by members of an anti-Christian and anti-foreign vegetarian sect. Nevertheless, the numbers of Christians grew rapidly now, and came to be greater in Fukien than in any other province or diocese. The Dublin University Mission undertook in 1896 the support of Church work in Funing.

In the north, work was begun at Tientsin in 1890. At first it was mainly chaplaincy work, and by 1891, no more than fifty persons had been baptized by Anglicans in all North China; in the following seven years, two hundred and thirty were baptized.

In the west, Horsburgh of the C.M.S., after a visit to West Szech'uan in 1888, began work in 1891 in the district north of Ch'engtu, and a diocese of West China, with W. W. Cassells as its bishop, was formed in 1895—hitherto the Church there had been in the jurisdiction of the bishop at Ningpo, several weeks' journey away. In 1899 the C.M.S. opened a centre at Songpan, on the border of Tibet.

Almost all pastoral work in Chekiang was by 1898 being done by Chinese clergy, of whom there were now about sixteen. Y. K. Yen died in this year. He was certainly the ablest of the Yangtze Valley Chinese clergy in the nineteenth century; besides helping to lay the foundations of the Church in Wuhan, he taught in the early years at St John's University, and was long in charge of the Church of Our Saviour in Shanghai.

Work in what was later the diocese of Kwangsi-Hunan began in 1899, when Louis Byrde of the C.M.S. reached Kweilin, hoping by that route to penetrate into the still closed and very anti-foreign province of Hunan.

Reform and an openness to external influences were now in the air; but first there came a last outburst of reaction with the so-called Boxer Movement, which was favoured by the Empress-Dowager and by some, though by no means all, of the provincial governors. This movement was primarily anti-foreign and only incidentally anti-Christian. It caused great alarm to missionaries and Christians all over China. The non-mission foreign community had been restricted by Chinese law to the Treaty-ports, and now missionaries mostly withdrew to the coast. Actual loss of life was restricted to the north. The Anglican community was very small relative to other Christian Communions, and its losses were proportionately small, though on the last day of 1899, a young English deacon, S. M. J. Brooks, of the S.P.G., was killed in Shantung; two English clergymen and several Chinese church people were killed at Yungts'ing, fifty miles from Peking; and all the Church's buildings at Peking and Yungts'ing were destroyed. Many church people in North China seem to have compromised with the Boxers, and either burnt incense or paid money to them.

When the Boxer storm was past, China as a whole was more favourable to influences from outside than it had ever been before, or was again to be, and Christianity of all sorts made great advances.

The Church not only grew in size but became more mature. So far, there had been the various Anglican missions, working usually in areas remote from each other, and without any organic link between them. In 1897, and again in 1899, the Anglican bishops had met informally to consider common problems, and had discussed what common Chinese name should be used for the Anglican Church, and another such meeting was held in 1903. At a meeting in 1907, besides the bishops, two clergymen from each diocese were present, all of whom were Westerners. A more formal conference in 1909, including representative Chinese clergy and laymen, accepted a tentative constitution and canons, and after the Churches in England and America had expressed their approval, these were formally ratified at the first meeting of the General Synod at Shanghai in April 1912. There were by now ten Anglican dioceses in China.

The name Chung Hua Sheng Kung Huei (Holy Catholic Church of China) was adopted as the Church's title: this followed the example of the Anglican Church in Japan. Since the Chinese language has no article, the title does not suggest that Anglicans alone constitute the Catholic Church. Bishop C. P. Scott was chosen as the first Chairman of the House of Bishops. One of the General Synod's first acts was to establish a Board of Missions; and a fraternal letter was sent to all Christians in China, expressing a desire for the unity of all Christian people.

By 1901, there were already several Chinese parishes in Hongkong that were completely self-supporting financially, and two years later, St Stephen's College was founded there.

The establishment of new dioceses during these years was one expression of the Church's growth. A diocese of Shantung was cut off from North China in 1901, with G. D. Iliff as its first bishop; and along the Yangtze, the Church had expanded so much that a diocese of Hankow was formed in 1902, for which J. A. Ingle was chosen bishop, being succeeded after his death the next year by L. H. Roots. Church work was begun in Ch'angsha in 1902, the capital of the long xenophobic province of Hunan, and in the lower Yangtze area also, the Church now began work in such important places as Soochow (1902) and Nanking (1910).

A diocese of Fukien was formed in 1906—this had theretofore been in the diocese of Hongkong. From Kweilin in Kwangsi the Church advanced to Lingling and Hengyang in Hunan, and in 1909 a diocese of Kwangsi-Hunan was established. Work was first begun in Kiangsi in 1901 at Kiukiang, and some years later at Nanch'ang. A diocese, at first called Wuhu, but soon renamed Anking, was set up in 1912, comprising the Church's work in the two provinces of Anhuei and Kiangsi.

Canadian Anglicans had undertaken to be responsible for initiating work in the province of Honan, where previously Anglicans had done nothing, and in 1909 a Canadian, W. C. White, was therefore consecrated bishop of a new diocese of Honan. White had previously worked in Fukien, and took with him from there several Chinese catechists, whom he soon ordained, and a number of Canadian missionaries. K'aifeng and Kweiteh came to be their main centres.

The wide scope of the Church's work is shown by a technical school opened in 1907 at Ich'ang, primarily for destitute boys; the idea originated with a Chinese clergyman, through reading a life of Dr Barnardo. Some years later as many as a hundred and sixty boys were learning various trades there.

It was in that year also that the Cathedral of Our Saviour in Peking was consecrated. It was designed by Bishop C. P. Scott, a connection of Sir Gilbert Scott, who used, which was then most unusual, Chinese art-forms and a Chinese architectural style.

After 1912 the Church grew mainly by working more thoroughly in areas where a footing had already been obtained. But even now work was started in some new areas: in Yunnan, for example, Anglican Christianity began about 1916. For long there was little but a Church hospital in Kunming, partly because other Communions were already active there. And in the same year, the C.H.S.K.H. Board of Missions began work in Sian, Shensi, the city to which Alopen, the first Christian missionary to China, had come in A.D. 635. The mission staff there were, and continued to be, all Chinese from the older dioceses; most of them came from the Yangtze valley, and found conditions of life, food, and climate very trying in Sian.

Our account of the Church in China during these years concludes fittingly with the consecration of the first Chinese Anglican bishop, Shen Tsai-sen, who was chosen Assistant Bishop of Chekiang in 1918.

The English bishops in China had urged the Church of England to undertake a mission in Korea, and it was eventually decided to appoint a bishop to inaugurate Anglican work there. In 1889 C. J. Corfe, a former naval chaplain, who had also done mission work in North China, was appointed, and reached Korea the next year. With him came an American doctor, E. B. Landis, who opened a hospital at Inchon, the port of Seoul. Next year a woman doctor and a nurse came, and a women's hospital was started in Seoul. Sisters of the Community of St Peter, Kilburn, joined the mission in 1892; they established an orphanage, and did nursing and other work; but it was long before there were any signs of vocation to the religious life among Korean women.

Corfe's plan was that the mission staff, while not taking any vows, were to be unmarried and live a common life; and that for the first five or six years they should refrain from direct evangelistic work, and prepare themselves by study of the language, literature, customs, and thought of the country. Till 1895, Korea was nominally subject to China, and after that increasingly subject to Japan, which in 1910 openly annexed it.

The first few Anglican catechumens were formally enrolled at Christmas 1896; the next year three of them were baptized and confirmed, and by 1900 there were about twenty baptized adherents and twenty catechumens. The staff did not expand as much as was hoped. What was founded as the Korean Mission Brotherhood, under H. H. Kelly, developed into the Society of the Sacred Mission at Kelham. Some Anglicans thought that since Roman Catholics had long been active in Korea, Anglicans should not intrude there, or else that it should be left to the Russian Orthodox; but of course there was scope, and indeed great need, for other Christian Communions also.

When Bishop Corfe retired in 1904, there were two hundred baptized Anglicans, including some Japanese, in Korea. He was succeeded as bishop by A. Turner, and during the next few years, many Koreans poured into all Christian Communions, including the Anglican, not a few of them chiefly from a desire to obtain help against the hereditary foe, Japan, which was increasingly controlling the country. Those who became Christians were mostly the poorer farmers. By 1900, there were over three thousand Anglicans, but after that came an inevitable reaction. Korean church people had from the first been impressed with the duty of giving to the Church, and under Turner a diocesan clergy fund was established for the payment of Korean clergy.

A. Turner was succeeded as bishop by M. N. Trollope (1911–30), who had been one of the original pioneers. Corfe's episcopate has been called a time of pioneering; that of Turner was marked by extension, that of Trollope by consolidation. In 1914 Trollope ordained the first two Korean Anglican deacons, and the next year Mark Kim became the first Korean priest.

In Japan it was only in 1889 that the Constitution explicitly granted religious liberty. During the eighteen-eighties, Western things had been very popular in Japan; there had even been talk of a national adoption of Christianity as the religion of the modern world. After this, however, there was something of a nationalist reaction from Western things and what were supposed to be such, and Christianity became less popular. Nevertheless, owing to the good foundations which had been laid, the S.K.K. grew rapidly; by 1897 it had six thousand adherents and in 1901 ten thousand.

Canadian Anglicans began a mission at Nagoya in 1889, and in this year the first Japanese, Imai, was ordained to the Anglican priesthood. Bishop Williams retired now, and was succeeded four years later by J. McKim.

The Anglicans in 1894 planned six dioceses to cover all Japan: the dioceses of South Tokyo, Osaka (including Kobe), Hokkaido, and Kyushu to be assisted by the English, those of Tokyo and Kyoto to be helped by the Americans.

Bishop Bickersteth's untimely death in 1897 was a great loss to the Japanese Church; he had a far-seeing mind and statesmanlike judgement. Through him, the Brotherhood of St Andrew and the Society of St Hilda (a religious community) came to Japan.

The three Anglican missions had each established some sort of a divinity school. These joined in 1911, and, with the aid of a big grant from the Pan-Anglican Congress, established the Central Theological College in connection with St Paul's University in Tokyo, where from henceforth nearly all the Japanese clergy were trained. Many Japanese Episcopalians were anxious to have Japanese rather than foreign bishops, but at the same time felt that the stipends of Japanese bishops should not come from abroad, so efforts were made to raise endowment funds for a Japanese episcopate.

In view of the provision by the goverment of primary schools, there was little place for Christian schools of this grade, but from 1905 not a few Church kindergartens were established. A diocese of Mid-Japan was set up in 1912, to be helped by the Church of England in Canada. The S.K.K. in 1914 had about twenty-three thousand baptized members.

III. AUSTRALIA AND NEW ZEALAND

As more and more of Australia, especially the west and north, was settled, the Church naturally expanded. In Western Australia also the population increased greatly after the discovery of gold in 1891, and the growth of the Church was marked by the formation of other dioceses. Bunbury (1903), North-West Australia (1907), Kalgoorlie (1914), and in 1914 an ecclesiastical Province of Western Australia was established.

The mission in New Guinea, begun in 1891, was organized into a diocese in 1898. New dioceses had been set up in Queensland (1878), Rockampton (1892), and Carpentaria (1900), and a province of Queensland was formed in 1905, with the diocese of New Guinea included in it.

In the older districts, as well as in the newer areas, the church had been growing and new dioceses were established. By 1905, there were in Victoria five dioceses, Melbourne, Ballarat, Bendigo, Gippsland, and Wangaratta, and an ecclesiastical Province of Victoria was set up. After 1914, the original Province of Australia was represented by the Province of New South Wales. Up till 1900, Sydney was the primatial see, but it was then decided that the Primate should in future be chosen from among the existing Metropolitans.

The General Synod in 1901 set up the Australian College of Theology to promote higher standards of theological study than were otherwise available.

IV. AFRICA

In Nigeria, Samuel Adjai Crowther died in 1891 at the age of eighty-five, after twenty-seven years as bishop. The experiment of appointing an African diocesan bishop seemed, as things were then, not to have been altogether successful, and Crowther was succeeded by a European,

J. S. Hill, with two African assistant bishops, S. Phillips and I. Oluwole. The title of the diocese was changed to "Western Equatorial Africa". Hill died soon after reaching West Africa, and was replaced by H. Tugwell.

Discipline was gradually restored and the Church continued to grow. Another African, James Johnson, was appointed assistant bishop in 1900, with the Niger Delta as his special sphere, and the Church there became virtually independent of C.M.S. help. It was about this time, too, that the Church first spread to the strongly Muslim region of Northern Nigeria, though here its growth has been very slow.

By 1914, there were in Nigeria about fifty-two thousand baptized Anglicans: the great majority were in the Yoruba country in the west, a number on the Niger, Ibos, and only five hundred in the north. There were relatively few Christians other than Anglicans in this region.

Division of the diocese of Western Equatorial Africa became necessary, and in 1919 the larger and western part of Nigeria, with most of the north, was constituted the diocese of Lagos, with F. Melville-Jones as its bishop; while the south-east was formed into the diocese of the Niger, for which B. Lasbrey was consecrated.

In the early days, few of the clergy in Liberia were negroes, but for thirty-one years till his death in 1916 a negro, S. D. Ferguson, was bishop. He moved the see-city from Cape Palmas to Monrovia, and founded Cuttington College at Cape Palmas, to train clergy, catechists, and teachers. The 576 communicants of 1890 had by 1915 increased to 2,501. Ferguson was succeeded by a white American.

After a long lapse, Anglican mission work on the Gold Coast resumed in 1904, when the S.P.G. again undertook work there, and a bishop, N. T. Hamlyn, was appointed, at first as a suffragan in the then diocese of Western Equatorial Africa. A diocese of Accra, covering the Gold Coast, was founded in 1909.

A conference of Anglican bishops in West Africa as early as 1906 advocated the formation of an ecclesiastical province, but this was not to come for many years.

In South Africa, white settlement extended considerably towards the north during this period, not least with the discovery of diamonds and gold on the Witwatersrand: this was a challenge of immense importance to the Church. And the Church of the Province of South Africa continued in this period to grow both extensively and intensively. An English priest, W. Greenstock, made his way to Bulawayo in 1876, some time before this area came under British rule, and had an interview with the great chief Lobengula who agreed to allow a mission to be started among his people. Next year the S.P.G. agreed to undertake this, but was prevented by the first Boer war. Knight-Bruce, recently appointed Bishop of Bloemfontein, trekked north to Bulawayo, Mashonaland, and the Zambezi in 1888, on a pioneer tour of investigation. Two years later Southern Rhodesia came under the British flag, and in 1891 the Provincial Synod decided to establish a missionary diocese of Mashonaland and the adjacent territories, and chose Knight-Bruce as the first bishop, with Umtali as the first diocesan centre. But in 1894, after another long tour round the area, Knight-Bruce had to resign with his health shattered. For the first few years there was little to show, though there were Church centres at Bulawayo, Salisbury, and elsewhere, and the industrial mission of St Augustine's, Penhalonga, was started near Umtali. Since the London Mission was active in Matabeleland, the Anglicans did not at first attempt anything there; later, however, when many British settlers, most of whom were Anglican at least in name, came there, the Anglicans could not but minister to them; and later they also extended the Faith among the Matabele. From 1915 to 1951, this diocese was known as Southern Rhodesia.

The South African Church Railway Mission was started in 1892 to shepherd both those who worked on the railway and the scattered settlers living near the line.

Bishop West Jones suggested as early as 1875 that a diocese of Lebombo should be constituted in Portuguese East Africa, where many of the Rand miners had their homes, and in 1893 W. E. Smyth, doctor as well as priest, was consecrated for this diocese, being at first the only clergyman in it. All services here had and have by law to be in Portuguese, the vernacular African language being forbidden.

A. Hamilton Baynes was in 1893 consecrated bishop for "Natal and Maritzburg", and from 1894 was known as Bishop of Natal. The Colenso group had failed to procure a successor to Colenso; they called themselves "Church of England in South Africa", and were alarmed by the fact that, according to the Constitution of the Church of the Province, a cleric who would be acquitted in England might in South Africa be condemned for heresy, and vice versa. Some of them returned to the Church of the Province when the Lambeth Conference, though declining to create an authoritative and binding Court of Appeal, agreed to establish a Consultative Body.

The occupant of the see of Cape Town had from 1897 the title of Archbishop. In the Pretoria diocese, where in 1878 there had been, besides the bishop, only three priests and two deacons, by 1899 the clergy numbered thirty-two, but during the Boer war, Anglican work in the Transvaal had for the most part to be suspended.

A Bantu Methodist minister named J. M. Dwane led a considerable number of Bantu Methodists to secede from their Church and set up what they called the Ethiopian Church; claiming to be descendants of Ethiopians who gradually worked their way through Africa to the South, they represented a revolt against the denationalization of Africans. After a time Dwane asked the Church of the Province to receive him and his followers, numbering about ten thousand, into the Church, and the bishops agreed to form them into an "Order of Ethiopia" within the Church to be under the direct control of the bishop in each diocese; most of them were in the Grahamstown diocese. Dwane himself was ordained in 1900, and the group later increased in numbers.

The diocese of Pretoria was strengthened by help from the Community of the Resurrection in 1903. Michael Furse became bishop in 1909, when W. M. Carter was translated to Cape Town, and the diocese grew rapidly. When Furse returned to England in 1920, he was succeeded by Neville Talbot. Two new dioceses were established in 1911: George being cut off from Cape Town, and Kimberley and Kuruman from Bloemfontein.

In Uganda, after some further opposition, this period saw tremendous advance. The Muslim chiefs got control for a time in 1888, and the leading Christian chiefs were either put to death or expelled from the country, but when Mackay died of a fever in the capital in 1890, the worst of the repression was over. Alfred Tucker became bishop in this year.

There was a fresh outbreak of persecution in 1897, and George Pilkington, the best linguist of the mission group, who was mainly responsible for the translation of the Bible into Luganda, lost his life in an internal disturbance. But on the whole Tucker's episcopate (he resigned in 1911) saw something of a mass movement to the Church in Uganda. While in 1890 there were hardly two hundred baptized, by 1914 there were ninety thousand baptized Baganda Anglicans. On Trinity Sunday 1893, six Baganda were made deacons, the first Anglican clergymen of their race. A cathedral seating about two thousand persons was built about 1895 on Namirembe, "the Hill of Peace", at Kampala; most of its cost being contributed by Africans.

The diocese of East Equatorial Africa, which comprised Uganda, Kenya, and so much of what is now Tanganyika as was not in the U.M.C.A. sphere, was divided in 1897, Tucker choosing to stay on as Bishop of Uganda, while W. G. Peel became Bishop of the diocese of Mombasa.

After 1901, when the railway from the coast reached the Lake, Uganda became very much more exposed to modern and Western influences, by no means all good; but the Church went forward. Tucker was a statesman, and prepared a Constitution for the diocese which was finally adopted in 1907. Till 1924, all education was left to the Anglican and Roman missions.

Meanwhile, to the south, the U.M.C.A. mission too was going forward. The first African priest in this area was ordained in 1890, and a new diocese of Nyasaland was established in 1892, with W. B. Hornby as the first bishop; the rest of the U.M.C.A. area was now renamed the diocese of Zanzibar and East Africa. The centre of the Nyasaland diocese was on Likoma Island in Lake Nyasa, where a cathedral was built on ground which had been used for the burning of witches. Frank Weston was Bishop of Zanzibar from 1908. Another diocese, Northern Rhodesia, was formed in 1910.

In Madagascar, a cathedral of St Lawrence was consecrated in 1889. During the following decade, Church work was much disturbed by French invasions, and a number of Christians were murdered in wars between the Malagasy tribes, and many village churches destroyed. G. L. King succeeded Cornish as bishop in 1899. French rule now put many obstacles in the way of the Anglicans, and no new church might according to law be built unless at least eighty people petitioned for it. But if the Church suffered in consequence as regards numbers, it gained in quality; the number of clergy rose to eight English and twenty-two Malagasy, and by 1914 there were fourteen thousand Anglicans baptized. A constitution and canons were adopted in 1918.

In Egypt, though the C.M.S. maintained some schools, and a medical mission had been started at Old Cairo in 1888, progress in building up a Christian community was exceedingly slow, and, mainly because of the existence of the large ancient Egyptian or Coptic Church, Anglicanism has never been active there on a large scale.

When the Sudan first came under British administration at the end of the nineteenth century, the British authorities would not allow mission work for fear of provoking Muslim riots. Before 1914, however, the

C.M.S. had been able to start medical mission work in Omdurman, and had opened several schools in and around Khartoum. In the Southern Sudan, where most of the population was not Muslim but pagan, there was not the same difficulty in starting mission work. It was not, however, much before 1914 that the C.M.S. began in this area.

In North Africa, elsewhere than in Egypt, there has been virtually no Anglican work, except for a few chaplaincies for British residents. At the end of the nineteenth century, an archdeacon supervised the chaplains in the Canary Islands and Madeira, both of which were then in the jurisdiction of the Bishop of Sierra Leone.

6

1920–1956

SINCE the Lambeth Conference of 1920, Anglicanism has not extended to any new large area of the world. In many areas, however, its numerical strength has increased greatly, and so new dioceses have been established. In the Younger Churches of Asia and Africa, as happened earlier in the English-speaking countries outside Europe, the great bulk of the clergy and bishops have come to be nationals of the country concerned, rather than expatriates from the British Isles or America. Nearly everywhere the Anglican Communion has clearly, whether or not it has greatly increased in numbers, become much stronger and more firmly established. On the other hand, opposition to it, whether in the form of sheer indifference to anything except material well-being, or of a nationalism antagonistic to anything which seems to come from Europe or America, or as a revival of old non-Christian religions, or as the rise of such a new religion as Communism, has also increased greatly. If the Anglican Communion is to-day more strongly rooted than ever before, it is also faced by more menacing and powerful rivals than ever before.

I. AMERICA

Because of difficulties and expense of transport, the Provincial Synod of the West Indies has so far consisted only of one house, that of bishops[1]. The diocese of the Windward Islands first had a bishop of its own in 1927—till then it had been administered by the Bishop of Barbados. The Church in Barbados is now in process of being disestablished; and the financial aid hitherto received from the Government is to cease.

[1] A meeting has now (1957) been planned to include, for the first time, besides the bishops of the Province, clerical and lay representatives from each diocese.

A large proportion of the population of the West Indies is now at least nominally Christian, and much of it is Anglican, though in Trinidad, which long belonged to Spain, Roman Catholicism is still dominant. Many of the clergy in the West Indies still come from England, but the numbers of the coloured clergy are increasing. Of the eight bishops, three are themselves West Indians, and the Bishop of Nassau an American. The Church is to a large extent self-supporting financially, but in recent years, because of the decline in the sugar-cane trade, the West Indian islands have become poorer; moreover, they constantly suffer great damage from hurricanes, so the Church's financial position is very difficult.

In the same area are six dioceses established by the missions of the American Protestant Episcopal Church: Cuba, Haiti, Puerto Rico, the Dominican Republic, the Panama Canal Zone, and the Virgin Islands. The diocese of Cuba uses a Spanish, the diocese of Haiti a French, translation of the American Prayer Book. These dioceses have not joined the ecclesiastical Province of the West Indies, but count as an integral part of the American Church, and are represented in its General Convention. In the West Indies there are well over a million Anglican church people.

The Anglican Church is numerically relatively small in the U.S.A., Roman Catholics, Baptists, Methodists, Lutherans, and Presbyterians, in this order, being more numerous, especially the first three; it has between two and three million baptized members, and a clergy of seven thousand, but its influence is much greater than its numbers would suggest. It has always included many prominent people—nine Presidents of the U.S.A. have been Anglicans, considerably more than have belonged to any other Communion. In the past, it has sometimes seemed to be a Church of the upper classes, and has neglected the less educated; but this position is changing. It is strongest in the towns of the eastern states, and in New York City alone has over a hundred parishes. In the south, where it was the established Church before the Revolution, it never regained its prominent position, and has long had relatively few adherents. It includes, like the Church of England, those who stress specially the Catholic aspect, and others who stress especially the Evangelical and Liberal aspects, of Anglicanism.

The Canadian Church had long been becoming more and more completely independent financially of the Church of Engand, and now is so completely: help from the C.M.S. ceased in 1920, from the S.P.G. in 1939. For a number of years it has helped the work of the Church in what is now the diocese of Amritsar in North India with staff and finance, and formerly it supported a diocese in both China and Japan.

Till 1955, the Anglican body in Canada was called the Church of England in Canada. But such a name was a handicap to its growth, inasmuch as many of the inhabitants of Canada are descendants of immigrants from the European Continent rather than the British Isles; and therefore the General Synod then formally changed the Church's name to "the Anglican Church in Canada". Anglicans form only about one-seventh of the population of Canada—they number about one and three quarter millions—compared with five million Roman Catholics, and two and a quarter million adherents of the United Church of Canada. The Anglican Church has four provinces and twenty-nine dioceses. Newfoundland stood aside when a Province was formed in 1861, but in 1948 rejoined the Church of England in Canada. Its clergy numbers seventeen hundred and sixty.

There are in Canada about a hundred and ten thousand Red Indians among whom Anglicans helped by the English C.M.S., have done considerable work. About a quarter of them are Anglicans, and some have been ordained. Most of the fifteen thousand Eskimos scattered over Northern Canada have become Anglicans, indeed, in Canada's Far North, only the Anglican and Roman Churches attempt anything. The Bible and the Prayer Book have, of course, both been translated into the languages of the Red Indians and (in part) of the Eskimos.

The number of British residents and of Anglican church people in South America had tended to decline in recent years, and the two English Anglican dioceses were united in 1946. The American diocese in Southern Brazil was in 1949 divided into three dioceses, two of which now have Brazilian bishops.

II. ASIA

The situation in Palestine after the First World War was very unlike what it had been before. The country was no longer part of the Turkish Empire, but was administered by Britain, under League of Nations Mandate, and there was a steady flow of Jewish immigration which came radically to transform the country. In contrast with the previous period, the Muslim law of apostasy was no longer effective, and there was in theory, and to a large extent in practice, complete freedom of religion, including the right to change one's religion. Nevertheless, there continued to be many cases when Muslims or Jews who became Christians were cruelly ill-treated by adherents of their former faith. Jewish, Muslim, and other children worked happily together, even at times of great racial tension, in the Anglican schools, and these were one of the few reconciling influences; indeed, till the end of the Mandate in 1948 secondary education was largely an Anglican responsibility.

During the fighting between Jews and Arabs which followed the end of the Mandate, the Church suffered great loss and was much disorganized. The partition into Israel and Jordan, and the removal of great masses of Arabs, among whom Christianity had made much more headway than among the Jews, greatly handicapped the Church's work. Owing to the great Jewish immigration and the high Muslim birth-rate, Christians of all sorts are a diminishing part of the population, and have in recent years declined from ten per cent. to less than eight per cent., the great majority of them belonging to the Orthodox or Lesser Eastern Churches, or else to the Roman Church. In Israel and Jordan together there are about four thousand baptized Anglicans, the great majority of whom are Arab by race.

After 1920, the Anglican diocese of Jerusalem[1] no longer included the Anglican mission in Egypt. But in 1931 the Anglican chaplaincies in Iraq were added to the jurisdiction of the Bishop in Jerusalem, who was already responsible for such Anglican work as there was (only a few chaplaincies) in Cyprus and Syria. In Jordan especially, the Anglicans have given not a little help to the Orthodox, chiefly with their schools.

In Iran, as in most predominantly Muslim countries, the Church has found it exceedingly difficult to make much progress, and has remained very small. The Anglicans have about twelve hundred adherents, of whom about half are baptized; the majority are ex-Muslims, while a considerable minority were Jews or Armenian Christians.

Anglican work is in five main centres, Isfahan (the diocesan centre), Teheran (the capital), Shiraz, Yezd, and Kerman. Some years after the First World War, the B.C.M.S. undertook work in Iran, and the Church Missions to Jews have been active in Teheran and maintained large schools there. But most Anglican work was supported by the C.M.S. which conducted eight hospitals. J. H. Linton succeeded C. Stileman as bishop in 1919, and was succeeded by W. J. Thompson in 1935.

In 1941, all Christian schools, including the well-known Stuart

[1] A new Archbishopric of Jerusalem has been formed (1957) with jurisdiction over Anglican work in Egypt and Libya, Iran, the Sudan, Jordan, Syria and Lebanon, as well as Jerusalem, Israel, Cyprus, and the Persian Gulf.

Memorial College at Isfahan, had to be closed or handed over to the government. In 1953, during the period of tension between Iran and Britain, the bishop was expelled, and no Anglican clergy of any nationality were allowed to enter the country; eighteen months later, however, the bishop was allowed back.

As communications improved, a growing desire was felt, especially since Christians were relatively so few in number, for unity between the Anglicans, mainly in south Persia, and the Presbyterians, mainly in the north. A scheme was worked out, somewhat on the lines of the Church of South India. But in 1947 the Presbyterians broke off negotiations; a majority of them had originally been Assyrian Christians, and were fearful of episcopacy in any form.

For Anglicans in India, one of the chief events of the twentieth century was the organization of the Church of India, Burma, and Ceylon as a fully self-governing member of the Anglican Communion. The bishops, it is true, had long urged the establishment of Church government by synods, and diocesan conferences or councils had been set up, but these were purely deliberative bodies, and had no legal status. Up to 1930, Anglicanism in India was legally a part of the Church of England, and was bound by all the rules and regulations of the English Church. For example, translations of the Prayer Book into Indian languages had to reproduce, down to the smallest detail, the Prayer Book of 1662. In some respects, indeed, Anglicanism was even more closely associated with the State of India than it was in England. In order that British residents should not lack spiritual care, the government paid the salaries of three bishops, and in part of three other bishops, of a number of arch-deacons, and of about a hundred and forty chaplains.[1] Those bishops were appointed by the British Crown under Letters Patent, on the recommendation of the Secretary of State for India.

Its establishment had long been a handicap to Anglicanism in India. Political authority was, from the early years of the century, transferred by degrees from the British government to Indians; but it was clearly impossible to transfer control over the Church to secular councils composed mainly of Hindus and Muslims. Consequently, the Anglican leaders in India themselves proposed a severance of the tie, and in 1927 the Indian Church Measure was passed by the British Parliament, and took effect in 1930. The government continued, indeed, to pay the

[1] It has to be remembered that over a quarter of the professing Anglicans in India were then Europeans, not Indians.

salaries of a number of chaplains; but the Church became free of control by the government, whether British or Indian. An endowment fund was started to make good so far as possible the loss of salaries previously paid by the State. The new Indian Church Constitution, after being considered by the new diocesan synods, was finally approved by the General Synod in 1928. After this all bishops were elected by representative bodies, overwhelmingly Indian in membership, and with a strong lay element, and Indians, in consequence, began to feel as never before that the Church was really Indian.

Anglicans in India received and receive help in staff and finance not only from English Anglicans; the Scottish Episcopal Church has long given regular help to the diocese of Nagpur, and the Church of Ireland, through the Dublin University Mission, to the diocese of Chota Nagpur. The area which is now the diocese of Amritsar and was formerly in the diocese of Lahore has been greatly helped by Canadian Anglicans, and Australian Anglicans have helped, for example, in Hyderabad. The American Episcopal Church in 1931 undertook to give regular help to the Church in India, and in 1933 its first representative came to the Dornakal diocese. On the other hand, more and more the Indian Church has been coming to rely on itself, as regards both leadership and finance, and Indian Anglicans had a considerable share in the Indian Mission of Fellowship to Britain in 1932, the leader of which was Bishop Bannerjee.

A number of new dioceses formed during these years witness to the growth of the Church; and, most significantly, it has come to be somewhat exceptional for a priest from overseas to be chosen bishop. A new diocese of Nasik was cut off from the diocese of Bombay in 1930; Canon Tarafdar, an Indian, was consecrated in 1935 to be Assistant Bishop of Calcutta; a diocese of Bhagalpur was cut off from Calcutta in 1943; C. K. Jacob was elected Bishop of Travancore, its first Indian bishop in 1945; N. K. Biswas, an Indian who before ordination had reached a high position in the medical world, became Bishop of Assam in 1946, and on his death in 1948 was succeeded by J. Amritanand. In April 1947, a new diocese of Delhi was formed, comprising an area which had been partly in the Lahore diocese, partly in Nagpur, and A. N. Mukerjee, who in 1940 had been appointed the first Indian head of the Cambridge Mission to Delhi, became the first bishop. In 1950 Mukerjee became Bishop of Calcutta, and so was the first Indian to be Metropolitan. A diocese of Amritsar was set up in 1953, comprising that part of the former Lahore diocese which is now in the Indian Union; it elected a Canadian priest, C. R. H. Wilkinson, as its bishop.

Numerically, the chief strength of the Indian Church was for long in the four southern dioceses of Madras, Travancore and Cochin, Tinnevelly, and Dornakal. By the time of the Second World War, there were in the diocese of Tinnevelly alone well over a hundred thousand baptized Anglicans, and the Indian clergy, numbering about a hundred, were almost entirely financed by their own church people. The Church's growth there had been more before 1900 than in the following half-century.

Dornakal diocese, however, grew phenomenally in this century; almost all the Christians there were of outcaste origin. By 1941, when the centenary of the start of Anglican work in that area was kept, there were, including unbaptized catechumens, two hundred and twenty-two thousand Anglicans, three-quarters of whom had become Christians in the last twenty-five years, with a clergy of a hundred and sixty Indians, and ten Europeans. In January 1939 eight bishops from Japan, Africa, Britain, and India met at Dornakal to consecrate the new cathedral. The architecture of this church was a notable attempt, designed by Bishop Azariah himself, to blend the Saracenic and Dravidian styles, symbolizing the Muslim and Hindu traditions of India, which find their reconciliation and goal in Christ. It combined the big open square of a Muslim mosque with the pillars and ornaments of Hindu temples, surmounted with crosses. Bishop V. S. Azariah died in 1945 at the age of seventy. He was succeeded by an English diocesan with an Indian assistant bishop.

As we shall see when we consider Anglican worship, Anglicanism had in India, and more especially, perhaps, in the southern dioceses, probably gone further than Anglicanism elsewhere (or, for that matter, than other denominations anywhere), to express itself in Eastern forms. Various ashrams were founded whose inmates lived a monastic or community life under Indian forms. A number of Indians lived as Christian sannyasis or sadhus, or Indian holy men, wandering from place to place in the utmost simplicity, and with no fixed provision for their needs, proclaiming the Faith wherever they went. Sundar Singh, by birth a Sikh, who is believed to have lost his life in Tibet, or in the Himalayas while trying to enter Tibet, in about 1929, was an outstanding example of this form of Christian devotion.

When in 1947 India became independent, government grants for chaplains inevitably ceased, and much difficulty resulted for the Church as regards both finance and staff. But the new government undertook to continue the previous regime's policy of religious freedom, and this it is in fact for the most part doing. Many threats had been made by groups of Hindus that, when independence was achieved, non-Hindus would be massacred. In one area, in consequence, while some Christian villages remained faithful many others apostatized. Elsewhere, though it had been expected that at least half the Church community would under threats at once deny the Faith, none in the event did so.

The four Southern dioceses, comprising a majority of the Anglican Christians in India, in 1947 entered the new Church of South India (formed in that year of those who had been Anglicans, Methodists, Congregationalists, and Presbyterians) and so ceased to belong to the Anglican Communion. They form about half the new Church. About thirty thousand, however, in the Nandyal area of the former Dornakal diocese, with three deacons and eighteen priests, preferred to continue as Anglicans, and it was arranged that a commissary appointed by the Metropolitan should be responsible for their pastoral supervision. More recently the Commissary has been consecrated, and has the status of a bishop assistant to the Metropolitan. Before the C.S.I. was set up, there were in India about a million Anglicans (in twelve dioceses); now there are about four hundred thousand.

In Pakistan, the numbers of church people have continued to be relatively small; out of a total population of seventy millions, only about half a million are Christian at all. There are in West Pakistan about eighty thousand, in East Pakistan about seven thousand five hundred, baptized members of the Church of India, Pakistan, Burma, and Ceylon, the former constituting the diocese of Lahore as it is now, while for the latter a new diocese of East Pakistan has been formed.

Though the S.P.G. has given some help at Lahore and Rawal Pindi, mission work in Pakistan has been mainly the concern of the C.M.S., which for long maintained a notable chain of hospitals along the North-West Frontier, partly to influence and aid Afghans who might cross the border. An Indian, J. S. C. Bannerjee, was in 1931 appointed Assistant Bishop in the Lahore diocese.

At the time of the partition of India, the Church rendered great services to the refugees, both Hindu and Muslim. The Church in Pakistan had an anxious time then, and in some places church people are said to have starved rather than deny their Master, as their Muslim neighbours pressed them to do. Pakistani church people, or their ancestors, seem in origin mostly to have been low-caste Hindus, and are economically a very under-privileged community; comparatively few of them are literate. A number of Hindus, too poor to leave Pakistan at the Partition, apparently thinking it impossible to be Hindus in a Muslim state, have become Christians; but the Church cannot hope for much new strength from this, except from the children of these people. The Christian educational institutions have declined to teach the Qu'ran, as they were asked to do, but for the present at least they are allowed to continue.

The Anglicans in Ceylon in 1933 joined with the Free Churches in a united evangelistic campaign in Colombo, which was later imitated in other parts of the island, and in a Five Year Forward Movement, launched in India in 1935 but extending to Ceylon, and carried on largely by the laity.

M. B. Carpenter-Garnier, who had been bishop since 1924, resigned in 1938, and was succeeded by C. D. Horsley, who in turn was followed in 1948 by A. R. Graham-Campbell.

A division of the diocese had for some time been desired, and as a step towards this Lakdasa de Mel was in 1945 consecrated Assistant Bishop, with charge of the Kandy district. In 1946 it was decided that a new diocese of Kurunagala should be formed, and this was done in 1950. De Mel became bishop of the new diocese, which covered a mainly village area in the interior, and had about twenty priests and five thousand church people. The two dioceses together had in 1953 a clergy of about a hundred and forty, of whom only about ten were Europeans. The 1951 census showed eight hundred thousand Christians in a population of eight millions, including sixty thousand Anglicans; this was about eight thousand more than Church statistics claimed, the balance presumably being church people who had moved to districts with no organized Church life. Anglicans outnumber the adherents of all the Free Churches put together.

Unlike in India, where Christianity has spread largely among the outcastes, in Ceylon the Gospel has attracted all classes equally. Anglicanism, indeed, has tended here to be a Church of the intelligentsia, and to suffer from lack of contact with, and understanding of, the manual workers. However, one consequence has been that church people have been the more able to finance their Church without aid from overseas; and in the thirties the diocese took over responsibility for almost all the work previously financed by the C.M.S. and the S.P.G. The Church, too, became more firmly rooted and naturalized in Ceylon. This was to be seen partly in Sinhalese forms of Church worship, and also, for example, in the chapel of Trinity College, Kandy, where both the architectural plan and the carving of wood and stone were in the ancient Sinhalese style.

Aggressive and nationalistic Buddhism has caused increasing difficulty to the Church, and most of all perhaps to Church schools. Non-Christian children may not now attend Christian worship or instruction without the written consent of their parents. Nearly all Anglican and other Christian primary and secondary schools have entered the government's free education scheme; but St Thomas', Colombo, Trinity College, Kandy, and Ladies' College, Colombo, remain independent. The opening of a new Christian school, other than Roman Catholic, has been made virtually impossible.

Partly because of the pressure of revived Buddhism, Anglicans have as we shall see in a later chapter, since 1932 been negotiating concerning Church unity with Methodists, Presbyterians, Baptists, and the North Ceylon district of the South India United Church, originally mainly Congregationalist and Presbyterian, which since 1947 has been included in the Church of South India.

A mission among the Kachins and Shans, hill-tribes in the North of Burma, was begun by the B.C.M.S. in 1924. A plan to divide the diocese of Rangoon was frustrated by the Second World War; by that time the diocese had about fifty clergymen, and including English and Indians, about twenty thousand baptized members, the Baptists, the main and almost only Free Church body, being much more numerous. The Asian clergy were trained at the College of the Holy Cross in Rangoon.

The Church in Burma suffered greatly during the War. Some church people were prevailed upon to renounce the Faith, though many faced death or torture in remaining loyal to their Lord, and some Church buildings, including the Cathedral, were desecrated. Services, which could not be held in church, were held in the homes, and when that was impossible, in the jungle.

A Burman, John Aung Hla, and a Karen, Francis Ah Mya, became assistant bishops in 1949–50, the first Asian bishops in Burma.

Anglican work in the Singapore diocese has never been strongly staffed. In 1924 there were, besides four Tamil priests and two Tamil deacons, three Chinese priests and two Chinese deacons, and a dozen European priests, but only one of the latter devoted all his time to mission, as distinct from chaplaincy, work. Nor had any considerable effort been made to win Malays to the Faith.

During the Second World War, though the European clergy were interned, Church services and activities could continue, and after the war, Anglicans, Methodists, and Presbyterians established a united theological college. In 1947 there were about fifteen thousand Anglicans in Malaya, out of a total of a hundred and twenty thousand Christians.

In Borneo there had for a number of years been one or two Chinese priests when the first Sea Dyak was ordained an Anglican priest in 1924. Much use was made of a mission launch for visiting centres to which the only approach was by river.

The establishment of an Oriental clergy was now stressed, but provision of adequate training for them was a difficult matter. The Community of the Resurrection opened a theological college at Kuching in 1934, but this had to close in 1937, by which time the Anglican community in the diocese numbered about twelve thousand five hundred. Considerable progress had been made in taking traditional customs, for example with regard to honouring the dead, into Church use, and the whole New Testament had by now been translated into Sea Dyak, though not yet into Land Dyak. In that same year, the Oriental clergy in this diocese first outnumbered the European clergy.

Services were faithfully maintained, though often under great difficulties by Asian clergy and church people, under the Japanese occupation during the war, when great damage was done to churches, schools, and other church property. After the war, when North Borneo, Labuan, and Sarawak were unified as a British colony, the diocese was given a new designation, as the diocese of Borneo. Church services have to be held in at least six different languages: Hakka and Hokien Chinese, Malay, Sea Dyak, Land Dyak, and English. The diocese now has a ministry of about eleven Europeans, five Sea Dyaks, four Chinese, and two Land Dyaks.

Mosher succeeded Brent as Bishop of the Philippines in 1920. The Anglicans were more active than any other denomination among the important Chinese community, and maintained a leading hospital in Manila, St Luke's, with which an orphanage and other institutions were associated. Among the Moros, the Church of St Francis in Upi was the centre of a promising work, and by 1939, the diocese as a whole had seventeen thousand baptized Anglicans, including of course a considerable number of Americans.

The Church and church people suffered severely during the war and enemy occupation, and many church buildings were destroyed in the fighting or in air-raids. From death and other causes, the number of church people decreased considerably. The destruction of the war was afterwards slowly made good.

The Philippine Independent Church[1], which had seceded from the Roman Church when the Americans occupied the Islands, in 1946 petitioned the Episcopal Church for valid orders (which they had lost), with a view to achieving intercommunion with it, and ultimately complete union. This was granted in January 1948. In this year, the Anglicans had twenty-four thousand baptized, and in 1949, a clergy of thirteen Filipinos and nineteen Americans.

In China, Anglican Christianity began relatively so late that the years since 1920 form a large part of its entire history. Certainly they have seen anything but a quiet and uneventful development.

An anti-Christian movement broke out in 1922, primarily in reaction from a World Student Christian Federation conference held that year in Peking, and for some years greatly hindered the spread of Christianity. The anti-Christian feeling revived in 1925–7, there was bitter opposition to the Church, and some church people lapsed. However, the Church was in some ways purified and strengthened as a result. From this time the heads of all recognized educational institutions had by law to be Chinese, and attendance at religious instruction and worship in them had to be voluntary. Probably neither of these requirements really harmed the Church. After 1929, and especially after Chiang Kai-shek was baptized as a Methodist in 1930, general feeling was much less unfavourable to Christianity.

Work was now begun by Anglicans in some new areas. In Tat'ung, Shansi, the S.P.G. in 1922 established a mission centring in a hospital. Next year the newly-founded B.C.M.S. began enterprises in East Szech'uan, and at Nanning in a region of Kwangsi hitherto untouched.

A Central Theological School was established at Nanking in 1922 to serve all dioceses of the C.H.S.K.H. and provide theological training of a higher standard than was available in diocesan theological institutions. Two years later a medical college was opened in connection with the very big Kwang Chi hospital maintained by the C.M.S. at Hangchow. In this year the small Anglican Boone University joined with two Free Church colleges, to form Huachung (Central China) College, with Francis Wei Tso-min as President. During the next twenty years, of the

[1] This has over two million members.

86

fifteen Christian universities and university colleges in China, St John's in Shanghai was purely Anglican, and while in several others Anglicans had a share, only at Huachung was their share a dominant one. These two institutions, both supported from America rather than England, produced nearly all the Chinese bishops.

The time for the creation of new dioceses was now almost past. A plan for a new diocese of Shansi and Inner Mongolia could not be carried out, for lack of resources in staff and finance. But in 1936 the unwieldy diocese of West China was divided into two dioceses, of East and West Szech'uan.

The Church's advance now was to be seen as much as anywhere in the growth of a Chinese episcopate. Ing Ong-ting, consecrated in 1927 as Assistant Bishop of Fukien, was only the second Chinese to be an Anglican bishop, but in 1929 two Chinese were appointed Assistant Bishops in the West China diocese, Ku Ho-ling and Song Ts'eng-tsih, while in the same year Lindel Tsen Ho-p'u became Assistant Bishop in the Honan diocese.

Lindel Tsen was in 1930 the first Chinese to attend a meeting of the Lambeth Conference. This meeting formally recognized the C.H.S.K.H. as a self-governing Church of the Anglican Communion. T. K. Shen in 1934 became first bishop of the missionary district of Shensi (previously administered by the Bishop of North China), and after this the Church made great progress there. In the following year, Lindel Tsen became diocesan bishop of Honan, the first Chinese to be a full diocesan bishop.

When the Sino-Japanese War broke out in 1937, the C.H.S.K.H. had twelve dioceses and one missionary district, one Chinese, three American, and eight English and Irish diocesan bishops, one Chinese missionary bishop and four Chinese assistant bishops, two hundred and seventy-two Chinese and eight-two Western priests and deacons, nearly forty thousand communicants, nearly eighty thousand baptized and catechumens.

During the Sino-Japanese War, the C.H.S.K.H. naturally suffered greatly. Many church people were scattered to remote areas and could not be shepherded, and so lapsed from the Church. Much Church property was destroyed, and many endowments lost through inflation. In consequence the movement for financial self-support was put back greatly in all dioceses. The C.H.S.K.H. was, however, established in some new places, especially in Ch'ungk'ing and the South-West; and so Y. Y. Tsu was in 1940 appointed assistant bishop in the Hongkong diocese, with special responsibility for work in Yunnan and Kweichow.

Some parts of China, especially the North China and Shantung dioceses, suffered greatly from the civil war between the Nationalists and Communists after the end of the Sino-Japanese War. In the course of this the Shantung cathedral at T'aian was in 1946 razed to the ground, and for many years the diocesan synod there could not meet, nor could the bishop visit the parishes. In both dioceses a number of parishes for years had no priest, and no organized religious activity, and even communication with some of them was for years impossible.

The number of baptized and catechumens had fallen considerably since 1937, and in 1947 was about sixty-six thousand, while the communicants had fallen to under thirty-two thousand. The numbers of the Chinese clergy were about the same as ten years earlier before the War; the number of Chinese bishops, however, had increased to eleven, and West Szech'uan (1938) and Fukien (1944) now had diocesan bishops. Over a quarter of the membership of the C.H.S.K.H. was in Fukien, and this diocese was probably more advanced than any other in financial self-support.

A meeting of the General Synod, the first for ten years, was held in 1947. This cut the Nanning area off from the Hongkong diocese as a missionary district, and established a new diocese of Yun-Kwei (covering Yunnan and Kweichow) with Quentin Huang as its bishop. Lindel Tsen was elected Chairman of the House of Bishops—in effect, Metropolitan, the first Chinese to hold this position—and T. K. Shen was chosen as its secretary. It was now decided that the C.H.S.K.H. should join the World Council of Churches. The Hankow diocese next year elected its first Chinese bishop, Stephen Tsang Hai-song.

At the end of 1949, the Communist armies had achieved control of most of China. By this time out of fourteen dioceses and missionary districts, six had Chinese diocesan bishops, and the remaining foreign bishops were replaced by Chinese soon afterwards. The Church's foreign staff was forced to leave China in 1950–1.

The C.H.S.K.H., however, like other Christian bodies, continued. As in the Soviet Union, the Communist policy in China was now no longer to eradicate religion by force, but to use education or propaganda to achieve the same end. Church services might for the most part continue, but otherwise Church activities were greatly restricted; the Church was not allowed to maintain any educational institutions, and in practice its hospitals also were taken from it. Church people, because of their contacts with the West, were regarded with great suspicion as being traitors and agents for foreign governments, and many completely baseless charges were brought against them; several of the diocesan bishops were imprisoned. Financial help from the West had to be completely renounced, and in practice all contact and communication, however trivial, with the West had altogether to cease. It is, however, known that the Church has continued, in spite of terrific difficulties and handicaps, though numbers of church people have, in the Communist phrase, "cast off the burden" of religious faith.

The diocese of Korea had in 1924, besides an English bishop, ten European and six Korean priests, one Japanese priest and a Korean deacon; of thirteen parishes, six were in charge of Korean clergymen, and there were about five thousand baptized Anglicans. Except for work among Japanese at Pusan in the south, and a new piece of work at Pyongyang in the north, all Anglican activity was in central Korea. There were three hospitals, but no big educational institutions, and it was claimed that, apart from the cathedral in Seoul (consecrated in 1926), all buildings, including foreign staff residences, were very unpretentious and such as Korean church people might themselves build. An assistant bishop was appointed in 1926. Cecil Cooper succeeded Trollope as bishop in 1931.

Christianity in Korea has had its ups and downs more than in most countries, and in the decade after the First World War, the numbers of Anglicans, as of other Christians, declined. Between 1928 and 1938, however, the Church grew greatly; in the latter year there were nearly ten thousand baptized, and by 1940 there were twenty-four Korean and nine European priests.

Since Korea is about the size of England, and communications were relatively poor, there had for some time been a desire to divide the diocese into two, as the nucleus of an ecclesiastical province. This was officially approved in 1939, but owing to the War could not be implemented. In 1932 the first Korean woman made her profession in the Sisterhood of the Holy Cross.

The years after the outbreak of the Sino-Japanese War were increasingly difficult for Christians in Korea, partly on account of the participation in Shinto rites which the government demanded. In 1940–1, there were much the same developments as in Japan with regard to handing over of responsibility by Westerners and departure of Western staff. Bishop Cecil Cooper did not resign, but left, after appointing the Japanese assistant bishop, John Kudo, as vicar-general. There was no serious persecution, but Christian activity during the War was severely curtailed; often worship was allowed only on Sunday evening, after the day had been given to War work.

After the war, in the North or Communist zone, the Church met difficulty and even persecution. Direct attack on the Church was after a while replaced by indirect attack and vigorous propaganda; no missionary was admitted to the Northern zone, and even correspondence was impracticable. The Anglican clergy in this zone could not attend diocesan meetings in Seoul, nor could the bishop visit them or send them financial help, and the clergy as such were not allowed any rations.

The invasion of South Korea by North Korea, and the resulting war, for the time being only made matters worse for the Church. The bishop was captured by the North Koreans and taken back with them when they retreated, and held prisoner till the truce was concluded, and two other missionaries were taken prisoner and died under the rigours of captivity. Tremendous harm was done to church people and destruction to church buildings, as to the country in general.

After the First World War the S.K.K., like other Christian Communions in Japan, made steady progress till 1931. An evangelistic campaign held in 1927 to commemorate the fortieth anniversary of its constitution had encouraging results. At the same time, the attempt to become financially independent of the Churches of the West was a great strain, and sometimes distracted attention from the task of extending the Church. The Japanese Church in 1925 assured a personal delegate from the Archbishop of Canterbury that help from the Churches of the West was still desired.

The chief event of this period was the election in 1923 of the first two Japanese bishops, J. S. Motoda for the diocese of Tokyo and J. Y. Naide for Osaka, after these dioceses had achieved the number of financially independent parishes required as a condition of this by the canons of the S.K.K. On Motoda's death in 1928, he was succeeded by P. Y. Matsui. A new diocese of Kobe was formed in 1925. Christian evangelism through articles in the secular press was an interesting feature of Anglican, as of Free Church, work now. The American Anglicans maintained the outstanding St Luke's Hospital, which later became the International Medical Centre, in Tokyo; but otherwise there was virtually no place for medical work by the Church as such.

On account of the revival of intense nationalist feeling, and the consequent pressure to attend the ceremonies at the Shinto shrines, the years after 1931 were a time of increasing difficulty for all Christians in Japan, but especially for the Sei Ko Kwai, because of its British connections. This was more than ever so after the speech in 1937 by the Archbishop of Canterbury in the Albert Hall criticizing the Japanese attack on China. Nor did this decade see any noticeable increase in the numerical strength of the S.K.K. By 1940, it had a nominal membership of forty-three thousand baptized, but its actual practising membership, partly owing to much moving about, was only twenty-seven thousand. The clergy numbered nearly two hundred and fifty Japanese (including some in Manchuria and Formosa), and about thirty foreigners.

The Brotherhood of St Andrew was introduced to Japan from the U.S.A. in 1932, and did much work among men and boys. The S.K.K. had three religious communities, the Cowley Fathers for men, and for women the Epiphany Sisters and a new Japanese order, the Community of Nazareth. In 1935 the diocese of Mid-Japan received a Japanese bishop, P. S. Sasaki. The celebration of the fiftieth anniversary of the S.K.K. in 1937 was made the occasion for a time of self-examination and re-dedication, followed by a year of intensive evangelism.

The foreign bishops of the S.K.K. resigned in 1940-1, under pressure from the government and their Japanese colleagues, and were later replaced by Japanese; Bishop Naide of Osaka was elected Presiding Bishop, and a great amount of property was handed over to the Japanese Church by the missionary societies. The S.K.K. declined any future financial help from overseas, and the mission staff left the country, since their presence was in the circumstances then obtaining merely an incubus to the Church.

By the time of the outbreak of the Pacific War in December 1941, there were only two Churches in Japan recognized and authorized by the government, the Roman Catholic Church and a partially unified Protestant Church. Bishops Naide and Matsui, both well on in years, and the assistant bishop of Osaka, threw in their lot with the latter. But the bulk of the S.K.K. (a hundred and sixty-two out of two hundred and thirty-nine parishes) felt that it could not join the government-sponsored Protestant Church, since this did not maintain the historic creeds and ministry. In 1942 it was refused official recognition, and was in consequence legally dissolved as a corporate body. Each local congregation was under the strict and unsympathetic control of the local authorities, and the S.K.K., since it had no official recognition, suffered now more than other Communions.

Sasaki became Presiding Bishop after Matsui's resignation in 1943, and was translated to Tokyo. He and another bishop were imprisoned for four months on account of an attempt to hold a meeting of S.K.K. leaders. Several priests were also imprisoned, and some had been arrested at the outbreak of the Pacific War on charges of disloyal association with enemy aliens.

Churchmen and Church institutions inevitably suffered much from the Allied air-raids in the later part of the War, the more so since they were nearly all in the towns rather than the villages. Between a quarter and a third of S.K.K. churches were destroyed or severely damaged; in the diocese of Tokyo, twenty-three out of twenty-eight churches were reduced to ashes.

After the War, the S.K.K. had much lost ground to make up, and all its endowments had been lost. Most of those who had left it to join the united Protestant Church returned, and the way was made easy for them; bishops they had consecrated were eventually received back as bishops without jurisdiction, and the reconciliation was sealed by the election in 1947 of one of the seceding bishops as Bishop of Osaka. The Church declared that the time had passed for foreigners to undertake pastoral and evangelistic work, but that it would welcome the help of foreign experts in educational and social work, and financial aid for reparation of its losses during the War.

P. S. Sasaki died in 1946, largely as the result of hardship suffered during the war, and T. Sugai succeeded him, but he too died soon, as the result of imprisonment and strain during the War years. M. H. Yashiro, Bishop of Kobe, was elected in his place. In 1947, the number of S.K.K. baptized had decreased to one-third of the figures in 1940, while the communicants had declined to a half.

III. AUSTRALIA AND NEW ZEALAND

There are now in the Commonwealth of Australia twenty-five dioceses, of which three, Adelaide, Willochra, and Tasmania, are not included in any province, and a clergy of about seventeen hundred. Forty-four per cent. of the population claim to belong to the Church of England, a much larger proportion than in any other country except England and New Zealand. There has not yet been a native-born Australian Primate. A new constitution for the General Synod, giving it more authority, is in process of adoption.

Many areas in Australia are only very thinly populated, and pastoral care of church people there consequently constitutes a great problem. The Church's work in such districts has been greatly helped by Bush Brotherhoods, the first of which began at Longreach in Queensland in the closing years of the nineteenth century, an example since followed at Dubbo and elsewhere. Each of these Brotherhoods consists of a number of priests who have promised to remain unmarried for a period of years; they work in remote areas, and are continually on the road, and at regular intervals meet at the Brotherhood's headquarters to counteract their spiritual isolation.

The Australian aborigines, a very primitive people, number only about seventy thousand, and are declining in numbers. The Church of England has much work among them, and the first of them was ordained deacon in 1925.

The Australian Church is responsible for helping the diocese of New Guinea, which now has about ten thousand baptized Anglicans, with thirty white and twelve coloured priests and deacons. It has also contributed much to the spread of the Gospel among non-Christian peoples through the English Anglican missionary societies; in 1926–7 it assumed responsibility for the new diocese of Central Tanganyika in East Africa, and more recently it has begun to help the diocese of Borneo.

When the Church first came to New Zealand, the Maori tribes were decimating their numbers by warfare and by inter-tribal blood-feuds. Now, however, their numbers are increasing. Most belong to some Christian Communion, and about one-third of them the Church of the Province of New Zealand, which has for some time had a Maori assistant bishop in the Waiapu diocese and has about thirty Maori clergymen.

A new diocese of Waikato was formed in 1925 from the southern part of the Auckland diocese. The missionary diocese of Polynesia (established in 1908) was in 1923 associated with the New Zealand province, and receives help in staff and finance from the dioceses; it has over five thousand baptized members, with ten white and two coloured clergymen. The diocese of Melanesia has grown notably, and now has fifty thousand baptized, with twelve white and eighty-four Melanesian clergymen. It receives help from England, through the S.P.G., and from Australia as well as from New Zealand. The Church in New Zealand also helps the Church in eastern Asia through the English missionary societies; it has itself for long received no help from outside. Thirty-eight per cent. of the population belong at least nominally to the Church of the Province.

The Church in West Africa has continued to grow both in numbers and otherwise. The Order of the Holy Cross in 1922 began work in the far interior of Liberia. This diocese had many ups and downs, and Cuttington College was closed for some time before it was reopened in 1949. In 1929, of a total population of about one million, fifty thousand were Christians, about fifteen thousand of whom were Anglicans. Since 1945 the diocese has again had a negro bishop, D. W. Harris, and appears to be making great progress. Education is still the responsibility almost solely of the missions.

On the Gold Coast, the Church has been more active in the second quarter of this century than it was before. St Augustine's College was founded at Kumasi, the capital of Ashanti, in 1928, to increase the supply of African clergy, and the African clergy of the diocese have all been trained there. An African, E. D. Martindale, was consecrated in 1951 as Assistant Bishop of Accra. The diocese now has a ministry of about thirty-four, nearly all of whom are Africans, and twelve Sisters of the Order of the Holy Paraclete, besides several women missionaries.

It had become clear by 1933 that the Rio Pongas mission must either be strengthened or closed down. The West Indies Church, which was responsible for it, resolved that the former must be attempted, and, with the backing of the S.P.G., a new diocese, of Gambia and the Rio Pongas, was set up in 1935, with J. C. S. Daly as its bishop. At Bathurst there was a strong body of church people, mostly originating from Sierra Leone; St Mary's Church, Bathurst, was built about 1901, and from there one or two outposts had come into existence. In 1940, a Christian settlement, Kristi Kunda, "Christ's Town", was founded three hundred miles up the river Gambia, and a boarding-school was transferred there, but the diocese faced many obstacles, and remained very small. In 1953 it had in addition to the Bishop only seven clergymen.

The Church in Sierra Leone, which had early become largely self-governing and financially independent, did not later on maintain its growth. But in Nigeria the Church continued to grow greatly. The first of the Ibo race (in Eastern Nigeria) to be consecrated bishop became in 1937 Assistant Bishop on the Niger. Melville-Jones was succeeded by L. G. Vining in 1940 as Bishop of Lagos. Lasbrey was succeeded in 1946 as Bishop on the Niger, by C. J. Patterson, with his see at Onitsha; and there were said then to be more churches in that diocese than in any diocese in England.

In April 1951 the Archbishop of Canterbury preached at the inauguration of a West African Province of the Anglican Communion. The Province included the dioceses which had come into existence as the result of the work of the Church of England, namely Sierra Leone, the Niger, Gambia and Rio Pongas, and Accra, but not Liberia, which was founded by and tied to the American Church. The inauguration took place in St George's Cathedral, Freetown, Sierra Leone, this being the senior diocese of those concerned. The Archbishop of Canterbury relinquished the jurisdiction which he had hitherto had over these dioceses, and the Bishop of Lagos, L. G. Vining, was elected the first Archbishop.

The two Nigerian dioceses were divided that same year into six dioceses—Lagos, Ibadan, Ondo-Benin, The Niger, The Niger Delta, and Northern Nigeria. Three of them received African diocesan bishops, and they were served by a ministry of over three hundred, almost all of them Africans. There were in Nigeria over three hundred thousand baptized Anglican church people, more than three times as many as in China and Japan together.

Since 1920 the Church in South Africa has progressed steadily. The large diocese of Pretoria was divided in 1922, and A. B. L. Karney became Bishop of Johannesburg. An important part of the work of this diocese, which covers the Southern Transvaal, has been a remarkable Christian settlement in the heart of the African location of Sophiatown on the outskirts of Johannesburg, and many welfare activities, besides a great church. A diocese of Damaraland in South-West Africa was cut off in 1924 from Cape Town and from Kimberley and Kuruman, and a diocese of Basutoland in 1950 from the diocese of Bloemfontein. It was now a question not of establishing the Church in new areas, but of relieving over-large dioceses. The Church has always been in the forefront of the struggle against *apartheid*.

In Southern Rhodesia, the population, both African and European, had grown immensely since 1891; and while in 1891 there was only one Bantu priest in the diocese, by 1951 there were twenty-five, and also two Bantu deacons. And so a new diocese of Matabeleland, with its centre at Bulawayo, was constituted; the remaining part of the diocese of Southern Rhodesia resuming the original name of Mashonaland, with its centre at Salisbury.

When the new ecclesiastical Province of Central Africa was set up in

1955, the Church of the Province of South Africa gave up to it two dioceses, namely Mashonaland and Matabeleland. The South African Province now has fourteen dioceses, about 780 clergy, of whom some 260 are non-Europeans, and nearly eight hundred thousand church people. About five parishes call themselves "Church of England in South Africa", and perpetuate the Colenso schism.

The Church continued now to extend in East Africa. So much of the Uganda Protectorate as is not in the kingdom of Buganda was, on account of the growth of the Church, cut off in 1926 from the diocese of Uganda to form the diocese of the Upper Nile or Elgon. This lies for the most part to the east of the river Nile, the Uganda diocese to the west of it. The Southern Sudan was at first included in the Upper Nile diocese, but difficulties of transport prevented the area becoming a unity, and so the Southern Sudan was again attached to Khartoum. In the area of this diocese there were in 1900 no Christians; it was evangelized in large part by Baganda clergy. Now, of a population of two millions, over two hundred thousand are Anglican adherents (not all baptized).

A diocese of Central Tanganyika was cut off from the Mombasa diocese in 1926–7. It receives help from overseas chiefly from the Australian C.M.S. In 1927 there were only two African clergy here, while now there are about forty-eight. The cathedral is at Dodoma.

To the south, where the U.M.C.A. works, the diocese of Masasi, set up in 1926 on the coast south of Zanzibar, grew from the settlement of freed slaves made in 1876. W. Lucas was its first bishop, and the number of church people increased greatly after this area was formed into a diocese. The diocese of South-West Tanganyika (formed in 1952) contains so much of the former Nyasaland diocese as was in Tanganyika territory.

The first East African to become an Anglican bishop was consecrated in October 1947, when Canon A. K. Balya became Assistant Bishop of Uganda. For this occasion the cathedral at Kampala, which normally holds two thousand, accommodated over three thousand, while another thousand people stood outside. Another East African became Assistant Bishop of the Upper Nile diocese in 1952, and there are now six African assistant bishops in the various East African dioceses. Nearly a third of the population of Uganda are now either Anglicans or Roman Catholics (there are no other Christians there), and these are about equal in numbers. The important chiefs are mostly Anglicans, and the Kabaka, who is an Anglican, was crowned in the cathedral by the bishop in addition to the traditional coronation ceremony. The two dioceses of Uganda and the Upper Nile had in 1953 over five hundred and fifty thousand baptized members, with 208 African and twenty-seven European clergy.

There has been much discussion concerning the formation of an ecclesiastical province in East Africa, and so long ago as 1927 seven out of the then eight dioceses accepted a scheme for this, the Mombasa diocese alone being opposed. One obstacle has been the fact that the dioceses resulting from the work of the C.M.S. were strongly Evangelical, while those which have had connections with the U.M.C.A. are strongly Catholic. Recently, however, a more serious obstacle has been the feeling of many Africans that the scheme for an ecclesiastical province was somehow connected with the proposal for a political federation of the East African territories, which is very unpopular among them.

However, a Central African Province was inaugurated by the Archbishop of Canterbury in May 1955, comprising the four dioceses of Nyasaland, Northern Rhodesia, Matabeleland, and Mashonaland, the last two of which had previously been in the South African Province.

In Mauritius, the C.M.S. ceased to give help early in the twentieth century. Anglican work here has been mainly among Indians and Chinese. The population is so mixed that services have to be held in a great variety of languages, including English, French, Tamil, Telugu, Hindu, Bengali, and Chinese; but French is the lingua franca of the island, and the French version of the Anglican Prayer Book is mostly used. Some of the staff of the diocese have been sent to Mauritius by the Church in India. The diocese has now about seventeen clergymen, of whom only four are from England; it includes the Seychelles, a thousand miles from Mauritius, and also the islands of Rodriguez and Réunion, with small Anglican communities.

In Madagascar, R. S. M. O'Ferrall was bishop from 1926 to 1940. By this time the clergy comprised sixty-five Malagasy and only five Europeans. Since the word "Anglican" was especially liable to misunderstanding in a French colony, the Synod in 1928 decided to adopt the name "Malagasy Episcopal Church". A division of the diocese had been proposed as early as 1928, and, as a step to division, an assistant bishop was appointed for the eastern part of the island in 1938. The Church suffered greatly in a revolt against French rule in 1946–47; the rebels attacked Christianity as a foreign importation, many churches were destroyed, and Church leaders persecuted. A Malagasy, Jean Marcel, was made Assistant Bishop in 1956.

The Church Missions to Jews worked for a time in Ethiopia after the First World War; the B.C.M.S. also works there, and aims at a reformation in the old Coptic Church, and in 1927 a priest was sent out by the S.P.G., partly as chaplain to the British residents, partly to cultivate friendly relations with the Coptic Church. Such few Anglicans as are in Ethiopia are under the jurisdiction of the Bishop in the Sudan.

The small Anglican work in Egypt was till 1920 under the jurisdiction of the Bishop in Jerusalem. In that year a diocese of Egypt was formed, with L. H. Gwynne as its bishop. Some development followed, and the Muslims were becoming less unapproachable. The first Egyptian was made deacon in 1924, and the next year Anglican work in Egypt was organized as "the Episcopal Church of Egypt in communion with the Church of England". At this time, about twenty Muslims a year were being baptized by Anglicans. A new cathedral of All Saints was consecrated in Cairo in 1938. Even now, the number of Anglicans in Egypt is only about two thousand; the Anglicans, unlike Free Church missions there, have always been careful not to proselytize the Copts, though the C.M.S. has helped the Coptic Church to open schools for its children.

In the Sudan, churches were built in several places during this period, and a cathedral in Khartoum. The Sudan was cut off from Egypt in 1945, and constituted a diocese with A. M. Gelsthorpe as its bishop.

A diocese of North Africa was formed in 1936, including such Anglicans as there were in Tunis, Algeria, Morocco, and the Canary Islands; but on the resignation of the bishop in 1955, the Bishop of Gibraltar was given responsibility for this area. The B.C.M.S. attempts to win Muslims to the Faith in Casablanca and elsewhere, but otherwise Anglican work here consists chiefly of chaplaincy work among British residents.

PART TWO

7

Anglicanism and the Bible

THE Anglican Communion throughout the world, as we shall see below, is not bound together by any formal organization, nor has it a defined constitution; and it is in fact not easy to say exactly what does hold it together. Clearly, however, one bond linking Anglicans throughout the world is the Bible and a common attitude to it, an attitude, moreover, which differs from that of at least some other bodies of Christians.

It is significant that Anglicanism emphasizes, as no other Communion does, the reading of the Bible in public worship. A sermon, for example, is no necessary and invariable part of either the Eucharist or Morning or Evening Prayer; but each of these services involves the reading of two passages from the Bible. The Anglican lectionary, moreover, ensures that almost the whole of the Bible, not merely such excerpts as any particular priest may specially value, is in due time read.[1]

Use of the Bible in the vernacular is an Anglican characteristic (a vernacular translation is for that matter a precondition of widespread and constant use of Holy Scripture), and one that is fully in accord with the practice of the Church in its early centuries. Parts of the Bible were translated into English very soon after the founding of the English Church, and Bede, early in the eighth century, is said to have translated into English the Gospel according to St John.

However, it was not till the fourteenth century that John Wycliffe and his disciples Nicholas of Hereford and John Purvey first translated the whole Bible into English. They translated it not from the original languages, which were then virtually unknown in England, but from the

[1] In the sixteenth century, the plan of the lectionary was that both Old and New Testament were read through at the rate of one chapter each day; so the O.T. was read once a year, the N.T. three times a year. This somewhat mechanical arrangement lasted in England till 1871.

Vulgate Latin version. At that period the Church of England, like the rest of the Western Catholic Church, though it did not altogether prohibit the reading of the Bible by lay people, certainly did not encourage this. Wycliffe, however, wanted all church people, including the less educated (for whom in particular his translation was made) to be able to read the Bible. This translation was eventually proscribed as erroneous by the ecclesiastical authorities of the time.

Wycliffe and his followers, the Lollards, in some respects like the later Puritans, regarded the Bible as the source of all religious truth, and held that every good man could and should interpret it for himself, and needed no guidance or help in this. They also came to oppose many Church customs simply on the ground that the Bible did not prescribe them.

It was not till the sixteenth century that the Bible was translated into English from the original languages, first of all by William Tyndale. Unfortunately Tyndale limited its usefulness by adding notes of an extreme protestant character. Another translation, by Miles Coverdale, was published in 1535, which was less scholarly than Tyndale's translation, though good from the literary point of view. The version of the Psalms in the English Prayer Book comes from Coverdale's Bible. Three years later, the so-called Great Bible was produced, based in part on Tyndale's version, in part on Coverdale's; and a copy of this Bible was in 1538 ordered to be placed in every church. From this time, reading of the Bible was not only permitted to all, learned or unlearned, but was encouraged. The first English Prayer Book restricted reading at public worship to the canonical Scriptures, and the reading of medieval lives of saints, usually legendary and fantastic, ceased.

English Anglicans were responsible for the so-called Authorized or King James version of the English Bible in 1611, and largely so for the Revised Version of 1881-5. Naturally Anglicans have also played a part in other English translations, both in Britain and America, and have also translated, or helped to translate, the Bible into many other languages; for example, the American Schereschevsky did more than any other one person to translate the Bible into both literary Chinese and the national Chinese language (Mandarin or Kuo Yü).

Many of the greatest Biblical scholars, such as Lightfoot, Westcott, and Hort, have been Anglicans, and the Russian Orthodox theologian Bulgakov recognizes[1] that Anglicans and Protestants have been specially distinguished for their study of the Bible.

[1] *The Orthodox Church*, p. 27.

The English Reformers, in opposing corrupt doctrines and practices in the sixteenth-century Church, appealed to the authority of both the Bible and the ancient Church. The Thirty-nine Articles (1571) declare that the Bible contains all things necessary to salvation: nothing not included in, or based on, the Bible may be required as necessary, nor may the Church ordain anything which is contrary to the Bible (Articles 6 and 20). This is still the attitude of the Church of England; the other Anglican Churches, most of which do not retain the Articles, include in their written constitutions fundamentally the same principles.

Though Calvin himself perhaps did not insist on an explicit Biblical command for everything, the Puritans in the sixteenth and seventeenth centuries on the whole wanted to forbid all customs not explicitly sanctioned by the Bible, and this in fact was the main issue between them and the Anglicans. The Puritans accordingly forbade the observance of Christmas and other traditional festivals and holy days (apart from Sunday, which they identified with the Jewish Sabbath); the use of organs, the surplice, and Eucharistic vestments; and such practices as kneeling at the Communion, and the sign of the Cross in baptism and at other times. Richard Hooker (1553–1600) firmly opposed such a narrow-minded use of the Bible, and claimed that the Bible did not forbid everything except what it explicitly sanctioned, but allowed all that it did not clearly forbid. In this matter, the Free Churches, the representatives to-day of the Puritans, seem to have largely come round to the Anglican attitude. Anglicanism, following Hooker, holds that the Bible does not aim to set forth in detail all permissible customs and practices. God has given man reason, and he should use it; God's revelation is to supplement reason, not to take its place, and if a custom is reasonable, it need not have an explicit basis in Scripture. The Bible contains not all things, but all things which are necessary.

Hooker set out what has come to be the Anglican attitude with regard to the Bible, as to so much else. He declared that Scripture, the Church's tradition, and reason, each have authority, and that Christian doctrine must be based on all three, and must not neglect any of them, since they are as it were a threefold cord linking the Churchman to Christ. Scripture (and equally the Church's traditional thought and practice) is to be tested by reason, and should not be explained to teach what reason shows to be certainly untrue. Hooker's attitude was typical of that of the classical Anglicanism of the seventeenth century, as we shall see further in regard to the controversial question of the interpretation of the Bible;

and William Chillingworth's well-known phrase about the Bible only in its original context was quite in harmony with it.

The Lollards and Puritans held that each individual could and should interpret the Bible for himself; they assumed that its meaning was crystal-clear, even to the completely untrained person. Anglicans, in distinction from this, held that the individual Churchman needs the Church's help and guidance to understand the Bible, like the Ethiopian eunuch mentioned in Acts 8.30,31 (cf. 2 Pet. 3.6).

Anglicanism has always refused, in interpreting the meaning of the Bible, to ignore Church tradition, that is, to say the general consensus of church people. Scripture is to be continually interpreted in the context of the Church's life. This is the characteristic attitude of the ancient Church; Tertullian, for example, declared that Scripture must be interpreted according to the standard of faith which the Apostles delivered to the Church, and which was handed down from generation to generation in the Churches founded by Apostles. The sense of Scripture is determined by the Creeds and, at least for English Anglicans, by the Articles and Catechism.[1]

Experience shows that individual interpretation of the Bible often produces through misunderstanding, strange and perverted doctrines and conduct. For example, certain Americans understood Rom. 12.16 to forbid high schools, and founded a new sect, whose chief characteristic was its prohibition of high schools. Negro slavery was long defended by reference to the Bible, and numerous schismatic African Churches uphold polygamy as sanctioned by the Old Testament. The Anglican attitude is often summed up in the phrase of Hawkins, Provost of Oriel: "the Church to teach, the Bible to prove." From a purely chronological point of view, indeed, the Church is prior to a Christian Canon of Scripture, which is in fact the product of the Church's faith. Because Anglicanism has always emphasized the Church's responsibility of interpreting the Bible, it could accept more easily than many Protestant Communions the new study of the Bible (the so-called Higher Criticism) in the nineteenth century.

The Anglican attitude thus differs somewhat from the historical Free Church attitude (though in our own day the Free Churches seem to be coming much closer to Anglicanism in this connection). It also differs somewhat from that of the other great Christian Communions. The Eastern Orthodox go further in laying stress upon the importance of

[1] So J. W. C. Wand in *Anglican Congress*, 1954, p. 35.

Church tradition for the understanding of the Bible; and hold that the Church, not the (written) Word, is primary in the work of salvation. The Bible, they say, is given to us by the Church; the Bible is God's gift to the Church, and is a means of grace which the Church uses in the work of man's salvation. The Church, under the guidance of the Holy Spirit, has received from God authority to explain, interpret, and even complete, the teaching of the Bible. They claim that this does not mean that the Church can add to the Christian Faith elements which contradict the Bible. Reverence, for example, for our Lord's mother and the saints, which is very prominent in Eastern Orthodoxy, does not conflict with the teaching of the Bible. However, the Orthodox regard Church tradition as a standard and authority for the Christian faith almost, if not quite, as important as the Bible.

The Roman Catholic Church since the Council of Trent (1545-1563) definitely regards Scripture and tradition as equally important sources and standards of Christian faith. The German Roman Catholic theologian Karl Adam says that Rome, unlike all other Churches, accepts the entire Old and New Testaments and neglects no part of the Bible. Nevertheless, he continues, Romanists derive their faith not from the Bible but from the Church. The Gospels give us only a fragmentary record concerning Jesus, and not a complete picture; we learn to know the complete Jesus only from the life of the whole Church. The Gospels themselves are based on oral tradition, and the New Testament is only one expression of the Apostolic tradition which the Church preserves. Living faith cannot be adequately described in dead writing; it is much better set forth by the living Church. The New Testment was originally written only to supplement the oral teaching of the Church. Rome is extremely cautious in using modern methods of Biblical study, and practically supports the theory of the Bible's verbal inspiration.

A result of this is that Rome has developed many doctrines without any basis in Scripture. In some respects, Rome seems to be conservative; but fundamentally she is more modernist than any other Communion, since she holds that the Church may develop new doctrines regardless of the Bible, such as that of the Bodily Assumption of the Virgin Mary to Heaven, which the Pope proclaimed in 1950, declaring that acceptance of this doctrine is necessary to salvation.

In contrast to this, Anglicanism maintains the sufficiency of Scripture. As Jeremy Taylor put it, the Bible, and nothing else, is the Word of God. It contains all teaching necessary to salvation; the Church may not require any man to believe, or regard as necessary to salvation, any doctrine not taught by the Bible nor based on it. Every Anglican priest at his ordination acknowledges that the Bible contains all doctrine necessary to salvation, and both the Chicago–Lambeth Quadrilateral and the Lambeth Appeal involve acceptance of the Bible as the rule and ultimate standard of faith.

The Anglican attitude here follows that of the ancient Church Fathers, who regarded tradition as having authority only to interpret the Bible, not to add new doctrines. The fact is that the earliest Church tradition, that closest to Christ and the Apostles, is contained in the New Testament. The ancient Church, before it became divided in the eleventh century, did not hold any doctrine not clearly based on the Bible.

The Church canonized certain early Christian writings, thus forming the Bible as we know it, mainly so that untrustworthy oral tradition should not, as it now does in the Roman Church, take the place of early well-authenticated evidence. For Anglicans, the Bible is the final criterion of truth, while Rome has substituted for this a theological will o' the wisp, "the living mind of the Church".[1] The Bible should be interpreted in the way it has always been interpreted by the main body of Christian thought and practice. In a real sense, the Bible is the Church's criterion and judge.

The Lambeth Conference in 1930 declared that it is not the purpose of the Bible to give information concerning matters within the sphere of natural science, and that the Biblical account of the creation of the world is not to be understood literally; its object is to declare the sovereignty of God and the goodness of Creation. Adam is not to be understood as a historic person. Not a few persons in the ancient Church recognized this, and regarded the early chapters of Genesis as allegory. The theory of evolution does not necessarily conflict with the Bible; rightly understood, it indicates the means by which God creates the universe.

Not all parts of the Bible, however, are to be regarded as having equal authority.[2] Some early parts contain a very primitive conception of God, very different from Christ's revelation; it records God's progressive revelation of Himself, and Christ is the climax of this revelation. Anglicans in general see no reason to suppose that Moses wrote the Pentateuch —much, if not all, of it was written after Moses' time. Naturally the Gospels, which record the life on earth and teaching of Christ, are felt to

[1] Cf. R. P. C. Hanson in *Theology*, October 1954.
[2] *Lambeth Conference 1930: Report*, p. 76.

have special authority. The Old Testament cannot be put on the same level as the New Testament; this was already recognized in the fifth century by Augustine. But there can be no question of discarding the Old Testament; it represents the preparation for Christ, and records God's gradual revelation (or perhaps it would be better to say, man's gradual apprehension of God's revelation). The Church's teaching has to be based on the general sense of the Bible, and not on texts isolated from their context. Article 8 declares that the Apostles' and Nicene creeds are to be believed since they can be proved by "most certain warrant of Holy Scripture".

The Church is a witness to, and keeper of, the Bible. The fact is that the Bible and the Church with its tradition belong together. Father A. G. Hebert expressed the Anglican viewpoint well when he wrote that the two can never be separated: the Bible can never be rightly understood apart from that tradition of the Israel of God out of which it arose. On the other hand, apart from the Bible and the living Word of God spoken through it, the Church becomes hierarchical and sacerdotalist in a wrong sense, or worldly, or pietistic. The Bible recalls the Church to the acts of the living God, and where the Bible is shut out, the Church lacks the wellspring of life.

Like other Christian Communions, Anglicanism holds that both the Old and the New Testament are inspired by God. Many Jews held that God's Spirit possessed the Old Testament writers, and spoke through them as mechanical and purely passive instruments, so that every word was directly inspired by God and was infallible. Some Christians even now, hold a similar view of the inspiration of the Bible, and in the past many did so, including not a few Anglicans. But the New Testament writers do not claim such inspiration; and Anglicans hold that God inspired, not every word of the Bible, but the writers of it. He did not use them as purely passive tools. Inspiration is not regarded as superseding or annihilating individual characteristics in the person inspired; his outlook, temperament and knowledge remain as before, and if he is inspired to write, his writing reveals his individual characteristics. The Bible has authority not because it was inspired by God in some miraculous way (as Moslems believe in regard to the Koran), but because it is the unique and classical record of the revelation of God in His relation to and dealings with man.[1]

A consequence of this is that Anglicans do not now regard the Bible

[1] *Lambeth Conference 1948*, II. 85.

as infallible; so to regard it is to misunderstand its purpose. The chief purpose of inspiration is not to give detailed information concerning the future,[1] nor is it either to teach natural science, or to prescribe detailed rules of conduct; its function is to record the progressive self-revelation of God in history, culminating in Jesus Christ. Only the Bible does this, and in this respect it is entirely reliable.

The message of the Archbishops to the Bible Reading Fellowship on its twenty-fifth aniversary declared that if the Church is the household of grace, it is the Bible which anchors the Church to the true Word of God and which equips Christians for their warfare. To speak of the Bible itself as the Word of God may be misunderstood to imply that every word of it is directly inspired by God and therefore infallible. Christ Himself is the Word of God, and the Gospel also may clearly be called the Word of God. Nevertheless, since the Bible is not chiefly the record of man's search for God, but through it God speaks to man, it may rightly be called "the Word of God".[2]

NOTE

The Roman Church at the Council of Trent gave to the Apocrypha the same authority as the canonical Old Testament writings. The Protestant Communions, on the other hand, mostly do not regard the Apocrypha as Scripture in any sense. As so often, Anglicanism follows a middle way: passages from the Apocrypha are prescribed in the lectionary for reading on some days at Mattins and Evensong[3] and Article 6 clearly says that these are to be read for example of life and instruction of manners, but are not to be used to establish any doctrine.

Anglicans accept the Canon of Scripture used by the great majority of Christians: they differ, however, from the Assyrians (the Church of the East or Nestorians), who reject 2 Peter 2 and 3, John, Jude, and Revelation, and from the Monophysites, who to the Catholic canon add a number of books such as Enoch.

[1] *Doctrine in the Church of England*, p. 29.

[2] Ibid., p. 28.

[3] The Church of Ireland, unlike other Anglican bodies, does not in its lectionary include passages from the Apocrypha, although it accepts Article 6 with its statement about the Apocrypha.

8

Doctrine

THERE are no particular Anglican doctrines which other Christian Communions do not hold, or even to which Anglicans attach much greater importance than other Christians. Anglicanism is characterized rather by its general attitude in regard to doctrines held by most Christians.

The Anglican Communion claims that it holds the doctrines held by the undivided Church in the first five centuries, and that these are preserved in, and witnessed to, by the Apostles' and Nicene Creeds. The supreme authority for doctrine is the Bible, to which the Creeds are definitely subordinate. The Church may not declare that it is necessary for salvation to believe any doctrine which is not based on the Bible; and maintains the teaching of the Bible as interpreted by the ancient Church Fathers and General Councils of the Church. The Book of Common Prayer is also an important witness to, and standard of, Anglican doctrine.[1]

So far as the Church of England is concerned, the Convocations in 1953 agreed to a draft canon stating that its doctrine is grounded in the Holy Scriptures and in the teaching of the ancient Fathers and Councils of the Church agreeable to the same, and is particularly contained in the Thirty-Nine Articles of Religion, the Book of Common Prayer, and the Ordinal. Except for the reference to the Articles, this statement would no doubt be accepted by the other Anglican Churches.

Cranmer, after the break between the English and the Roman Churches, drew up Forty-two Articles (issued in 1553), to set forth the Faith of the Church of England. In 1563 these were reduced to Thirty-nine, and were approved (as the Forty-two had not been) by

[1] Cf., e.g., *Lambeth Conference 1930: Report*, p. 29, Encyclical Letter.

Convocation. From 1571, the Church of England clergy had to subscribe to them, but since 1865 only a general assent has to be given. Lay readers must assent to them, but otherwise the laity need not accept them, though until 1871 all members of the universities of Oxford and Cambridge had to assent to them.

In Wales, the clergy are bound by the Articles just as in England. In Scotland they are not printed in the Prayer Book, but the clergy must assent to them. The Church of Ireland accepts them, and so do the Anglican Churches in Australia, New Zealand, and Canada.

When the American Anglican Church was formally organized towards the end of the eighteenth century, Bishop White and some others wanted a thorough revision of the Articles; but in 1801 they were adopted, with the omission of Article 21 (about General Councils meeting only by the authority of princes) and with some change to Article 35 (concerning Homilies). Individual clergymen and lay people in the American Church need not sign them, but they are printed with the American Prayer Book.

The Lambeth Conference in 1888 declared that outside England Anglicans need not accept the Articles. The Church in Uganda accepts them as one among other sources and standards of its doctrine, but some other African dioceses do not retain them, nor does Anglicanism in China or Japan, nor the Church of India, Pakistan, Burma, and Ceylon.

Many of the controversies to which the Articles refer belong only to the sixteenth century. Some questions they deal with are not important now, and on some subjects their attitude is ambiguous, with the result that they are, or may be thought, valueless. So some hold either that they should no longer be regarded as a standard of Anglican doctrine, or at least that they should be revised. In points where their teaching is not clear, they have to be interpreted in accordance with the Prayer Book,[1] and it is clear that, except possibly in England, the Prayer Book is more authoritative that the Articles in regard to Anglican doctrine.[2]

Nevertheless, in some respects the Thirty-nine Articles are still of value, and plainly set out Anglican doctrine, in distinction from medieval abuses on the one hand, and Anabaptist tenets on the other. Articles 6 and 20, for instance, declare that the Bible is the supreme standard of Anglican doctrine, and that the Church may not teach any doctrine as

---

[1] Cf., e.g., *Lambeth Conference 1930: Report*, p. 135.

[2] Ibid., p. 55, and *Lambeth Conference 1948: Report* I.23.

necessary to salvation which is not based on the Bible; this is in sharp contrast to the attitude of Rome. Others also, for example Article 8 about the Creeds, Article 24 about the vernacular Bible and worship, Article 25 about the sacraments, Article 32 about the marriage of priests, and Article 34 about traditions and ceremonies, do unquestionably set forth the Anglican standpoint.

The Anglican Communion regards the Apostles' and Nicene Creeds also as standards of its doctrine and as witnessing to the faith handed down by the Apostles. The eighth Article declares that they should be thoroughly received and believed, inasmuch as they may be proved by the most certain warrant of Scripture. And those Anglican Churches which have written constitutions have in them similar statements. Not all Anglicans are agreed as to the exact relation of the Creed to the Bible; some regard it as only a summary of the teaching of the Bible, and as authoritative only if it faithfully sets forth the Bible's teaching, while others regard it as the authorized interpretation of the Bible. In general, of course, most Christians, and not only Anglicans, accept the Creed as representing accurately the teaching of the Bible, but Anglicans regard the Creeds as subordinate to the Bible.[1]

It is not claimed that the historic creeds completely set forth the whole Christian faith, but they are regarded as indispensable witnesses to and safeguards of the historic Christian truths. Such phrases in them as "ascended into heaven" and "sitteth on the right hand of God" are clearly metaphorical, but it is readily agreed that, essential as the historic creeds are, no external or written standards can suffice without inward and personal Christian experience and belief.[2] Anglicans would endorse the statement of the Dominican Gerald Vann, that Christians believe not in a creed but in the reality behind the creed.[3]

The Creeds, which were sanctioned by the still undivided Church, may not be altered by any of the separated or local Churches.[4] The whole Church could, at least in theory, agree to change the wording, but not the general sense. When the American Episcopal Church was being organized, it was at first proposed to omit the phrase "he descended into hell" from the Apostles' Creed, and even to jettison the Nicene Creed; but it was soon realized that the historic creeds should be retained, and

[1] L. Hodgson, ed. *Convictions*, p. 181.
[2] Ibid. p. 180.
[3] G. Vann, O.P., article "Symbol and Religion" in *The Listener*, 9 Sept. 1954.
[4] *Lambeth Conference 1930: Report*, p. 154.

those proposals were abandoned.[1] Preservation of the two creeds is one of the four indispensable conditions from the Anglican standpoint of a united Church, and the Lambeth Appeal of 1920 spoke of the Nicene Creed as a sufficient statement of the Christian faith, declaring that either it or the Apostles' Creed should be used as the baptismal confession of faith.

The Apostles' Creed is essentially a creed of the Western Church, and the Nicene is essentially the ecumenical creed—the Eastern Orthodox have only this creed, and use it at baptism as for other purposes. The Orthodox use the creed in its original form, omitting the words "and from the Son (filioque)", and are strongly opposed to this insertion. The Lambeth Conference committee in 1920 upheld this addition, but representatives of the Church of England, commenting on the reports of the Lausanne conference on Faith and Order, expressed the view that a re-united Church should affirm the original form of the Creed, while allowing those who wished to do so to retain the insertion.[2]

The "Athanasian" Creed or *Quicunque vult*, the third of the so-called Catholic creeds, was in origin not a creed, but a hymn setting forth the orthodox doctrine of the Trinity chiefly for the instruction of the clergy. It was not written by Athanasius, but was composed after his death, about A.D. 400. It has never been used in the Eastern Orthodox Church. The Lutheran and Calvinist Churches retained it at the Reformation, and the German Lutherans, commenting on the Lausanne Conference on Faith and Order, which declared that a united Church should accept the Apostles' and Nicene Creeds, urged that the Athanasian Creed also should be kept. The Church of England at the Reformation kept it (so Article 8), and in the Prayer Book prescribed that on certain fixed Sundays it should be recited at Morning or Evening Prayer. The first American Prayer Book (1789) omitted this creed, not meaning to deny its doctrine of the Trinity, but because much of its language is too technical for general use and the damnatory clauses especially are liable to misunderstanding. Since 1928, its use in England has been optional, as is also the case in Canada. The Scottish Prayer Book prescribes its use, the Irish Prayer Book includes it but does not prescribe its use. The Church of India, Pakistan, Burma, and Ceylon prescribes it, and so does the Korean

[1] In reciting the Apostles' Creed, American Anglicans are allowed by their Prayer Book to substitute "went into the place of departed spirits" for the misleading words "descended into hell".

[2] L. Hodgson, ed. *Convictions*, p. 180.

Church, while China and Japan do not recognize it. Whether or not they think it suitable for use in public worship (and neither Roman Catholics nor Orthodox use it so), Anglicans probably maintain substantially the doctrine taught in it.

It seems to some Christians that Anglicans are too much concerned with the creeds and doctrine. Some Free Churchmen, for instance, would claim that Christianity is not a creed but a life. And indeed Anglicanism does not regard the question of right or wrong doctrine as trivial or unimportant. The distinction between truth and falsehood is always important, and moreover, wrong doctrines often have unfortunate practical results (so history shows how the heresy that matter is evil all too often leads men either to be absurdly ascetic or to be morally irresponsible). Further, since man is endowed with reason, he must seek to define his faith and give it intellectual expression; and doctrines are but the intellectual expression of faith.

There is, as we have seen, no special Anglican system of theology, in the sense that, for example, there is a Calvinist system; nor is any one doctrine given such overwhelming importance as Lutherans give to the doctrine of justification by faith alone. Anglicanism maintains the doctrines of the ancient and undivided Church, and rejects medieval developments, such as the doctrine of transubstantiation, and modern Roman Catholic doctrines such as the Infallibility of the Pope and the Assumption of the Blessed Virgin Mary, which have no basis in the Bible. In regard to many questions, for example the Atonement, no one definite interpretation is laid down in Anglican formularies. Anglicans have, consequently, as compared with members of many Christian Communions, a wide freedom with regard to the intellectual formulation of the Faith. Anglican doctrine is in fact a synthesis; it upholds on the one hand respect for the authority of tradition and revelation, on the other hand freedom for the individual to follow his conscience and to search for truth; and it is this attitude which is distinctive of Anglicans compared with other Christians.

In the latter part of the sixteenth century, Anglican theology was for a time a good deal influenced by Calvinism, and the Church of England sent delegates to the Calvinist Synod of Dort in 1618. Lord Chatham once remarked that the Church of England had a Calvinist Creed (the Articles), a Catholic liturgy, and an Erastian clergy. There is a little truth in this, but that the Articles are not thoroughly Calvinist is proved by the repeated attempts of Calvinists in the sixteenth and seventeenth centuries to change them. Cranmer's aim in the Articles was merely so far as possible to satisfy the Calvinists and keep them in the Church of England.

In the early seventeenth century, which is often regarded as the golden age of the Church of England, many Anglicans, such as Laud, were Arminians; that is, as against Calvinism, they stressed the availability of God's grace for all men, and man's responsibility to accept or reject God's grace. John Wesley, too, was an Arminian. And for long there has been more ground for accusing Anglicans of going to the opposite extreme from Calvinism, and following Pelagius.

The truth is that both the Church of England and the Anglican Communion in general, while insisting on certain fundamental doctrines, such as the Incarnation and the Trinity and the use of the historic creeds and sacraments, allows much freedom in regard to doctrinal belief. Cranmer's aim was to exclude on the one hand purely medieval Roman doctrine, and on the other thoroughgoing Calvinism and extreme Protestantism; so as to enable both moderate Catholics and moderate Calvinists to accept the Articles and remain within the Church of England.

Anglican theology follows a middle way between Rome and Protestantism. This is clear, for example, in regard to the doctrine of the Eucharist. The Thirty-nine Articles reject the Roman or medieval doctrine of transubstantiation (Article 28); but at the same time, though some Anglicans hold the Zwinglian theory and regard the Holy Communion as no more than a memorial of Christ's death, the general Anglican tendency has been to reject this, and to see a much fuller and deeper meaning in the Eucharist.

In contrast to Roman Catholic custom, Communion in both kinds is allowed to the laity (Article 30). And it is emphasized that Christ on the Cross made a complete and perfect and final sacrifice for the sins of the world. The sacrifice on Calvary does not need, as many Romanists hold, or at any rate held in the sixteenth century, to be supplemented by the sacrifice of the Eucharist. Article 31, which teaches this, rejects the medieval custom of the sacrifice of Masses, with a view to diminishing the suffering of relatives or friends in Purgatory. But it does not deny that the Eucharist is a sacrifice. The English Archbishops, in their reply to Pope Leo XIII in 1897, clearly stated that the Church of England does hold the doctrine of Eucharistic sacrifice, and set out the meaning of this. The Eastern Orthodox had previously been doubtful of Anglican teaching in this respect, but in 1930 their representatives declared themselves satisfied with that statement, as being in accordance with Orthodox doctrine. The use of the name "Mass" for the Eucharist or Holy Communion is not forbidden, and indeed the first English Prayer Book used this name.

More than one theory is held by Anglicans as to the exact manner of Christ's Presence in the Eucharist. Some regard Christ as Present primarily in the whole service of the Eucharist, others see the Presence chiefly in the consecrated elements. The rule that at the end of the service the priest should reverently consume the remains of the consecrated elements (not throw them away or use them again at the next service, as would be reasonable on the purely Zwinglian view) shows that Anglicanism does maintain that consecration effects a change in the elements.[1] Anglicanism rigidly keeps the rule that only those ordained by the bishop in the historic succession may celebrate the Eucharist.

The ancient and general Church practice of infant baptism, which some (relatively few) Christians in recent centuries have discarded, is retained. Baptism is the door into the Church, and confers regeneration or new birth. In emergency, it may be performed by a layman and, provided it is with water and in the name of the Trinity, is accepted as valid. Properly baptized members of other Communions, therefore, if they become Anglicans, are not baptized again. Since in baptism only the proper intention is required, Anglicans follow the Western tradition in accepting even a baptism performed by a person not baptized; though some are dissatisfied with this attitude, as apparently denying that the sacraments are sacraments of the Church.[2]

The sacraments are declared in Article 25 to be effectual signs[3] of God's grace. They are, that is, effective instruments by means of which grace is given. The Catechism defines a sacrament as an outward and visible sign of an inward and spiritual grace given unto us; and as means of grace the sacraments have always been regarded as highly important, though it is not denied that God can and does give grace apart from the sacraments. The effectiveness of a sacrament does not depend on the worthiness or unworthiness of the minister who performs it.

[1] Cf., also *Lambeth Conference, 1930: Report*, p. 135.
[2] Cf., *Doctrine in the Church of England*, p. 133.
[3] The word "sign" is here used not in the sense of a mere empty symbol, not, that is, in the sense in which the Royal Standard flying over Buckingham Palace is a sign that the Queen is in residence, but in the sense in which certain fittings are a sign that electric light and power are available in the house. The flag does not bring the Queen, but the wiring is the actual means by which the power is conveyed. Cf. Wand, *What the Church of England Stands For*, pp. 67-8.

With regard to the number of sacraments, Anglicanism distinguishes between the Eucharist and Baptism, on the one hand, which were ordained by Christ, and the five others (Confirmation, Penance, Holy Orders, Matrimony, and Unction) for which Dominical Institution is not claimed. The first two are generally necessary to salvation, the other five are not (all Christians admit this: the laity and unmarried can be saved). As a result of medieval abuses, Article 25 is distinctly negative: but it is not denied that these five rites may be regarded as sacraments, and none of them is to be forbidden. The Eastern Orthodox were perplexed about Anglicanism in this respect, and their representatives asked a sub-committee of the Lambeth Conference of 1930 whether Anglicans regard Holy Orders as a sacrament or not. They were told that the term "sacrament" is used in a special sense of Baptism and the Eucharist, but that if the significance of a sacrament lies in its being the outward and visible sign of a spiritual gift, Holy Orders would be considered a sacrament. It was, moreover, stated that if there were any ambiguity in the Articles, they were to be interpreted by what the Prayer Book itself says.[1]

The traditional view of the Church is maintained as being characterized by the four notes of Unity, Holiness, Catholicity, and Apostolicity. It is one, for it is the Body of Christ, and it must seek to recover outward unity both in order and in the expression of its faith; the Church's unity is not confined to the present world. It is holy, as being a body set apart for God, and owing its existence to his will; the Church's first duty is to maintain the faith and life entrusted to it. It is catholic, both as the main guardian of the Christian tradition, and as potentially universal and all-inclusive, being entrusted with a mission to all mankind; the Church is supra-national, and links in fellowship the citizens of every rank in every nation. It is apostolic in that it preserves the essential tradition of the apostolic preaching and teaching, and maintains, as a safeguard of that tradition, a duly appointed order of ministers, who derive their commission in historical succession from the original apostolate.[2]

The Church is defined in Article 19 as a congregation of faithful men, in which the pure Word of God is preached and the sacraments are duly ministered according to Christ's ordinance. While Roman Catholics and Eastern Orthodox each regard their own Communion as alone constituting the true Church, no Anglicans hold this of the Anglican Com-

[1] *Lambeth Conference 1930: Report*, pp. 134–5.
[2] *Doctrine in the Church of England*, pp. 106–11.

munion. Some Anglicans regard bodies of Christians who have abandoned, or at least lack, the Church's historic order, as no true part of the Church, and certainly it is not easy, among the many Christian sects, more or less orthodox and unorthodox, to know where to draw the line. But in a general sense all those who believe in our Lord Jesus Christ and have been baptized in the name of the Holy Trinity are regarded as being members of the universal Church of Christ.[1]

Even General Councils of the Church, which some Christians regard as infallible, may err; and their decrees concerning what is necessary to salvation are authoritative only if they are based on the Bible (Article 21). In particular the decisions of the first four General Councils of the Church on matters of doctrine are held to be authoritative.

The Church has power to decree rites and ceremonies, and to make decisions in doctrinal controversies; but nothing may be maintained which is contrary to the Bible, nor may any belief not based on the Bible be insisted on as necessary for salvation (Article 20).

Anglicans would endorse Dr R. N. Flew's statement that the Church is the object of God's activity and also the instrument of his saving purpose for mankind; and would hold that its fundamental activity is worship.[2]

The conception of an invisible Church, which looms large in the outlook of some Christians, seems meaningless to Anglicans. It does not appear to them that anyone in the New Testament would be considered a Christian who was not a member of the visible society, the Church. The Church is not co-terminous with the elect, and not all members of the Church are saved, nor are all who are not members of the Church damned.[3]

It goes without saying that Anglicans regard Jesus as God Incarnate; the great majority accept also the traditional belief in his Virgin Birth. The Incarnation, as a unique event, may reasonably have used a unique method. The Jews, unlike many ancient people in Western Asia and Europe, honoured marriage highly, and so there is no reason why the early Christians should have invented a belief in Christ's Virgin Birth if this was not a fact. However, a few theologians and other Anglicans are doubtful about this tradition, and think it more congruent with Christ's perfect humanity that he should have been born in the normal way. In

[1] *Lambeth Conference, 1930: Appeal to all Christian People.*
[2] R. N. Flew, *Jesus and His Church*, p. 33.
[3] R. N. Flew, ed., *The Nature of the Church*, L. Hodgson on p. 134 and L. C. Lewis on pp. 310–11.

general, the Incarnation is regarded as the fundamental fact, and given this, belief in the Virgin Birth is not insisted on. Bishop Lightfoot ordained Hastings Rashdall, knowing that he definitely disbelieved the Virgin Birth, on the assurance that he did believe the Incarnation. A minority of the Church of England Doctrinal Commission took Rashdall's line, and Archbishop William Temple, the chairman of that Commission, who himself accepted the Virgin Birth as an historical fact, fully recognized the position of those who sincerely affirmed the reality of Christ's Incarnation without accepting the Virgin Birth as an historical occurrence.[1]

There is a similar question about the exact manner of Christ's Resurrection, whether or not on Easter morning the tomb was empty, and whether or not Christ's physical body rose again. The historical evidence for the Empty Tomb is much stronger than for the Virgin Birth. It is very difficult to believe that the disciples made a mistake and went to the wrong tomb, or to see how, without the Empty Tomb, the disciples could have become convinced that Christ had risen and overcome death, and could have become, as they did, changed men. The Resurrection was the core of the Apostles' preaching, which the unbelieving Jews bitterly opposed. If the tomb was not empty, why did not the latter, to refute the Apostles, produce Christ's dead body? And so a majority of the English Doctrine Commission, including Archbishop Temple, together with the great majority of Anglicans, affirmed the belief in the Empty Tomb and Christ's physical Resurrection. Archbishop Temple nevertheless recognized the position of those who believed in the Resurrection without believing in the Empty Tomb.[2]

With regard to Biblical miracles in general, many Anglicans would hold that most, perhaps all, records of miracles in the Old Testament are misunderstandings of natural events, or are unhistorical traditions. The miracles, however, which Christ is recorded in the Gospels to have done, are another matter. The historical evidence alone can never decisively prove that these miracles did or did not take place. Some members of the English Doctrine Commission thought that God would never want to interfere with the system of natural law which he has established and work what we call miracles (that is, events not according to the usual

---

[1] *Doctrine in the Church of England*, p. 12. This Report was never officially accepted by the Church of England, and so it has only the authority which its many distinguished signatories give it.

[2] Ibid., p. 12.

natural order). Others, however, think that God would for special reasons, at times in carrying out his purpose, act not according to the normal order, but perform miracles. These, if they occur, would not be breaches of order, but would express, just as much as the normal order of nature, God's purpose. The Doctrine Commission was divided on the question whether God would or would not do miracles, but agreed that he could do so. It is thought reasonable to suppose that Christ, being God Incarnate, may have done miracles, but that they could not occur except by his agency. Archbishop Temple held that God would not always act according to natural law, but would use different ways of carrying out his purpose; that is, that what we call miracles have happened.[1]

The traditional doctrine of original sin is maintained by Anglicanism, though some conceptions which have been read into it are not accepted. Fundamentally, the doctrine means that man has an inborn tendency to evil and to self-centredness (which, as William Temple used to insist, is the central sin). This doctrine is not bound up with the historical truth of any story of a Fall. The story of the Garden of Eden, however, has deep spiritual truth, an explanation of man's universal sinfulness, which is an unavoidable fact of experience. The origin of sin cannot be attributed to God. Milton is wrong in suggesting, as Genesis does not, that man was created perfect in both intellect and virtue.[2] The mere process of producing children certainly is not sinful and does not convey sin.[3]

The individual person is not responsible for this inborn tendency to sin; so it cannot be held, as some Christians following Augustine have done, that man has original guilt.[4] Augustine was moved by his own personal experience to lay tremendous weight on the terrible power of sin, man's weakness, and the irresistibility of God's grace. But he exaggerated a little, and the Church has not approved the whole of his teaching on these subjects. It is not necessary to hold, as he did, that man before the Fall was perfectly righteous; rather, he was morally neutral, neither moral nor immoral, but amoral, primitive, and immature, so that the Fall was in a sense a Fall up. Article 9, indeed, implies both man's

[1] Cf. *Doctrine in the Church of England*, pp. 10–11 and 50–52, and Iremonger, *William Temple*, pp. 533–5.

[2] Gore, *Reconstruction of Belief*, p. 569.

[3] *Doctrine in the Church of England*, p. 62.

[4] Gore, op. cit., p. 573. But some members of the English Doctrine Commission did regard original sin as involving guilt: cf. *Report*, p. 67.

righteousness before the Fall, and his original guilt. But the Articles were more influenced by Augustine and Calvin than Anglicanism has been since then.[1]

Article 17 declares that predestination to life is God's eternal purpose; but it is studiously vague, and does not say, as Calvin did, that some men are predestined by God to damnation, so that salvation is not possible for them; this is clean contrary to the New Testament (e.g. John 3.16), and is certainly not the Anglican view. Nor does Anglicanism hold, as Calvin did, that man as a consequence of the Fall, is totally corrupt, though the universality and terrible nature of sin is fully admitted. Article 9 does not teach total depravity.

The doctrine of justification by faith is naturally accepted (so Article 11). It is not, however, stressed nearly so much by Anglicans as by Lutherans, and the latter fear that Anglicans tend to minimize it. They were very unhappy over the statement about justification made by representatives of the Church of England and the Rumanian Orthodox Church in 1935. Many Protestants seem to Anglicans to lay so much weight on justification that they ignore sanctification, the gradually becoming more faithful to Christ of those already Christian and therefore justified.

Various theories have been advocated to explain how Christ's death made atonement for men, and Anglicanism, while insisting on the fact of the Atonement, has not made authoritative any one interpretation of it.

The medieval Roman doctrine of Purgatory is rejected in Article 22. It was crude and terrible, and incompatible with the love of God; it was also too mercenary and mechanical—a man's sufferings in Purgatory were held to be diminished precisely in proportion to the number of Masses which a priest was paid to say on his behalf. Whether or not all conception of Purgatory is rejected depends largely on the precise meaning one attaches to Purgatory. Many Anglicans believe that even after death church people need further training and growth in the knowledge and love of God, and some would call this further training Purgatory; many, however, would think it better to restrict the term Purgatory to the medieval conception, which is rejected by all Anglicans.

It is possible, as Origen held, that all men may eventually be saved, and Christians may hope that this will be so; on the other hand, it is clear that

[1] Doctrine in the Church of England, pp. 61 and 69; and Gore, Reconstruction of Belief, p. 569.

men have freedom to accept or reject the Gospel. Heaven and Hell are not places; the essence of Heaven is fellowship with God, the essence of Hell is exclusion from fellowship with God, and some may voluntarily choose the latter.

It is impossible to say whether or not there will be a Last Judgement, in the sense of an event after the end of this world's history; but certainly God's judgement on our earthly lives will be made manifest both to our neighbours and to ourselves.[1] There is great peril in the easy-going sentimentality of some modern forms of Christianity, which suppose all who have departed this life to be forthwith "in joy and felicity".[2] Belief in the Resurrection of the body means, as Origen declared, not resuscitation of the particles of flesh and blood which compose men's earthly bodies, but the eternal life of the complete personality.

Because in the Middle Ages men had an unworthy and mechanical conception of prayer for the dead, many Christians since the Reformation have rejected it altogether. The early Church, however, did pray for the dead, and the practice never entirely died out in the Church of England. It is doubtful to what extent the 1662 Prayer Book implies prayer for the departed; the Prayer for the Church is restricted to the Church Militant here on earth as distinct from the Church Expectant or Triumphant, already in Heaven. But the Prayer of Oblation was said by the English archbishops in 1897 (in their reply to Pope Leo XIII) to include the Church Expectant, when prayer is made that "we and all Thy whole Church may obtain remission of our sins". Anglicanism has never forbidden prayer for the dead, and recent revisions of the Prayer Book imply it much more clearly. If there is any such fellowship of living and departed as Christians have always believed, there can be no theological objection in principle to prayer for the departed.[3] Admittedly, in praying for the dead, it is not possible to do much more than commend them to God's care, since we can know so little about the conditions of their life.

It may be regarded as legitimate to ask for the prayers of departed friends, as we might ask for their prayers while still in this world, and this was done in the ancient Church. But there is, as Gore pointed out,[4] no support for this in the New Testament, and still less is there evidence there of direct invocation of saints. And so the tendency among Anglicans

[1] *Doctrine in the Church of England*, p. 206.
[2] Ibid., p. 217.
[3] Ibid., pp. 215–16.
[4] Op. cit., p. 932.

has been to abandon this; and it (or at least the Roman doctrine of it) is explicitly ruled out by Article 22.

Anglicanism is criticized by many Christians, especially Eastern Orthodox and Lutherans, for being too lax and ambiguous in doctrine. It cannot but seem vague and confused, since it is at once liberal and traditional, and has connections and common convictions on the one hand with the more Evangelical or Protestant or Free Churches, and on the other hand with the more Catholic Churches. But fundamentally the Anglican attitude is certainly not just to allow anyone to hold any belief, so as to be completely "comprehensive"; it is by no means vague and uncertain in regard to true doctrine. On the contrary, it emphasizes the wholeness of the Christian Faith, it loyally upholds the historic creeds and the Faith handed down from the Apostles, and it believes that the Holy Spirit will in each age lead it to understand and explain the historic Christian Faith; it certainly does not want a new Faith in each new age.

9

Worship

ANGLICAN worship is of course based on the Book of Common Prayer. This is not exactly the same in all English-speaking countries; and while some of the many translations into other languages are word-for-word translations of one or other English version, other versions incorporate not a few changes. Nevertheless, the various Prayer Books used in the Anglican Communion are very similar to each other, and the Book of Common Prayer is in fact one of the great bonds which link the self-governing Anglican Churches; it may even be said that the real Anglican unity is liturgical.[1] The Prayer Book is a very important standard of Anglican doctrine and order,[2] and the ethos of Anglicanism is in a very real sense exhibited in the Prayer Book.

In the sixteenth century, the Church's worship needed reform no less than other aspects of its life. Some of its forms of service implied doctrine that was far from the faith of the Bible and ancient Church, or even downright superstitious. Some tended to be too elaborate and long-winded, and much of it lacked real spiritual meaning. During recent centuries English had come increasingly to be a literary language, and those who knew Latin were never more than a minority.

Providentially, Thomas Cranmer, who had been a don at Cambridge and was now Archbishop of Canterbury, had a great gift for composing forms of worship, and was also a master of the English language. He first composed the English litany, based on many ancient litanies; this was published in 1544. He continued to compose reformed forms of worship in English, and in 1549 Parliament ordered the use of the first English

[1] Bishop S. C. Neill in *East and West Review*, April 1948.
[2] Cf. *Lambeth Conference, 1930: Report*, p. 162, and *Lambeth Conference, 1948 Report*, Part I, p. 23.

Prayer Book, which was probably for the most part his personal work.

The basic principles on which this first English Prayer Book was composed are still those of the Book of Common Prayer in all its forms and in all the languages in which it exists.

In the first place, it had much in common with the worship of the ancient undivided Church and links also with the Eastern Orthodox tradition; it retains much which was used in the medieval Western Catholic Church and is now also used in the Roman Church.

Secondly, it was thoroughly Biblical, both as being based on and according to the teaching of the Bible, and as making great use of it. Medieval worship had departed far from Biblical standards and the Bible had been relatively little read in worship (and then in Latin); instead legends of the saints had been read, and other passages from uncanonical books, parts of which had all too little value and were sometimes misleading, or actually wrong in their teaching. In contrast to this, apart from the Epistle and Gospel at the Eucharist, Morning and Evening Prayer consist very largely of passages from the Bible—Old Testament and New Testament lessons, Psalms, and some of the Canticles.

Thirdly, it simplified worship very much. The old services had become very elaborate and complicated and lengthy, and the rubrics and rules most involved. This simplification, incidentally, often meant a return to the usage of the ancient Church.

Fourthly, instead of Latin, as theretofore, the English vernacular was used, so that all could understand and share in the service.

Fifthly, services were to be more congregational. They were to be audible to the congregation, who were also to have an active share in the service, by saying some parts with the priest, and reciting other parts responsively. The use of the vernacular of course greatly helped this.

Sixthly, the Prayer Book was both Catholic and Evangelical, and remains so in its various forms, though these vary a little in where they lay the greater stress.

To emphasize the Church's unity, all parishes were to use the same Prayer Book, instead of retaining a great variety of local usage. Though this Prayer Book was a splendid achievement, many were dissatisfied with it. In some districts there were demonstrations against it by crowds who said that they understood the old worship better; others were influenced by Continental Reformers to demand more thorough changes.

So Cranmer in 1552 produced the Second English Prayer Book, and this was prescribed by Parliament for use in all parishes. A number of medieval ceremonies hitherto retained, especially in the Occasional Offices, were abandoned. The Introduction (exhortation, confession, absolution) was added to Morning and Evening Prayer. The Canon, or central part, of the Eucharist was broken up, so as to be less like the Roman Mass. The *Gloria in Excelsis* was transferred from the beginning to the end of the service, a change which has been well called "a sublime stroke of liturgical genius".[1] The surplice was ordered to be used in place of the traditional eucharistic vestments. The Prayer for the Church was to be only for the Church militant here on earth, with no thought of the faithful departed. At the Administration, in place of the words in the first half of the present long combined form ("The Body, Blood, of our Lord Jesus Christ . . .") was substituted the second half of this (Take and eat this . . ." "Drink this . . ."). How much, if any, change of doctrine was implied continues to be debated; Cranmer himself claimed that there was no change.

Very soon after this, during the reign of Mary Tudor, the medieval Latin services were restored. When Elizabeth came to the throne, the Third English Prayer Book was issued. This changed a little, in the Catholic direction, the form of 1552; for example, the Ornaments Rubric prescribed again the use of eucharistic vestments, including the alb and chasuble or cope. For the Administration the phrases used in 1549 and in 1552 were combined (as they remain in the English Book of Common Prayer). The Black Rubric, declaring that kneeling at Communion did not imply adoration, was omitted, and so was the petition in the Litany for deliverance from the Pope. The aim of those chiefly responsible for this book, Elizabeth and Archbishop Matthew Parker, was to satisfy moderate men of all groups.

However, Puritan feeling was increasingly strong in England during Elizabeth's reign. The Puritans were strongly opposed to the use of eucharistic vestments (so that their use in fact died out till the nineteenth century), and even to the wearing of the surplice, kneeling at Communion, the sign of the Cross (including its use at baptism), organs, the ring in marriage, observance of holy days other than Sunday (for example, Christmas and Good Friday). The Puritans argued that such things could not be reconciled with worship in spirit and in truth, and were wrong both because they are not clearly ordered in the Bible and because they are used by the Roman Church. In opposition to them,

[1] S. C. Neill in H. Martin, ed., *The Holy Communion*, p. 52.

Richard Hooker characteristically argued that customs were not necessarily bad simply because they were followed by Rome, and that what was not contrary to the Bible was permissible, even if not directly ordered by it. This has become a fundamental Anglican principle.

Anglicans were able to maintain most, though not all, of these historic usages. For some time the Holy Table was an ordinary table, often moved about and sometimes used for secular purposes, till Laud ordered that it should be left permanently at the East End of the church. A few small additions were made to the Prayer Book in 1604.

Under the Commonwealth and the Puritan ascendancy, the use of the Prayer Book was forbidden (in 1644), and the observance of Christmas, for example, was made illegal. After the Restoration, attempts were made at the conference at the Savoy Hospital in 1661 to reconcile the Puritans to the Prayer Book; but they were conscientiously opposed to much in it, and now left the Church of England, mainly because of this.

The Prayer Book was again revised in 1662, and many changes, mostly small, were made. Commemoration of the dead was restored in the Prayer for the Church at the Eucharist; the so-called State Prayers were added at Mattins and Evensong; and so were various thanksgivings, including the General Thanksgiving, which had been composed shortly before this by Reynolds, Bishop of Norwich. The work "priest" was several times substituted for "minister". This Prayer Book, unlike earlier ones, was formally sanctioned by the Convocations.

A futile attempt was made in 1689 to rewrite the Prayer Book in such a way as to satisfy the more moderate Nonconformists, and in 1772 there was an unsuccessful movement to revise it in a liberal direction. During the nineteenth and early twentieth centuries, partly but by no means wholly as a result of the Oxford Movement, the Prayer Book of 1662 was increasingly felt to be not completely satisfactory, and to need enrichment in various directions. And not a few unauthorized enrichments and changes were in fact made.

The Church Assembly and Convocations in 1927–8 sanctioned a revised Prayer Book. This made many changes of varying importance, some more and some less controversial. It allowed the use of our Lord's Summary of the Law instead of the Ten Commandments, and many other alternative usages; a number of new occasional Prayers were provided; an alternative form of Holy Communion had a new Canon (or central part), and Reservation of the Sacrament, though only for the Communion of the Sick) was allowed. The book, however, was violently opposed by both extreme wings of the Church, and the prospect of its bringing peace and order seemed remote. It was rejected by the House of Commons. Most of the Bishops then courageously declared that they would allow the use of the new Prayer Book, but would try to stop such practices as were not sanctioned either by it or the 1662 book. Parts of the new book have come to be very widely used.

The Welsh Church, which from the twelfth century till its disestablishment in 1920 was part of the Province of Canterbury, still uses the 1662 Prayer Book, and has not sanctioned the 1928 revision or made any other revision. The English Prayer Book was translated into the Welsh language soon after the Reformation.

The Church of Ireland used the same Prayer Book as the Church of England till it was disestablished in 1870. Unfortunately it was not translated into the Irish language, which most Irish spoke in the sixteenth century, till 1608. A revision was made after disestablishment, and again in 1929; but liturgical development seems to have been permanently arrested. Thus the Eastward position for the Eucharist, wafer bread, candles on the altar except when necessary to give light, coloured stoles, and the sign of the Cross (except at baptism), are all forbidden. In other respects, however, the Irish Book has its merits, not least a revised translation of the Psalter, which clears up many obscurities.

The Scottish Prayer Book has always kept closer to the 1549 book than later English Prayer Books have done. In the Eucharist the Prayer for the Church is part of the Canon, an unbroken central prayer, which includes an Epiclesis, or invocation of the Holy Spirit; but in contrast to the 1549 book, the *Gloria in Excelsis* comes at the end. The Church of England Prayer Book is, however, also authorized and widely used in Scotland.

Until 1783 Anglicans in North America used the Church of England Prayer Book. In view of American Independence, this was naturally revised, and the Prayers for the Sovereign omitted; but the Preface to the American Prayer Book still states that there is no intention to depart from the Church of England in any essential point of doctrine, discipline, or worship. It was at first proposed to omit both the Athanasian and Nicene Creeds, and also the "descent into hell" from the Apostles' Creed and all phrases implying baptismal regeneration, and to make use of the sign of the Cross in baptism optional. However, when the Prayer Book was finally sanctioned by the General Convention in 1789, it included the Nicene, though not the Athanasian, Creed. The form for the Eucharist was based on the Scottish Rite, not that of the 1662 English Book and was thus closer than the latter to the 1549 Book and to the Eastern Orthodox tradition. This American book was revised in 1892 and 1928, and made somewhat more flexible; in the latter year the Lord's Prayer and Prayer of Humble Access were put immediately before the administration of Communion. The American Church now has a standing Liturgical Commission to consider what changes in the Prayer Book may from time to time be necessary.

The Lambeth Conference of 1930 explicitly recognized, as previous Lambeth Conferences had done implicitly, the right of other branches of the Anglican Communion to make suitable changes in the Prayer Book, and not to be bound by the usage of the Church of England. The Church of England in Australia is by its own rules committed to the exact usage of the Church of England, except that it has its own book of Occasional Services; and so is the Church in New Zealand.

The English Book of Common Prayer has been translated into many languages. In the sixteenth century it was put into Latin for use in the universities, and in Ireland (where most of the clergy at that time did not understand English). In the following century it was put into French for use in the Channel Islands. A French version of the English Book is now used in Mauritius, while the American book has been put into French for Haiti and elsewhere. In Cuba and elsewhere a Spanish translation is used. The Book of Common Prayer, in whole or in part, has also been translated into about 200 of the languages of Asia, Africa, and other parts of the world. Some of these versions are word-for-word translations; others contain numerous, usually not very important, changes: some are based on the 1662 book; others are closer to the 1549 version, or follow the Scottish or American use.

The Indian Church was till 1930 tied to the usage of the Church of England. It then prepared its own Prayer Book, and three forms of the Eucharist are provisionally authorized in the Church of India, Pakistan, Burma, and Ceylon: a form similar to the English 1928 form but, for example, containing a litany as an alternative to the Prayer for the Church; the form of 1662; and a "Liturgy for India" which attempts to give a more specifically Eastern form[1]. A special Ceylon liturgy has been sanctioned for use only in Ceylon, which, like the "Liturgy for India", makes considerable use of forms derived from the old Eastern Churches.

South Africa also has its own book, which began as a series of Alterna-

---

[1] It is doubtful, however, if this third form will receive final authorization.

tive Forms of the various Services and was issued finally in 1954 as a complete Book of Common Prayer authorized for the whole Province. It includes many enrichments approximating to those in the 1928 Book, extra Occasional Offices appropriate to local conditions, and Collects, Epistles, and Gospels for minor Feasts and Fasts; and has been translated into the major vernaculars.

In China the Prayer Book has been translated into the national spoken language (Kuo Yü or Mandarin), the old literary language, and the lesser languages used along the south-east coast. Some versions have been made from the 1662 book, others from the American, while others have made not a few changes. The various dioceses up to the present use different Prayer Books. The desire had often been expressed for a standard Book to be used by all dioceses, so the General Synod of C.H.S.K.H. resolved in 1947 that steps should be taken towards its preparation. In Japan one Prayer Book, a blend of the 1662 and American books, with some adaptations and alternatives, is used throughout the Church; and a revised Eucharistic liturgy has been provisionally authorized. The Korean Prayer Book is for the most part a translation of the English 1549 book.

The Anglican Reformers in the sixteenth century wished the Eucharist to continue to be the main service each Sunday, as it had always been; and it is because of this that the Prayer Book mentions the possibility of a sermon only in the Communion service, not at Mattins or Evensong, which were intended as daily services, not specially for Sundays.[1] They also wanted the congregation to understand the language of the service, and to receive Communion more frequently. Before the Reformation, the minimum rule for receiving Communion was once a year, and in fact actual Communion was rare. The Anglican Reformers laid down as a minimum three times a year, of which Easter was to be one. They also restored to the laity the chalice, which had in the Middle Ages gradually come to be denied to them.

Both in England and elsewhere there has been much controversy in recent times concerning the rightness or otherwise of Reservation of the Sacrament, whether for Communion of the Sick or for Devotions before the Reserved Sacrament. For the latter there seems in most parts at least of the Anglican Communion to be no particular authorization. The 1928 English Prayer Book sanctioned in a guarded way Reservation

[1] The sermon is now regarded as having an essential place in worship, though it is not the chief or central part of an Anglican service.

for the Sick (the fact that it did so was one of the chief reasons for the opposition to it); but no service, such as Benediction or Devotions, in connection with the Reserved Sacrament is allowed, nor may the Sacrament be exposed. The Scottish Prayer Book explicitly allows Reservation for the Sick, and so does the revised Eucharistic liturgy put out by the American Liturgical Commission for study purposes. Archbishop William Temple was convinced (as Charles Gore had been) that the Church should not sanction organized worship in the presence of the Reserved Sacrament, because of two great spiritual dangers involved: those who learn to rely on the help of Christ's sacramental Presence may find it more difficult to apprehend his Presence when there is no sacramental medium at hand, and they may easily slip into some form of superstitious belief in an actually localized Presence of Christ.

Intinction, instead of administration from the chalice, is allowed for hygienic reasons in some American churches; the American Liturgical Commission's Rite allows it and directs that the diocesan bishop should determine the manner of it. The Lambeth Conference in 1948 recommended that administration from the common chalice, being scriptural and having symbolic meaning of great value, should continue to be the normal method of administration, but that there was no objection to intinction where conditions required it; the manner of intinction was to be regulated by the Province and not left to the individual priest.

Fasting before Communion is not obligatory upon Anglicans, but is regarded as a laudable ancient custom, and its observance is a link with the historic Church; it is a reminder of the need of self-discipline for worthy reception of Communion, and of the facts that Communion should not be left to the last (so giving priority to things which are really less important), and that through it God's grace is received for the tasks of the day. As in the Roman Church now, fasting is not necessarily held to mean abstinence from food and drink since the previous midnight, but rather for a limited period before Communion.

In accordance with an old canon, and also the recently approved rules for Church membership, attendance at public worship each Sunday is one of the duties of Church people and the minimum obligation for receiving Communion thrice a year.

It is an Anglican characteristic to stress reverence in worship. This is entirely in line with modern psychological teaching concerning the interrelatedness of the outward and the inward. Most ceremony originates from some practical necessity, but in time comes to have a value independent of this. Ceremony is a link both between worshippers gathered in one place, and also between them and church people separated from them in place or time. Beauty, moreover, is divine, and therefore has to be considered in the arrangement of worship. Robes and vestments both strengthen corporate feeling, and, since they do not vary with the economic status of the individual, are democratic. The reverence of its worship is unquestionably in all countries one of the features of Anglicanism most attractive to non-Anglicans.

The usual Anglican custom is to stand for praise of God (for example, when singing hymns), to sit when receiving instruction (the lessons and sermon), and to kneel for prayer. Incidentally, this last is not quite in accordance with the practice of the early Church, which was to stand for prayer, except in times of special crisis or in penitence[1]; kneeling probably came to be usual because of our Lord's example in Gethsemane. Kneeling and standing both, in distinction from sitting, imply respect and reverence.

In general, Anglicanism allows great freedom in ceremonial, as in doctrine, and on many points there is no rule. Many Anglicans bow towards the altar when passing in front of it, and at the mention of Jesus' name in the Creed (or at all mention of it), but some do not. Some bow or kneel at the recital of the facts of the Incarnation in the Creed, as the central mystery of the Christian Faith. Some make the sign of the Cross (chiefly in the Eucharist at the end of the Creed and before the Gospel, at the Blessing and perhaps Absolution, perhaps at the beginning and end of private prayer). But all these and similar acts of reverence are for Anglicans purely optional and left to the discretion of the individual.

The Anglican use of liturgical (or fixed) forms of worship was in the past often criticized by the Free Churches as being formal and lifeless. Even to say together the Lord's Prayer was in the past regarded by Presbyterians, and is perhaps still regarded by some conservative Presbyterians, as an Anglican peculiarity. But the objection to liturgical forms is steadily disappearing even among Free Churchmen. They are indeed virtually a necessity if a congregation is to take an active part in worship; without them, worship depends entirely on the minister; the use of the Prayer Book transcends the failings and limitations of the minister and checks individualism. The use of traditional forms of worship, such as are in the Prayer Book, links the Church of to-day with the Church which has gone before, from which the Prayer Book has been inherited, and

[1] So the twentieth Canon of the Council of Nicaea (A.D. 325) forbade kneeling and ordered standing for prayer on Sundays.

indeed with many non-Anglican Christians to-day who use similar forms (such as the Eastern Orthodox and Roman Catholics); while the Prayer Book is of course one of the chief of the bonds which unite Anglicans in different countries.

Bishops may, and do, authorize both special forms of service and special books of prayers, and it is generally recognized that clergy have wide freedom in choosing suitable prayers for use after the Third Collect at Mattins and Evensong. And, where this is appropriate, opportunities may be given for silent prayer during Anglican services. In worship, as in other ways, Anglicanism combines order with freedom and variety.

Anglicans have never objected, as the early Presbyterians and Congregationalists did, to the use of music in worship, though it is true that Hooker was so far influenced by the Puritan atmosphere of his time as to regard music in worship as just a concession to human frailty. The Prayer Book does not mention hymns, and till the middle of the nineteenth century Anglican liturgical worship included virtually no hymns, singing; apart from the canticles, was restricted to the metrical psalms. In England the first edition of *Hymns Ancient and Modern* came out in 1861, and the situation was much the same in the other Anglican Churches. Charles Wesley was the first of many distinguished Anglican hymn-writers.

The Book of Common Prayer is a great bulwark and guardian of the historic Faith. It can be, and should be, revised from time to time; but, being relatively fixed, it does not merely reflect whatever theological or ecclesiastical opinion may be fashionable at any particular moment; it sets forth the fundamental truths of the Bible, and prevents, or at least discourages, the substitution of faith in man for faith in God. So Dr Reinhold Niebuhr regarded the Prayer Book as having done more than episcopacy to save Anglicans from Pelagianism and rationalism. Successive Lambeth Conferences have all declared that the Prayer Book is a most important standard of, and witness to, Anglican faith and order.

The fundamental nature of Anglicanism as both Catholic and reformed or evangelical is well expressed in the Prayer Book.[1] As we have seen, it was originally composed in such a way that clergy and church people of either Catholic or reformed sympathies could happily use it. Its links with the worship of Eastern Orthodoxy and the Roman Church are obvious. On the other hand, it is reformed as being in the vernacular, stressing preaching, making great use of the Bible, and rejecting the necessity of doctrines without a Biblical basis. It appears that the Pope

[1] Cf. *Lambeth Conference 1948: Report*, Part II, p. 83.

would have been willing to sanction the Elizabethan Prayer Book as Catholic, if Elizabeth had been willing to receive it as from him. The Preface to the 1662 book well explains the object of the Book of Common Prayer as being to reconcile Catholic and Evangelical, to combine order and freedom, and "to keep the mean between the two extremes, of too much stiffness in refusing, and of too much easiness in admitting, any variation from it." Because Anglicanism is united by loyalty to the Prayer Book, it has been able to allow more freedom than other Communions in regard to doctrinal opinion.

Successive Lambeth Conferences have recognized, with ever-increasing clarity and emphasis, that, though the authority of the Book of Common Prayer should be maintained as the standard of Anglican doctrine and practice, the Prayer Books of the various Churches of the Anglican Communion need not be entirely uniform. This is the old Anglican principle enshrined in Article 34—every national Church has authority to ordain change and abolish ceremonies or rites of the Church ordained (not by Christ or the Bible but) only by man's authority, provided that everything is done for the edification of church people. As we have seen, the Prayer Books used in different countries do in fact have certain differences.

Moreover, the Anglican tradition of worship allows a wide freedom for the use of Oriental or African customs and ceremonies in worship.[1] And in India, for example, where the marriage service of the English Prayer Book seems very short and bare, Indian ceremonies are added to it. In China, too, there have been adaptations in the marriage service: in the North China diocese, for example, the banns are called before the engagement rather than just before the wedding; in one prayer, reference is made to the ancestors of the bridegroom and the bride; to "Who giveth this woman?" is added "Who giveth this man?"—that is, both families must recognize the marriage to make it valid; and the signing and sealing of the certificate of marriage are done publicly as part of the marriage. Some dioceses in China have a special form of service for use when a dead person's body is put into the coffin, while special forms of service for the commemoration of the faithful departed, perhaps in connection with corporate visits to the Christian cemetery, are not uncommon.[2]

[1] Cf. H. P. Thompson, *Worship in Other Lands*.

[2] Cf. further my article "A note on some Church customs in China" in *The East and West Review*, Oct. 1946.

How much uniformity in public worship is desirable is a difficult question. It is held by some that the great divergence to be found in worship in Church of England churches is one of the causes of the decline of church attendance; and how far a self-governing Church of the Anglican Communion could depart from the traditional Anglican pattern of worship without leaving the Anglican Communion has never been made clear. J. S. Burdon (Bishop of Hongkong and South China 1875–97) suggested that the Church in China should in the Eucharist use rice and tea, as the equivalent in China of bread and wine in Palestine in the first century. It is hardly likely that such a dramatic break with Christian tradition, and one which involves such a loss in symbolic meaning, would ever be sanctioned. The position is that on the one hand much variety is permissible, while on the other there has never been any indication of what are the limits within which alone such variety is permissible. All would agree that especially in Asia and Africa there is need for more adaptation and enrichment of the Prayer Book and for some indigenization of Anglican worship. On the other hand, a high authority has held that some of the Anglican provinces are much too reckless in their liturgical departures from the standard Anglican pattern.

So far as England and some other English-speaking countries are concerned, desire for change and improvement of the Prayer Book is along two main lines. Not a few desire that the service of the Eucharist should be enriched by a larger element of thanksgiving and reference not only to Christ's Passion and Death but also to His Resurrection and Ascension, by an Invocation of the Spirit on the Eucharistic elements, or on the Communicants that they may receive the Sacrament worthily by a fuller provision of special Collects, Epistles, and Gospels and other variable parts of the service, by more prayer for the faithful departed, and commemoration of a larger number of saints. Recent revisions of the Holy Communion Service outside England mostly make more of the Offertory and of the oblation of the elements, make the Prayer for the Church more inclusive, with fuller reference to the faithful departed, and put the Prayer of Oblation and Lord's Prayer before the Communion. There is also a feeling that the Occasional Offices should be simplified, and that either there should be simpler and more popular alternatives to Mattins and Evensong, or possibly a series of services additional to those already in the Prayer Book. It may at the same time, however, perhaps be doubted whether it is really possible to provide a Prayer Book in which every service is wholly intelligible and edifying to every chance person who may happen to attend the service, and which yet bears balanced witness to the whole Christian Faith.[1]

The Lambeth Conference of 1948 declared[2] that the Book of Common Prayer has been, and is, so strong a bond of unity throughout the whole Anglican Communion that great care must be taken to ensure that revisions of the book shall be in accordance with the doctrine and accepted liturgical worship of Anglicanism. The committee of that Conference which was especially concerned with this question repeated[3] the declaration of previous Lambeth Conferences that Churches in Africa and Asia must have generous liberty of experiment in liturgy, and said that the time had come to examine those features in the Book of Common Prayer which are essential to the safeguarding of the unity of the Anglican Communion. The Lambeth Conference of 1958 will have more to say on this important subject.

The Anglican tradition of public worship is not only one of the chief bonds which unite Anglicans all over the world, but one of its greatest contributions to Christendom as a whole, and a treasure which the non-episcopal Churches are coming increasingly to appreciate and indeed to use; many being attracted by what they call its combination of reverence and devotion with lack of unreasonable mystification. It has even been suggested that it might suitably take the place of the Lambeth Quadrilateral as a basis on which Church Unity might be achieved.

[1] Cf. C. Dunlop, *Anglican Public Worship*, p. 72.
[2] *Report*, Part I, p. 46.
[3] *Lambeth Conference 1948: Report*, Part II, p. 86.

10

Order and Organization

ANGLICANISM, with its stress on the Church as the Body of Christ and on the corporate nature of Christianity, cannot but assign great importance to the Church's order. This is the case whether order is regarded as definitely subordinate to faith, or whether it is regarded as strictly speaking part of faith. And so the English Ordinal states that from the Apostles' time there have been in Christ's Church three orders of ministers: bishops, priests, and deacons; that no man may presume to exercise any of these offices till properly authorized to do so; and that these offices should be continued. The other Anglican Churches have substantially similar statements.

Historically, of course, the Church's order, like its Canon of Scripture and standards of faith, developed, though at an earlier date than these, in response to the needs of the early Church and the perilous situation in which it found itself. The Church's order was a safeguard of its unity, sound faith, and very existence, all of which were seriously threatened. This historic threefold order, which was common to all Christians till the sixteenth century, is retained by the great majority of Christians.

While Roman Catholics seem to regard the ministry as existing independently of, and as above, the Church, Anglicans would rather regard [1] a distinctive ministry as an orginal element, but not the sole constitutive element, in the life of the Church. A distinction corresponding to that drawn later between clergy and laity is there from the outset. It is not necessary to demand or expect acceptance of any one theory of the origins of the ministry. [2] But the ministry exists in succession to the original apostolate; the bishops were, and are, regarded as having taken the place

[1] *Doctrine in the Church of England*, p. 115.
[2] L. Hodgson, ed., *Convictions*, p. 185.

of the Apostles, except indeed that they are not in the same sense witnesses of Christ's Resurrection.

Maintenance of the threefold ministry and the episcopate is indeed one of the bonds which link together Anglicans in different countries; it is also a necessary condition of any united Church which Anglicans could enter. They adhere to episcopacy as the source and centre of their order.[1]

Many Free Church people are coming to admit that episcopacy is a convenient and suitable form of Church government. The great majority of Anglicans, however, regard episcopacy as much more than only a convenient form of administration. Though there is not complete agreement concerning the theory of episcopacy, it is valued above all as an organ of unity and continuity; bishops should have those functions which in the historic and catholic Church they have always had.

Bishops on the one hand help to link together church people in different places and parishes by visiting them, and in the House of Bishops and at other meetings link together their several dioceses; and on the other, they link the Church of to-day with the Church of past centuries and with the Apostolic Church. So, through their bishops, Anglicans, like Eastern Orthodox, Roman Catholics, and Old Catholics, maintain the Apostolic succession.

Historically the episcopate has certainly been a very valuable and effective check on schism, and has led those Churches that have it to stress not only individual religion but the body of the Church. Episcopal Churches, while not entirely free from schism, have in fact been much less prone to division than have the non-episcopal Churches, and the description of bishops as the cement or glue of the Church is true to life.

The functions of a bishop, apart from maintaining the Church's unity and continuity, have not always been the same. The only function which has always been restricted to bishops is that of ordaining clergy to administer the Church's sacraments and teach its doctrine (and in fact in the ancient Celtic Church bishops were monks who, apart from ordaining as needed, lived as ordinary monks). If the power of ordination were not restricted, schisms under self-appointed leaders and holding false doctrine would be encouraged.

The Anglican bishop is also a shepherd of shepherds. Clergy need a father-in-God who will guide and encourage and where necessary warn and discipline them, in a way that no chairman with an annual term of office can do. Through the administration of Confirmation, the bishop

[1] *Lambeth Conference 1948: Report*, Part II, p. 85.

is brought into pastoral relationship with the lay members of his flock, and he has a general responsibility for supervising the Church. His actual governmental powers and responsibility, for example in regard to the appointment of parish clergy, may and do vary very much, even in different dioceses of the same province. He has a *jus liturgicum*, in virtue of which he may issue forms of service and prayers for special occasions, though he may not alter any of the Prayer Book services.

Bishops also, in the Anglican view, which as usual is in accordance with Christian tradition, have a special responsibility for maintaining the purity of the Church's faith; and so, for example, in the English Church Assembly, no measure purporting to express the Church's teaching can be initiated except by the bishops. Stress on the episcopate is in fact closely related to concern for sound Christian doctrine.

Richard Hooker in the sixteenth century made the classical Anglican defence of episcopacy against the Puritans, who argued that the Bible insisted on the parity of ministers, or in fact presbyterianism. Hooker claimed that the Bible did not prescribe any one definite form of Church government, but that it was neither necessary nor convenient for all clergy to have precisely the same status and responsibility, and accordingly the historic threefold ministry should be kept. After the death of the Apostles, the bishops took their place. In opposition to Congregationalism, which was then arising, Hooker claimed that the clergy derived their authority not from the laity but from God.

Some Anglicans regard episcopacy as so indispensable that without it there is no true Church; others only claim that it is highly desirable. Since, however, all desire the highest for the Church, the difference here is not as great as is sometimes supposed. Anglicanism, though it nowhere explicitly declares that episcopacy is of the Church's *esse*, or that only ordination by bishops and celebration of the Eucharist by priests who have been ordained by bishops is valid, is certainly pledged to episcopacy in the sense that it will never join a non-episcopal Church.

Equally, all Anglicans in fact uphold the principle of Apostolic Succession, though some value it more highly than others. Dr Leonard Hodgson sets out[1] a characteristic Anglican attitude: in any earthly society, unity and continuity from generation to generation depend on two factors interwoven like two strands of a single rope, the outward continuity of organization and the inward continuity of spirit faith and practice; and we cannot rightly exercise less care in matters spiritual than

[1] In R. N. Flew, ed., *The Nature of the Church*, p. 142.

is required in matters temporal. Maintenance of the Apostolic Succession and the historic ministry goes with, and is a help to, preservation of the Church's historic doctrine.

Consecration of a bishop is regularly by three bishops, though consecration by one bishop would be valid in case of emergency. In most Anglican Churches a bishop is elected, in accordance with tradition, by the clergy and laity of his diocese, but the other dioceses in the province must usually express their consent to the choice made. Nomination, as in England, by the Sovereign on the recommendation of the Prime Minister, is by no means a necessary Anglican custom, and is due to fortuitous historical circumstances.

Most Anglican provinces are presided over by an archbishop. An archbishop is in point of order a bishop, and has no additional spiritual responsibilities inherent in his office; but the other bishops in the province promise canonical obedience to him. The Scottish Church, however, has not an archbishop but a Primus, who is elected for life, and the other bishops give their oath of allegiance not to the Primus, but to the Synod of Bishops. The American Church has no archbishop, but instead there is a Presiding Bishop of the House of Bishops; formerly he was the senior bishop by date of consecration, but since 1925 the Presiding Bishop is elected, and now on election he gives up his diocese and becomes a bishop without a see; the bishops at their consecration promise conformity and obedience to the doctrine discipline and worship of the Episcopal Church. In China and Japan any bishop may, while retaining his diocese, be Chairman of the House of Bishops, and as such is recognized by the Lambeth Conference as a Metropolitan.

The other two Anglican orders are those of priest and deacon, who on the one hand are ministers of the Word, authorized to expound the Church's teaching, and on the other hand are ministers of the sacraments and authorized to administer these. Article 23 declares that a man may not take up on himself the responsibility of either public preaching or administering the sacraments; only those may do so who have been authorized by those who have the responsibility of conferring this authorization, that is, the bishops, though in case of emergency a lay person may baptize. An archdeacon in the Middle Ages was usually a deacon; he was called the bishop's eye, and was responsible for the property and finance of the diocese; nowadays, an archdeacon is in point of order a priest responsible for supervising clergy and parishes in an area usually smaller than a diocese.

Some African dioceses make use of the traditional minor orders, such as subdeacon, acolyte, reader; but most provinces do not, or at any rate do not regard them as offices of holy order, though there is no definite objection to so regarding them.

Of recent years there has been considerable discussion in Anglican circles of the desirability of ordaining men who would depend for their living on, and give most of their time to, some so-called secular occupation, for example farming or engineering; or alternatively, of men already ordained undertaking some secular work. It is probable that during the first three centuries, before the Church was officially tolerated by the Roman government, most clergy and even bishops largely supported themselves by some outside occupation; but when the Church became stronger in numbers and its resources greater, it could provide for its clergy to give all their time to specific Church work. And eventually canons were made which prohibited the clergy from engaging in trade; since it had been found that if a priest was allowed to do so, it was only too easy for this to usurp his main interest at the expense of his ecclesiastical work. The clergy have, however, always been allowed to engage in teaching and to farm their glebe. The Lambeth Conference in 1930 considered this subject, declaring that[1] it could not recommend a widespread adoption of the proposal to ordain auxiliary priests who would continue in a secular occupation; but saw no insuperable objection to the ordination of such priests with provincial sanction and under proper safeguards.

The diaconate has in practice become but a step to the priesthood. It has, however, been urged that the permanent diaconate, which existed in the ancient Church and in effect still exists in the Orthodox Church, should be revived for men who, though unsuitable for the priesthood, could give good service as deacons. The Church should not fail to use the gifts they have. This would not involve any enactment, but could be put into effect, at least in the Church of England, by any bishop. In the United States, the canons were recently amended to allow of it. Some bishops have ordained not a few such men as deacons. It appears, however, that these deacons have in fact usually pressed after a time for ordination to the priesthood; moreover, such deacons would not materially relieve the shortage of clergy, since they can do virtually nothing which a lay reader may not do.

The ancient order of deaconess has been revived. It was recognized by

[1] Cf. *Report*, pp. 60 and 175–7.

the Lambeth Conference in 1930[1] as an order of the ministry, and in 1935 the Report of the (English) Archbishops' Committee on the Ministry of Women expressed the opinion that a deaconess is in Holy Orders; some, however, maintain that a deaconess is not in Holy Orders.

It is agreed that the order of deaconess is not just the feminine equivalent of the male diaconate. The Lambeth Conference in 1930 recommended[2] that the ordination of a deaconess should everywhere include prayer by the bishop and the laying-on of hands, the delivery of the New Testament to the candidate, and a formula giving authority to execute the office of a deaconess in the Church of God; but in the United States deaconesses are "set apart" but not ordained, and the English form of service has deliberately not been adopted.

The work of a deaconess is largely with women and children, and concerned with religious instruction. The rules concerning the work of deaconesses are not entirely the same in all countries, but a deaconess is usually authorized to prepare candidates for baptism and confirmation, to baptize in church, to conduct Morning and Evening Prayer, except for those parts reserved to a priest, and, with the licence of the bishop, to preach except at Holy Communion.

The Lambeth Conference of 1930 repeated the resolution of the previous Conference that no vow or implied promise of celibacy should be required as a condition for admission to the order of deaconess, though it is understood that the deaconess dedicates herself to a lifelong service; the Committee of the Conference declared that there is a real place for married deaconesses and much special and valuable work which they can do.[3] In the United States, however, they were till recently not allowed to marry; and in Canada they may not do so.

In most countries deaconesses do not automatically have, as clergy, a place in diocesan conferences or synods. In China, however, they do have such a place; and there, too, deaconesses assist at the administration of Holy Communion, and wear a stole while doing so.

The general tradition of the Church of not ordaining women to the priesthood is followed by Anglicans. The Chinese General Synod in 1947 asked the advice of the Lambeth Conference about whether it should for an experimental period of twenty years ordain women to the priesthood. The Lambeth Conference in 1948 declared that in its opinion such an experiment would be against Anglican tradition and order, and would

[1] Cf. *Report*, pp. 60 and 178. [2] Cf. *Report*, pp. 60 and 178.
[3] *Report*, pp. 61 and 179.

gravely affect the internal and external relations of the Anglican Communion.[1] In addition to the obvious practical objections, some feel that there are theological objections to the ordination of women as priests.

Anglicans emphasize more than most Protestants the importance of ordination and the ministry. The Lambeth Conference in 1930 pointed out[2] that our Lord showed the crucial importance of providing leaders by the care and patience with which he trained the Twelve, and that this ministry has been perpetuated from the first days until now. From the first there was in the Church a distinction corresponding to that between clergy and laity. Administration of the sacraments and teaching in the name of the Church are felt to be such serious responsibilities that they should be that work of persons trained, tested, ordained, and commisioned by the Church. The clergy are regarded by Anglicans, as by Eastern Orthodox, as the necessary framework of the Church, and as part of it, not (as Roman Catholics hold) apart from, and superior to, the Church.

The clergy is held to derive its authority not from the congregation, as the Puritans tended to think, but from Christ. Orders once given are indelible, they cannot be assumed and discarded at will. Article 26 declares that the unworthiness of a minister does not hinder the effectiveness of sacraments performed by him, which can be means of grace to those who receive them.

The religious orders lapsed in Anglicanism after the Reformation, but since 1841 there has been a gradual revival of the religious life (in the technical sense) in Anglicanism. Experience shows that some men and women are called by God to devote themselves to a disciplined and celibate life in community, and a considerable number of communities, some for men, such as the Society of St John the Evangelist (Cowley Fathers) the Community of the Resurrection, the Society of St Francis, and some for women, such as the Community of St Mary the Virgin, have been founded in the last hundred years. Most of the Anglican Churches have their own religious communities.

The two principles of order and freedom are both exemplified in Anglicanism, which indeed treats them as complementary. In technical language, in addition to the ministry of succession, there always remains the power of God to give to the Church prophets, evangelists, and teachers apart from the succession no less than within it[3] and Anglicanism

[1] *Report*, I, 52 and II, 119–20.
[2] *Report*, p. 30.
[3] *Doctrine in the Church of England*, p. 116.

140

gives much scope and responsibility to the laity. This is in harmony with Jerome's description of Confirmation as the ordination of the laity. Thomas Aquinas, similarly, taught that at Confirmation the layman is given "through the Holy Spirit, power and responsibility, not only to effect his own salvation, but also, by sharing in the priesthood of Christ, to act as His Apostle in the salvation of the world". It is not easy, however, to hold a right balance between the respective functions of the clergy and laity, and it has to be admitted that Anglicanism, like other Communions which maintain the ministerial succession, at times tends to clericalism and fails to make full use of the laity.

While the power of ordination is restricted to the bishops, no one can be ordained without receiving the approval of the laity (this is expressed in different ways in different countries: in England it is understood when no objection is raised in response to the "*Si quis*" clause in the ordination service). The laity have an important share in choosing bishops; indeed, in England the clergy's share in this is small. In most countries the laity have a very large share in the appointment of parochial clergy; and they may even perform some sacramental rites: lay baptism in an emergency is regarded as valid, and in a marriage it is strictly speaking the contracting parties who, by making the necessary pledges, perform the ceremony, the priest only acting as witness and adding the Church's blessing.

There are also definite offices, such as churchwarden and lay reader, in which the laity serve the Church. The office of lay reader was revived in the Church of England in 1866; it is not now regarded, as it was in the Middle Ages, as a minor order of clergy. The Church of England now has about four thousand readers, who are admitted to office without any laying on of hands; they are usually authorized to conduct those parts of Morning and Evening Prayer not restricted to a priest, and may also be licensed to preach. The Lambeth Conference in 1930 resolved[1] that it would not question the action of any bishop who, with the sanction of the national, regional, or provincial Church concerned, should authorize licensed readers to administer the chalice at the request of the parish priest. Some bishops, though not many, have acted on this.

The exact form of Church government by synods varies in the different Anglican Churches. In England a national synod met at Hertford as early as 672, and included members from the five Anglo-Saxon kingdoms into which England was then divided. English synods till the Norman Conquest included laymen, and indeed, there was no very clear distinction

[1] *Report*, p. 60.

between civil and ecclesiastical assemblies; but after the Conquest, the Convocations became purely clerical assemblies, meeting of course separately in the Provinces of Canterbury and York. It was early in the thirteenth century that the lower clergy were first represented in Convocation, and it was from the Church of England that the Mother of Parliaments derived the principle of representative government. Historically, indeed, the Convocations are part of Parliament.

In 1532 the Convocations undertook not to meet or make canons without royal authority. Till 1664, Convocation voted the taxes to be paid by the clergy, and it was only after that year that they were liable to the taxes voted by Parliament. The Convocations from 1717 to 1852 were prevented by the Government from meeting except purely formally, being always immediately prorogued. They were then revived, and a House of Laymen was established for the Province of Canterbury in 1886, and one for the Province of York in 1892, and these soon came to sit with the Convocations as the Representative Church Council. The Convocations are summoned by royal writ soon after the opening of each new Parliament, and are dissolved simultaneously with the dissolution of Parliament.

The historic Convocations of Canterbury and York, each containing a House of Bishops and a House of Clergy, still meet; but in 1919 after an Enabling Act of Parliament there was established the National Assembly of the Church of England, with three Houses, of Bishops, Clergy, and Laity. The Church Assembly may not issue any statement purporting to define the doctrine of the Church of England in regard to any theological question; and any measure concerning doctrinal formulae or services or ceremonies or the administration of the sacraments has to be debated and voted on by the three houses separately, and accepted or rejected in the terms finally proposed by the Bishops.

Diocesan synods of clergy are sometimes held in England, but are purely advisory, and cannot legislate or administer. This is the responsibility of the diocesan conferences, the first of which met in 1864.

In the United States, the organization of the Protestant Episcopal Church in distinction from the Church of England included the establishment of a General Convention of two houses, of Bishops and of Clerical and Lay Deputies, meeting triennially, and of diocesan synods, which include lay representatives. Each diocesan synod elects its own bishop, by methods which vary somewhat from diocese to diocese; usually a two-thirds majority of both clerical and lay deputies is needed.

Australia and Canada have had responsible diocesan synods since about 1850; provincial or general synods were organized at a later date. Elsewhere, too, the establishment of diocesan and provincial synods has been a regular feature of Anglican organization, though the process is not yet everywhere complete. In most synods and assemblies women may be elected as lay representatives, but this is not the case in the American General Convention.

Each self-governing Church normally has its own written constitution, canon law, and system of Church courts.

The fundamental unit of Church organization is the territorial diocese under the jurisdiction of one bishop,[1] in which, the bishop and (outside England) the diocesan synod are usually jointly responsible, though, for example in Africa, some synods are so far purely advisory; the diocesan synod consists of the clergy and lay representatives of the parishes, and is usually responsible for electing the bishop.

Individual parishes have considerable freedom, and may in some countries and dioceses, if they are financially self-supporting, choose their parish priest.

A diocese should not be isolated from the rest of the Church, and dioceses are usually grouped in provinces. The Lambeth Conference in 1930 recommended four as the minimum number of dioceses suitable to form a province. That conference also declared[2] that the balance between provincial authority and diocesan autonomy may vary from province to province, according to the constitutions agreed upon in each case, and this is the Anglican practice. It is an essential feature of a province that the bishops act corporately in dealing with questions concerning the faith, order, and discipline of the Church, and a normal feature also is the right to appoint and consecrate bishops for the province without reference to authorities outside the province.

In some areas, as Wales, Scotland, China, Japan, there is only one province, which thus coincides with the national Church. Elsewhere, for example in England, the U.S.A., Canada, and Australia, the national Church consists of more than one province. In such cases there are usually provincial synods, as well as the national synod or assembly.

The Anglican Communion is a league of fifteen self-governing Churches: in England; Wales; Scotland; Ireland; the U.S.A.; Canada; Australia; New Zealand; India, Pakistan, Burma, and Ceylon; China;

[1] *Lambeth Conference 1930: Report*, p. 157.
[2] *Report*, p. 57.

Japan; West Africa; South Africa; Central Africa; and the West Indies,[1] together with a number of scattered dioceses, for example in the Pacific. In all there are about three hundred and thirty Anglican dioceses, with perhaps thirty-seven million baptized and enrolled members. From the point of view, therefore, of numbers of adherents, the Anglican is not only much smaller than the Roman and Eastern Orthodox Churches, but smaller than more than one of the Protestant Communions.

The self-governing Anglican Churches are not bound together by any central legislative and executive authority, but "by mutual loyalty sustained through the common counsel of the Bishops in conference".[2] This is in complete contrast to the pattern of the Roman Church, but very similar to that of Eastern Orthodoxy, in which the Patriarch of Constantinople holds a primacy of honour. The Archbishop of Canterbury naturally presides at meetings of the Lambeth Conference, but has no authority outside the Church of England and missionary dioceses; he is therefore not a Patriarch. The Anglican Communion is a group of Churches bound together by very close ties of history and tradition, doctrine and practice,[3] in fact by a common attitude, not by any formal organization or written constitution. From time to time there have been proposals for a formal primacy of Canterbury, for a central Appeal Tribunal, and for giving the Lambeth Conference the status of a legislative synod; but such proposals have invariably by general agreement been rejected.

A Canadian synod in 1865[4] proposed that the Archbishop of Canterbury should invite a conference of Anglican bishops throughout the world for discussion of common problems; many Church leaders were perplexed over questions raised both in the volume *Essays and Reviews* and in the controversy connected with Bishop Colenso. Accordingly what proved to be the first Lambeth Conference met in 1867. There was considerable doubt in the minds of many as to the wisdom of such a conference, and fear that it might lead to episcopal autocracy and centralization. Out of a hundred and forty-four bishops invited, only seventy-six attended. The Archbishop of York stayed away, and Dean Stanley refused the use of Westminster Abbey for a service in connection

[1] Now (1957) increased to sixteen by the formation of the Jerusalem Archbishopric.

[2] *Lambeth Conference 1930: Report*, p. 55.   [3] Ibid., p. 26.

[4] The American Presiding Bishop, J. H. Hopkins of Vermont, as early as 1851 had expressed to the Archbishop a hope for a meeting of all bishops in communion with Canterbury.

with the Conference. Since then the Conference has normally, except during the two world wars, met at intervals of ten years, and its moral authority has gradually become very great, though it is purely advisory.

In between meetings of the Lambeth Conference, its Consultative Body can give advice, if asked to do so by one or other of the Anglican Churches; but it has of course no executive or legislative power. It includes a representative of each of the self-governing Churches, chosen after consultation with the Metropolitan concerned; the members number not less than eighteen.

Inevitably there is the possibility that any Anglican Church may become infected by a spirit of excessive nationalism, and this danger has to be guarded against. The Lambeth Conference of 1930 declared[1] that each Church must be on its guard lest the spirit of nationalism weaken its loyalty to the whole Catholic Church, lest it lend itself to unworthy political ends, and lest it exposes itself to undue interference by the secular state.

Whereas other Communions tend to lay almost exclusive stress on either order or freedom, Anglican order and organization is characterized by its combinations of these principles. It is of a piece with the Anglican stress on the Church as the Body of Christ, and the extension in time and space of the Incarnate Word of God. Anglicans emphasize continuity, because they regard the Faith as something given by God, and not as something thought out by men or a matter of "following the gleam".

Though maintenance of the Church's historic order is emphasized, it is at the same time freely admitted that this order, and the actual duties and status of bishops, priests, and deacons, have varied greatly within the continuity of a long historical development. Development in this respect has not necessarily ceased, and the threefold ministry may require further adaptation to the needs of the Church in a perpetually changing world[2]. The Lambeth Quadrilateral insists on the historic episcopate locally adapted, and some Anglicans would hold that the present form of episcopacy could conceivably be changed to a collegiate form of episcopacy if (though this is highly unlikely) it seemed likely to render better service[3]. Episcopacy can be combined with presbyterian and congregational elements; and, besides bishops, priests, and deacons, lay persons and local congregations all have their proper place and responsibility within the framework of the Church's order.

[1] *Report*, p. 162.
[2] *Doctrine in the Church of England*, p. 124. [3] Ibid., p. 122.

11

Christian Unity

DR VISSER 'T HOOFT, the General Secretary of the World Council of Churches, has said[1] that the Anglican Communion is more active in the cause of Christian reunion than any other Communion, and that this is no accident. This is indeed the case. It is true that it sometimes seems that Anglicans tend to propose some plan of Church unity, and then after long discussion raise many objections to it and finally reject it. This is largely because some unrepresentative Anglicans propose schemes which conflict with the essential Anglican attitude and therefore do not command general Anglican support. But the main division—and it is a gulf—between Christians is, as the Amsterdam conference of the World Council of Churches in 1948 declared, that between Catholics and Protestants. Anglicanism has, as no other Communion has, points of similarity and contact with both Catholics and Protestants, and is therefore specially fitted to mediate between them. This is very widely recognized by non-Anglicans.

At times, like other Communions, the Church of England has taken an isolationist attitude, and has neglected other Churches. But in 1534, when it made what was intended as a final and complete rejection of the Pope's jurisdiction, it did not mean to break Communion with the Italian Church; and the Pope's adherents continued to worship in Anglican churches, not only during the years of reaction under Mary Tudor, but until 1570, when the Pope ordered them to cease doing so. Later it desired to retain the Puritans, and even used what we now see to have been unsatisfactory and repressive measures to prevent schism.

Archbishop Laud in the seventeenth century discussed the question of Church unity with envoys from the Pope, but without practical result.

[1] *The Church and its Function in Society*, p. 36.

He, and a little later other Anglican leaders, discussed the question also with Eastern Orthodox representatives; but there was then little contact between the two Communions, and not much knowledge of each other, and consequently nothing came of the negotiations. At the end of the seventeenth century, Archbishop Tillotson suggested the recognition of Presbyterian orders and revision of the Prayer Book and Articles, to conciliate the Puritans, and bring them back to the Church of England; but his lukewarm attitude to the Anglican tradition was not widely shared, and the Puritans continued to be antagonistic to it, and so the division between Anglicans and Nonconformists has lasted till to-day.

Early in the eighteenth century there was an interesting attempt to bring together the French and English Churches: the Roman Catholic theologian, Du Pin, with the approval of the Archbishop of Paris, Cardinal de Noailles, corresponded with William Wake, Archbishop of Canterbury. The latter received a good deal of criticism for having dealings with Roman Catholics, who were thought to be superstitious and idolatrous. Du Pin admitted that the Pope was only the first among bishops, and had no higher grade; he was prepared to allow that the Anglican clergy should marry, and that lay people should receive Communion in both kinds. There was friction then between many French Roman Catholics and the Pope, but many Romanists, especially the Curialists, or adherents of the centralized Papal court, disapproved the negotiations, and these came to an end when Du Pin died in 1719. Wake also corresponded with leaders of the Protestant Church of Prussia.

One of the results of the Oxford Movement was to lead Anglicans to take more interest in the other historic Churches and to create a desire for Christian reunion. And so Anglicans, Roman Catholics, and Eastern Orthodox founded in England the Association for Promoting the Unity of Christendom (the Pope in 1864 forbade his followers to share in this); and in 1863 the Eastern Churches Association. J. M. Neale and other Tractarians both wrote books explaining Eastern Orthodoxy to Anglicans, and also translated many Greek hymns into English, which are now widely used by English-speaking Christians of many Communions, and have been translated into many languages of Asia and Africa. In 1906 the Anglican and Eastern Churches Union was founded.

The first Lambeth Conference in 1867 expressed its deep sorrow over the divisions of Christendom, and an ardent longing for its reunion.

Anglicans in the U.S.A. were as much concerned for Christian unity as were English Anglicans. About 1800 they had talks concerning unity both with the Methodists and with Lutherans, and in 1862 the American Episcopal Church appointed a committee to discuss intercommunion with the Russian Orthodox Church. As we have seen, the substance of what is now called the Lambeth Quadrilateral, first proposed as a basis of Church Unity by R. T. Huntington, Rector of Grace Church, New York, in 1870, was accepted by the House of Bishops at the General Convention in Chicago in 1886 (by the House of Deputies in 1892), and with some modifications by the Lambeth Conference in 1888. These four points were (1) the Bible as the standard of faith, (2) the Nicene and Apostles' Creeds, (3) the two sacraments of Baptism and Holy Communion, (4) the historic episcopate. It was not claimed that these four points completely set forth the whole apostolic Christian faith, but that their acceptance is a minimum indispensable condition of a satisfactory Church Union.

Towards the end of the nineteenth century there was an attempt, in which Viscount Halifax and the Abbé Portal were the chief agents, to bring the Anglican and Roman Churches together. The upshot was that in 1896 Pope Leo XIII appointed a commission to inquire into the validity from the Roman viewpoint of Anglican orders. Some of the members of the commission, like the great historian Duchesne, held that there was no flaw in Anglican orders, but the majority thought otherwise, and so the Pope in the bull *Apostolicae Curae* declared Anglican orders to be invalid, partly on the ground of defects in the Anglican form of ordination up to 1662, partly on the ground of defective intention on the part of those who drew up the Anglican Prayer Book. This decision was largely due to the influence of English Roman Catholic leaders who feared that, if Rome admitted the validity of Anglican orders, there would be no place for Roman clergy in England. Next year the two English Archbishops issued a reply, showing that Anglican clergy are validly ordained in accordance with traditional Church usage, and that the Anglican intention is to continue the historic ministry.

Since 1888, each Lambeth Conference has considered the question of Church Unity and passed resolutions in regard to it. Some Communions tend to ignore the Eastern Orthodox and Roman Catholics, but the Lambeth Conference in 1908 declared that no Church Union could be considered satisfactory which did not ultimately include the great Latin Church, with which in the past Anglicans had had such close contacts.

On the proposal of Bishop Charles Brent, Bishop of Western New

York and previously Bishop of the Philippines, the General Convention of the American Episcopal Church in 1910 resolved to invite all Christian Communions which confess Jesus Christ as God and Saviour to hold a conference on Faith and Order. This initiated the Faith and Order Movement, in which each Communion appoints delegates to explain its attitude to other Communions, and seeks to understand their standpoint, as a necessary preliminary to Church union. The plan for a world conference on Faith and Order was delayed by the First World War, but such conferences have been held at Lausanne (1927), Edinburgh (1937), and Lund (1952). Anglicans have always taken a great part in this movement, which helped to bring about the setting up of the World Council of Churches in 1948. The Lambeth Conference of 1948 cordially welcomed the establishment of the World Council, and the member-Churches of the Anglican Communion have all joined it.

The Lambeth Conference of 1920 drew up and issued the famous Lambeth Appeal for Church Unity. This [1] acknowledged all Christians baptized into the name of the Trinity as "sharing with us membership in the universal Church of Christ", and went on to express the belief that God desires Christians to form in this world a visibly united fellowship, such as does not at present exist. On the one hand there are other ancient episcopal Communions, to which Anglicanism is bound by many ties of common faith and tradition, and on the other there are the great non-episcopal Communions, standing for rich elements of truth, liberty, and life which might otherwise have been obscured or neglected. There should be a reunited Church, within which Christians now separated from one another would retain much that has long been distinctive in their methods of worship and service. The Church's visible unity would involve the whole-hearted acceptance of the Scriptures as the rule and ultimate standard of faith; the Nicene Creed as the sufficient statement of the Christian faith, and either it or the Apostles' Creed as the baptismal confession of belief; the divinely instituted sacraments of Baptism and Holy Communion; and a ministry acknowledged by every part of the Church as possessing not only the inward call of the Spirit, but also the commission of Christ and the authority of the whole body. The episcopate was claimed to be the one means of providing such a ministry. At the same time the bishops did not call in question the spiritual reality of the ministries of non-episcopal Communions, but thankfully acknowledged that they had been manifestly blessed and owned by the

[1] *The Lambeth Conferences 1867–1948*, pp. 38 ff.

Holy Spirit as effective means of grace. Anglican bishops and clergy would, if the other Communions desired it, willingly accept from them a form of commission or recognition.

This appeal was translated into the chief European languages (French, German, Russian, Latin, Italian, Greek), and a copy was sent to the head of each Communion. Its generous and sympathetic attitude made a great impression, though there was little visible result. Possibly it led some to think wrongly that the Church could easily and quickly be united, and that there were no vital differences of principle among Christians; nevertheless, it showed clearly that Anglicans did not want just to absorb the other Communions or insist that they should discard their valuable customs and characteristics. The English Free Churches, who were most directly concerned, felt, however, that they could not accept the proposals for episcopal ordination and recommissioning.

Official representatives of the Church of England, appointed to negotiate with the English Free Churches, in 1923 formally declared[1] that in their opinion "ministries which rest upon a long established order, which have been conferred by some solemn and authoritative act implying ordination to the ministry of the Universal Church and not merely commission to the ministry of a particular denomination, and which are regarded as involving a lifelong vocation . . . (are) within their several spheres real ministries in the Universal Church." Such ministries might, however, it was added, be in varying degrees irregular or defective. Although it was obvious that some ambiguity lurked in the word "real", it was felt by many that the statement marked a big step forward in mutual understanding.

For some years, beginning in 1921, there was another attempt to promote unity between the Anglican and Roman Churches. There were conversations, unofficial, but held with the knowledge and approval of the Pope and the English Archbishops, at Malines in Belgium between Roman Catholics, including Cardinal Mercier, Archbishop of Malines, and Anglicans, concerning the basis on which the two Communions could draw together. A Roman Catholic theologian suggested that the Pope might recognize the Anglican Communion as a Uniat Church, in Communion with Rome but retaining its own language, rites, and canon law. Thus Anglicans would have to accept the Papal jurisdiction and recognize the Pope's infallibility in regard to faith and morals, and Anglican clergy would be reordained in a body; but Rome could allow

[1] *Documents on Christian Unity*, ed. G. K. A. Bell, First Series, p. 158.

Anglicans to receive Communion in both kinds, use the vernacular for worship, have married clergy, and make only a few changes in the Prayer Book. Such is always a possible basis for union between the two Communions, but it is doubtful whether it commends itself to many in either Communion. The Pope eventually forbade the continuance of these conversations, and moreover instructed the Roman Catholic monastery of Amay in Belgium, which previously studied points of difference between Rome and both Eastern Orthodox and Anglicans, and sought to reconcile them, to concentrate its attention solely on the Orthodox.

We must now consider briefly the existing relations of the Anglican Communion with the other great Communions individually. It is clear that Anglicanism and Eastern Orthodoxy, which both reject control by the Pope but maintain the Catholic creeds, sacraments, and order, have much in common. They function mainly in different countries, and unity between them means primarily Intercommunion. On the Orthodox side, at least, this means that they must be satisfied both that Anglican orders are in the Apostolic Succession, and also that Anglican doctrine is orthodox.

The Ecumenical Patriarch of Constantinople in July 1922 issued an encyclical recognizing officially the validity of Anglican orders; but, though regarded as the leader of all Eastern Orthodoxy, he cannot legislate except for his own Patriarchate. The Patriarchs of Jerusalem and Alexandria, and the Orthodox Churches in Cyprus and Rumania, have also recognized Anglican orders, but other Orthodox Churches have not yet done so. The friendly relations which exist between Anglicans and Eastern Orthodox are illustrated by the united service which they held in Westminster Abbey in 1925, commemorating the sixteenth centenary of the Council of Nicaea.

Eastern Orthodox representatives met with a sub-committee of the 1930 Lambeth Conference to discuss various problems.[1] The Orthodox asked whether or not in Anglicanism, as in Eastern Orthodoxy and in traditional Church usage, the supreme authority in regard to doctrine lay with the bishops. The Anglicans answered that the final decision lay with the bishops, but that this did not exclude co-operation and consultation with the ordinary clergy and laity in the discussion of doctrine, since Anglicans greatly stressed the co-operation of the laity. In answer to other questions, the Anglicans assured the Orthodox that Anglicans could regard ordination as a sacrament and that, like the Orthodox, they always

[1] Cf. *Lambeth Conference 1930: Report*, pp. 48–9 and 131–140.

carefully preserved the Apostolic Succession. They set out the Anglican view of Christ's Presence in the Eucharist and of the Eucharist as a sacrifice, and the Orthodox agreed that the Anglican explanation on these points was in harmony with Orthodox doctrine. With regard to sacramental ministrations to Orthodox by the Anglican clergy when, as often happens especially in America, no Orthodox priest is available, the Orthodox declared that there is here no difficulty in respect to baptism and marriage; but since the two Churches are not yet in Communion it is irregular for members of one Church to receive Communion in the other, though this practice might continue till all the Orthodox Churches could meet and finally decide the matter.

Representative English, Irish, and American Anglicans in 1935 conferred at Bucharest with representatives of the Rumanian Orthodox Church (to which nearly all Rumanian church people belong). They issued an agreed report on the doctrine of the ministry, the Eucharist, tradition, and justification, which the Church of England a little later accepted as in accordance with Anglican doctrine. In the following year the Rumanian Church accepted the validity of Anglican orders.

A conference of the Russian and certain other Orthodox Churches held in Moscow in 1948 declared that they could not recognize the validity of Anglican orders till they had recognized as adequate Anglican doctrine in regard to the sacraments, especially ordination; but the general attitude of the conference to Anglicanism appears to have been friendly.

There are still many differences between Anglicans and the Orthodox, and not a few obstacles to unity. The latter stress the tradition of the Church far more than Anglicans do, and are not yet satisfied with Anglican doctrine; and they regard as authoritative the Seventh General Council, held at Nicaea in 787, which condemned any who refuse to accept all Church tradition, whether written or unwritten. Anglicanism has never accepted the judgement of this Council, and it is questionable whether it can be reconciled with the belief in the sufficiency of Scripture laid down in Articles 6 and 20. Anglicans are divided about whether the words "and the Son" (*filioque*) can be omitted, as the Orthodox insist, from the Nicene Creed, which originally said only that the Holy Spirit proceeds from the Father.

In general, relations between Anglicans and the Eastern Orthodox are increasingly close and friendly. The Anglican and Eastern Churches Association continues the work of the "Union" founded in 1906, and in 1928 the Society of St Alban and St Sergius was founded to promote understanding and friendship between Anglicans and the Russian Church. For many years in some countries where there was need for it there has been co-operation between Anglicans and Orthodox, and members of one Communion, when without clergy of their own, have received the sacraments from clergy of the other Communion. Anglicans also give not a little financial help to Orthodox schools, for example, in Jordan.

Anglicans have a great opportunity and responsibility to help the Orthodox and Protestants, between whom there is very little direct contact, to come to know and understand each other; and it would be a great pity, for the sake of a hasty union with one or the other, to relinquish this opportunity.

The Lesser (or Separated) Eastern Churches include the Assyrians (the remnant of the Nestorian Church, which formerly spread right across Asia), the Syrian Orthodox or Jacobite, the Coptic, and the Armenian Churches, which broke away from the Great Church in the fifth and sixth centuries, nominally because they adopted the heretical views of Nestorius or Eutyches. The Lambeth Conference in 1908 and again in 1920 proposed that if these Churches first declared that they no longer held the ancient heresy, their members might in case of need receive Communion at Anglican altars (occasional Intercommunion). The Lambeth Conference in both 1930 and 1948 declared that in many cases they no longer profess their ancient heresy, though perhaps they have never formally rejected it, and the Anglican Communion desires that their doctrinal beliefs should be made clearer, so that it may come into closer agreement and union (full Intercommunion) with them. In the last thirty years, owing to their disturbed conditions, there has been little progress with this, but the Church of India, Burma, and Ceylon in 1937 established limited and partial Intercommunion with the Mar Thoma Church in South India. English and American Anglicans have helped these Eastern Churches a good deal in such ways as training of clergy.

So far as the Roman Church is concerned, as we have seen above, something of an impasse has been reached. The Lambeth Conference in 1930 expressed its regret at the Pope's prohibition of Roman Catholic participation in Conversations regarding Church Unity, and declared once more that no Church Union would be complete which did not include the great Latin Church. This was repeated in 1948. During the Second World War, there was increased co-operation between Anglicans and

Roman Catholics, and the Lambeth Conference in 1948 expressed a desire for as much co-operation as Roman Catholics would approve.

Anglicans would probably agree with the suggestion of the Lausanne Conference on Faith and Order that a united Church should include both episcopal and presbyterian and congregational elements. It is a question whether it should also include (if Roman Catholics were on this condition willing to enter it) a papal element; that is, whether one bishop, no doubt the bishop of Rome because of his historic position, should have, not jurisdiction over the whole Church, but a primacy of honour as leader on earth of the whole Church. Some Anglicans would be willing to concede this for the sake of Church Unity; others are unwilling, and feel that there is no need for such a primacy.[1]

For many years relations between the Anglican and the Old Catholic Churches have been becoming closer. The Old Catholics are not numerous but are important because, like Anglicans, they hold a mediating position between Rome and Protestantism. Some of them left the Roman Church in 1723, some of them in 1871, because they would not accept the new dogma then proclaimed of Papal Infallibility in faith and morals. The Old Catholic Churches allow clerical marriage, and use the vernacular in their services, but in the main, like Anglicans, keep the Church's historic doctrine, worship, and order. The Anglican Communion was quite satisfied with the Old Catholic doctrine and ministry, while the Old Catholic attitude to Anglicanism was for long doubtful. But in 1925 the International Old Catholic Congress officially recognized the validity of Anglican orders, and consequently of Anglican Baptism, Confirmation, and Eucharist. A Joint Commission, representing the two Communions, met in 1931 at Bonn, Germany; it examined the doctrine of both Churches and concluded that there was no conflict, and recommended that each Communion should admit members of the other to its sacraments. Later in the same year, the Old Catholic Churches formally sanctioned Intercommunion with Anglicanism, and the Church of England sanctioned Intercommunion with Old Catholics in 1932, other Anglican Churches doing so soon afterwards. Since the Old Catholics are mainly in countries in Europe where there is no Anglican Church, such Intercommunion means in effect that the two Communions are now united.

The Philippine Independent Catholic Church, commonly called the

[1] Cf. *Doctrine in the Church of England*, p. 126, and K. D. Mackenzie, ed. *Union of Christendom*, pp. 376–8.

Aglipayan Church, was established in 1902, when a number of priests and many church people left the Roman Church, which in the Philippines was then dominated by Spaniards. The new Church desired to retain the historic episcopate, but it had no bishop, and it appeared that no episcopal Church was then willing to consecrate bishops for it. So twelve priests laid their hands on their leader Aglipay, who took the title Supreme Bishop, and consecrated other bishops. In 1946 this Church requested the American Episcopal Church to appoint bishops to consecrate for it bishops in the Apostolic Succession. After the Philippine Independent Church had shown that its faith and worship were in harmony with Church tradition, three American bishops ordained and consecrated three bishops for the Philippine Church, and through them all its clergy received canonical orders. Intercommunion is likely to be authorized soon between it and the Anglican Churches.

Anglican Churches have many times expressed the desire for union with the Protestant (or Free) Churches. In many countries there are both Anglicans and Protestants, and if they are to be united they must have a common organization. An obstacle to this, however, is the fact that the Protestants, at and since the sixteenth-century Reformation, abandoned the Church's historic order; some lost it unintentionally, others conscientiously rejected it, to emphasize their complete break with what they regarded as the totally corrupt medieval Church.

It has been clearly and authoritatively recognized at least by English Anglicans that Protestant ministries are spiritually effective. But it cannot be maintained that they are valid or regular, if by this is meant according to the Church's general custom and law. Anglicans, like Eastern Orthodox and Roman Catholics, regard it as important to follow the Church's historic custom in regard to order no less than in doctrine; and cannot but hope that, if only for the sake of Christian unity, the Protestant Churches will recover the historic threefold ministry. It is not that any Anglicans deny that grace is given through non-episcopal ministries; some indeed hold that we cannot be certain that God will not give grace through sacraments celebrated by those not canonically ordained by bishops. Many think that in fact God does give his grace through sacraments performed sincerely and with faith by Free Church ministers, and yet are convinced that ordination should be restricted to bishops.[1]

[1] A further question is whether or not Free Church ministries should (as A. G. Hebert and others hold) be regarded, though real and efficacious, as essentially different in meaning and function from the Anglican ministry.

Anglicans do not, like Roman Catholics and Eastern Orthodox, regard the Anglican as the only true Church. Some Anglicans hold that bodies which lack bishop's and the Church's historic order are not real Churches; but many would regard the non-episcopal Churches as real Churches, though deficient in order and therefore imperfect. The Lambeth Conference in 1920 recognized all who have faith in Christ and are baptized in the name of the Trinity as members in the universal Church of Christ; some would therefore speak of all schism among Christians as being schism within the Church, rather than of one body from another.

Four Anglican dioceses in South India left the Anglican Communion, with the blessing of the latter, in 1947, to form with Methodists and the South India United Church (composed of former Congregationalists and former Presbyterians) the new Church of South India. The formation of this Church was an event of extreme importance, as being the first occasion when a Church retaining Catholic order and doctrine united with a non-Episcopal Church. The new Church is in harmony with the principles of the Lambeth Quadrilateral, and of course preserves the episcopal ministry. At the same time it includes also what are called presbyterian and congregational elements, and its aim is to preserve all that is of value in the three uniting Churches. All clergy are to be ordained by bishops, but ministers ordained before union by persons not bishops may continue during a period of thirty years to function as ministers in the united Church, though they should usually not be appointed to work in a parish accustomed to a minister episcopally ordained. It is expected that eventually all clergy of the C.S.I. will have been ordained by bishops. Great freedom is allowed in regard to forms of worship and other matters. Anglicans hope that the new Church will eventually make a rule of Confirmation by bishops, but this is not a necessary condition of union. For this reason, and also because the new Church accepts no particular conception of episcopacy but only the fact, because it remains in communion with its parent bodies, not all of whom are in communion with Canterbury, and because its doctrinal orthodoxy was thought questionable, some Anglicans, both in India and in other countries, disapproved of the union. In the Nandyal area, thirty thousand Anglicans declined to enter the new Church, and continue as Anglicans. The new Church declares its aim to be to express under Indian conditions and in Indian forms the spirit, thought, and life of the Church Universal, and eventually to unite all Christians.

The Anglican Communion cannot be in full communion with the

Church of South India till all the clergy of this Church are, in accordance with the historic rule, ordained by bishops. The majority of the Lambeth Conference of 1948 accepted bishops and priests consecrated or ordained in the C.S.I. as true bishops and priests, while a minority felt it was not yet possible to pronounce definitely on the subject. The English Convocations, however, in 1955 unanimously accepted clergy consecrated and ordained in the C.S.I. as true bishops, priests, and deacons in the Church of God. Some Anglicans have been unhappy because the new Church does not prescribe the use of the creeds in public worship or confirmation.

There are somewhat similar schemes of Church unity between Anglicans and Presbyterians in Iran (though here for the present the Presbyterians seem to have rejected the scheme, and to be unwilling to accept any form of episcopacy), and Nigeria.

In Ceylon, Anglicans are negotiating for union with Methodists, Baptists, and Presbyterians. The Lambeth Conference of 1948 regarded this scheme as, on certain controversial points, a decided improvement on the South India plan. It is proposed that at the inauguration of union, those who have been elected bishops but have not received episcopal consecration should be consecrated by three bishops from outside Ceylon, representing different Church traditions and acceptable to all the uniting Churches; and after that all those elected to be bishops shall receive from ministers of all the uniting Churches a wider commission to exercise their ministry in the united Church. Each diocesan bishop will then receive into the presbyterate of the united Church the clergy of the uniting Churches in his diocese, with prayer and laying-on of hands. The ministry of the new Church will thus be unified from the start, and there will not be, as in South India, an interim period during which some clergy have received episcopal ordination, and some have not. It is clearly stated that the united Church will accept episcopacy as it was in the ancient Church, though no particular interpretation of it is imposed. Priests will not, as they may in the Church of South India, lay on hands at the consecration of a bishop. For the time being, other forms of service for admission to communicant status are to be accepted as equivalent to confirmation. There is a similar scheme in North India and Pakistan.

In the U.S.A., Anglicans and one of the big Presbyterian Churches ("the Presbyterian Church in the U.S.A.") for some years had negotiations aiming either at unity or a concordat; but the Anglicans were much divided concerning this, and it seemed better to wait till they could become more agreed. In Ireland, twenty-five years ago, there were discussions between Anglicans and Presbyterians, but they came to nothing as the latter insisted on preconditions that were impossible for Anglicans.

There have been conversations regarding unity between the Church of England and the English Free Churches intermittently ever since 1920. In 1938 *An Outline of a Reunion Scheme* between the Church of England and the Free Churches was published. The Free Church Federal Council in 1941 expressed itself unfavourably concerning this.

The Archbishop of Canterbury in 1947 proposed a new approach, suggesting as a first step that some of the Free Churches might each combine episcopacy with its own existing system. If this were done there could be Intercommunion between them and the Church of England, before complete unity was achieved, and no definite theory concerning episcopacy need be accepted. The Lambeth Conference in 1948 pointed out some disadvantages in this proposal: the scheme does not provide for a real growing together or assimilation of the different traditions; it seemed unlikely that the non-episcopal Churches would be attracted by it if the result would be not unity but only partial Intercommunion; and catholicity involves more than the possession of a valid ministry. However, exploration on these lines was not discouraged.

Since 1946 there have been renewed conversations, based on this plan,[1] between representatives of the Church of England and the Evangelical Free Churches. It has become clear that a crucial question needing consideration is what precisely are the functions of a bishop. These have in history varied greatly, and ordination has been almost the only constant episcopal function. The Anglican and Free Church representatives in these conversations declared that bishops should also have the responsibility of decision, in concurrence with clergy and laity, about suggested changes in matters of doctrine and polity, as well as pastoral oversight.

In some countries, for example Australia and Canada, it is suggested that, as a first step towards unity, the clergy of the various Communions should, by prayer and laying-on of hands, receive supplemental ordination or mutual recommissioning, and that the various ministries should thus be unified. This proposal is usually based on the view that in a divided Christendom all orders are defective, inasmuch as they do not have behind them the authority of the whole Church. An incidental

---

[1] More recently conversations have been held by The Church of England both with the English Methodists, and with the Episcopal Church of Scotland, and the Presbyterian Church of England (1957).

result of such a unification of the ministry, as it is usually presented, is that all ministers would then have received episcopal ordination, and could therefore be recognized without contravening historic usage.

The Lambeth Conference of 1920 recommended that there should be partial Intercommunion with the (Lutheran) Church of Sweden, which, unlike other Lutheran Churches, has retained the historic ministry and apostolic succession, so that members of one Church could receive Communion in the other, when out of reach of their own. The Church of Sweden agreed to this in 1922, since when Anglican bishops have taken part in the consecration of Swedish bishops, and Swedish bishops in the consecration of Anglican bishops.

Anglicans have also had conversations regarding unity with other Lutherans. The orthodoxy of Anglicanism is somewhat suspect to Lutherans, especially in regard to the doctrine, all-important in Lutheran eyes, of justification by faith alone, and also in regard to the Eucharist. Lutherans regard Church order as unimportant, and think Anglicans attach too much importance to this and too little to pure doctrine. In South India the Lutherans declined to join the new Church of South India, when this was formed, because they were doubtful about its orthodoxy.[1] Anglican and Lutheran conceptions of Confirmation also differ greatly: in the Lutheran view, it is not a sacrament, but fundamentally a profession of faith by the person receiving Confirmation, not the gift of God's grace and the Holy Spirit to him.

Naturally there are many unsolved problems in connection with the subject of Church Unity, or at least questions on which different opinions are held. One such question is whether episcopacy is necessary or only desirable (of the *esse* or only the *bene* or *plene esse* of the Church). Moreover, reunion schemes tend to prescribe episcopacy but at the same time declare that no particular theory of episcopacy need be held. This could imply the retention of episcopacy purely as a piece of mechanical mumbo-jumbo, but in fact it is assumed that the bishops will discharge the functions which they have had from the earliest times.[2]

There must in a united Church be agreement concerning the fundamentals of the faith, and liberty to differ in non-essentials; but it is not easy to decide just where the line has to be drawn, and how much

[1] More recently, however, the Lutherans have been more favourably disposed to the C.S.I. as this has been developing.

[2] Cf. *Lambeth Conference 1930: Report*, pp. 115–16. There is of course room for difference of opinion as to what precisely the historic functions of bishops are.

difference is compatible with fundamental agreement. Anglicans recognize that the creeds do not completely set forth the apostolic faith, and may allow some reasonable, but undefined, liberty in interpreting them. But, while some Protestants oppose the use of any creed, the Eastern Orthodox and Lutherans regard Anglicans as unjustifiably lax in regard to doctrinal unity. Again, while many Anglicans would regard order as of less importance than faith, others would regard order as itself part of faith.

With regard to the question whether Intercommunion should be the goal of unity, or the expression of unity already achieved, the Anglican attitude,[1] though there is a dissentient minority, is that, perhaps with partial and occasional exceptions, it should be the climax and goal of unity. In this it resembles that of some Protestants, as well as all the Orthodox Churches and the Roman Church. This does not result from regarding as irregular the celebration of the Eucharist by those not ordained by bishops; the fundamental reason is that the Eucharist is the supreme sacrament of unity, and to celebrate it where the unity is in fact broken is a mockery. Moreover, this would both encourage and express an acquiescence in essential disunion.

Not all Anglicans are altogether satisfied with the Lambeth Quadrilateral as a basis of Church Unity. Some hold that it should include the Prayer Book, or even that the Prayer Book should replace it, while others think that it is not clear enough in regard to the doctrine of the Church, which is the point of greatest division among Christians, and perhaps that it should recognize not only two but seven sacraments. Others again urge that it is satisfactory only if it is regarded as a symbol of the undivided wholeness of the primitive tradition that lies behind it. There is moreover some difference according as the Quadrilateral is regarded as a sufficient basis for unity, or rather as a starting-point in the progress towards unity; and there are various slightly different versions of the Quadrilateral.

However desirable and urgent Christian union may be, the Anglican standpoint is that it is not to be desired *at any cost*. If that were so, it would be easy enough: the names of the various Communions could all be put into a hat, and the name of one Church could be drawn, which all should previously have agreed to join; or alternatively all could join the largest of the existing Communions, namely the Roman. A union with purely political motivation, such as the National Socialists in

---

[1] Cf. *Lambeth Conference 1930: Report*, pp. 52, 113, 116–17; *Convictions*, p. 194; *Doctrine in the Church of England*, p. 139: Iremonger, *William Temple*, p. 405.

Germany and the military regime in Japan attempted a few years ago, with a view to making the Church a tool of the Government, would be equally unsatisfactory.

Nor can a united Church satisfactorily be based on ambiguous phrases which conceal fundamental disagreement. Sooner or later these are only too likely to lead either to charges of bad faith or to disappointment; and charity is not shown by indifference to questions of truth and order.

Anglicanism is often said to advocate and practise comprehensiveness; comprehension, that is, in one Communion of considerable divergences in both doctrine and worship. There is some truth in this, and up to a point this generous comprehensiveness is one of the glories of the Anglican Communion. At the same time, mere comprehensiveness cannot be the final standard either for Anglicanism or for a united Church. This should rather be "integrity" or "wholeness"—that is, the whole and complete Christian faith, as distinct from the one-sidedness and incompleteness characteristic of heresy. Certainly there can be no question of including all beliefs which Christians hold or have held—some of these are probably wrong, and certainly many of them conflict hopelessly.

It is probably a weakness in the Anglican Communion at present, and one which hampers its work for Church unity, that it is not very well unified internally; there is sometimes considerable tension between the various groups, and even threats of secession. Accordingly, a first step towards uniting with other Communions is that there should be more mutual understanding and sympathy between different groups in the Anglican Communion itself.[1] To concentrate on this for a time, and show forth better the reconciliation of Catholic and Protestant, may from a long-term point of view be a greater contribution to the unity of all Christians, than if Anglicanism in one country were to be absorbed in a Protestant Church, in another country in the Eastern Orthodox or Roman Church. The historic mission and divine vocation of Anglicanism is to reconcile these two sides, which have perhaps not yet been perfectly synthesized in it, and this task should not be impatiently rejected.

Many non-Anglicans recognize that because of its contacts with the Catholic or historic Churches on the one hand, and the Reformed Churches on the other, Anglicanism has a position of great opportunity in regard to Christian unity. For example, in the nineteenth century the well-known French writer, de Maistre, a Roman Catholic, wrote: "If

[1] Cf. *Lambeth Conference 1930: Report*, pp. 30 and 121; *Lambeth Conference 1948: Report*, Part I, p. 23.

ever, and everything invites to it, there should be a movement towards reunion among the Christian bodies, it seems likely that the Church of England should be the one to give it impulse. Presbyterianism, as its French nature rendered probable, went to extremes; between us and those who practise a worship which we think wanting in form and substance, there is too wide an interval; we cannot understand one another. But the English Church, which touches us with one hand, touches with the other those with whom we have no point of contact." The well-known French historian Guizot spoke similarly. No Protestant Church has links, as Anglicanism has, with the Eastern Orthodox.

This mediating position of Anglicanism is not just a prudent compromise between Catholicism and Protestantism, but a positive tradition. It is not an easy position to hold, and causes Anglicanisn to be much criticized by both sides. The metaphor of "bridge-Church" often applied to it is not entirely satisfactory. No one wants to stay permanently on a bridge; and is said that, if Anglicanism is a bridge, it is a bridge not quite in contact with the bank on either side. Nevertheless, there is a real truth in the metaphor. The Anglican Communion should treaure both parts of its inheritance, and promote contacts across the gulf between Catholic and Reformed. Eventually Anglicanism may die, that is, when all Christians are united; but it should not commit premature suicide, nor allow itself to be extirpated in a Protestant New Deal. As the Lambeth Conference of 1948 pointed out, it would be a betrayal of its trust if the Anglican Communion were to allow itself to be dispersed before its work, the reconciliation of Catholic and Reformed, were done.[1]

[1] *Report*, Part I, p. 23.

12

Conclusion

It has always been characteristic of Anglicanism to hold together the new and the old, so it has valued continuity. Its attitude has not been negative and destructive, rather it has treasured the Christian heritage while at the same time it has welcomed new light. At the time of the Reformation, great care was taken that the consecration of Matthew Parker should be in accordance with traditional usage. The more Protestant reformers often resigned their orders, and perhaps accepted a new ordination—indeed, this was often insisted on; for Anglicans, however, there was no question of a new ordination.[1]

Accordingly, Churches of the Anglican Communion maintain the Church's historic Scriptures, creeds, sacraments, and orders. Till the sixteenth century, it must always be remembered, these were common to all Christians. Certain groups of Christians since then have abandoned some of these, in some cases without really intending to do so; but most Christians still retain them; they are common to East and West, to the countries behind the Iron Curtain and to the free world. The Anglican Communion is thus on the one hand "catholic".

At the same time, Anglicanism gives more scope to the layman than does the Roman Church. It allows more freedom than the Roman Catholic or the Eastern Orthodox Churches, and does not stubbornly oppose all change. It upholds in due proportion on the one hand authority and order, on the other hand freedom. Like the Protestant Churches, it encourages the laity to read the Bible for themselves, which Rome, formerly at

[1] The writer once asked a recognized Congregationalist theologian whether nowadays a Roman priest who wished to function as a Congregational minister would have to be re-ordained. The answer was that he *need* not be but of course might *wish* to be re-ordained, to mark a break with his former ministry.

least, forbade. It regards the Bible as the supreme standard and source of faith, and denies the Roman contention that tradition has authority equal to that of the Bible. So Anglicanism is also "reformed" or "protestant" or "evangelical".

Moreover, Anglicanism welcomes new truth more eagerly than some Christian Communions do, and values learning and reason highly. It allows much freedom to the individual, and has a liberal and tolerant attitude. Richard Hooker, for instance, spoke of the Christian as bound to Christ by a rope with three strands, the Bible, tradition, and reason. Anglicanism, further, lays great stress on practical morality, and on following the Christian way of life. It claims to be at the same time catholic, apostolic, protestant, and reformed.

In general, the Anglican Communion is important chiefly because it combines, as no other Communion does, catholic and evangelical or protestant characteristics. It is for this reason that it is often spoken of as a bridge-Church, which unites Catholic and Protestant Communions otherwise separated by a deep gulf. So the American Presbyterian theologian Dr William Adams Brown wrote[1] that "in the Anglican Church, and in the Anglican Church alone, men who are genuinely Protestant and men who are consistently Catholic have been able to find a home side by side". On the other side, such Roman Catholic writers as Perè Congar O.P. and Fr. H St. John S.J. agree in regarding the Church of England as a microcosm of divided Christendom.

It has long been recognized that Anglicanism follows a middle way and that moderation and restraint are characteristic of it. This, however, does not by any means imply that it merely timidly avoids extremes, or that it practises an unworthy and unprincipled compromise.

Rather, its principle is to be what is sometimes called "comprehensive" but is better called "complete": that is, to maintain and show forth all the various aspects of Christian truth, and to hold a balance of opposites. Anglicanism holds that the values stressed by Catholicism, Evangelicalism, and Liberalism are not incompatible, but complement each other. The Catholic, if he is lacking in evangelical fervour, is very cold and formal; the Evangelical, without catholic order, is very narrow and shallow; the Liberal may be wanting in depth and devotion and fervour. The Anglican ideal is unity in diversity; its members may differ considerably in non-essentials, while in essentials they are united.

The Anglican attitude naturally has its dangers and drawbacks.

[1] In *Your Church and Mine*, p. 167.

Moderation and the middle way are not always good (cf. Revelation 3.15–16: "I would that thou wert either hot or cold"), they may only denote laxity and indifference and timidity. William James criticized Anglican moderation as totally unlike the fervour and wholehearted devotion of the New Testament and the early Church. Anglicanism, he wrote, is "so massive and all-pervasive, so authoritative and on the whole so decent, in spite of the iniquity and farcicality of the whole thing. . . . Never were incompatibles so happily yoked together. Talk about the genius of Romanism. It is nothing to the genius of Anglicanism, for Catholicism still contains some haggard elements that ally it with the Palestinian desert, whereas Anglicanism remains obese and round and comfortable, and decent with this world's decencies, without one acute note in its whole life or history, in spite of the shrill Jewish words on which its ears are fed, and the nitro-glycerin of the Gospels and Epistles which has been injected into its veins."

When Orchard was still a Congregationalist he wrote in a similar way. Anglicanism "is built on the system of compromise by which we Englishmen rule our lives: it is essentially the Church of 'good form' . . . an essentially conventional Church, it is the Church of all respectable people, is the gentleman's Church: it is snobbish, squiry, and a bit feudal, of course . . . but the chief thing is that it fits the average Englishman like a glove: it is decent, not fanatical, its devotion is reticent, and it knows better than any other Church in Christendom how to administer just enough religion to keep the soul quiet and contented: it has discovered exactly how much religion the Englishman can stand."

Such criticisms no doubt are grossly one-sided, and have less validity in regard to Anglicanism to-day than they would sometimes have had in the past. Nevertheless, they do point to possible dangers and corruptions of the Anglican ideal. An Anglican priest himself has pointed out that Anglicans seem so desperately afraid of getting excited about the wrong things that they manage not to get excited even concerning the right things.

And so an old gibe runs, "For God's sake don't touch the Church of England, it is the only thing that stands between us and Christianity"— as if Anglicanism were a sort of vaccine to prevent the real thing from catching on. In a similar way, Anglicanism has been called "a muffled Christianity". Not a few have thought Anglican worship to be too cold and formal. Anglicans themselves have attributed the alienation from the Church of so many manual workers to the rejection at the

Reformation of colour and warmth in the services. In general, some would agree with Blake's saying "The road of excess leads to the palace of wisdom", and therefore in principle criticize the restraint and moderation of Anglicanism.

In particular, Anglicanism is criticized for being too little interested in doctrine and faith and truth, and for being only concerned with practice; so it is said that Roman Catholics follow St Peter, Protestants St Paul, and Anglicans St James (cf. James 2.14 and 17). It is wrong, say the critics, to be vague and indecisive in regard to the truth, nebulousness and indecision are sins, and Anglican lack of interest in doctrine really displays a wrong scepticism. It is wrong, even for the sake of unity, to compromise in regard to the truth or to be ambiguous or illogical. Among many others, Continental Protestants and Eastern Orthodox specially tend to feel this about Anglicanism. And the criterion of truth for not a few Anglican theologians appears (it is said) to be not the Bible, nor even the Catholic Church, but simply "the mind of the Church of England".

The Anglican Communion is also criticized for including people with very different views and attitudes, which at least appear to be mutually contradictory. So it is said to be fundamentally not a really united Church but very much divided and at conflict within itself, a chaos of contending sects precariously held together in England by the fact of the Eastablishment. It has long been feared that Anglicanism will break up into several Churches. Because of its internal dissensions, Anglicanism is felt to be paralysed, so that it cannot take decisive action; and so inertia and stagnation come to be more than ever characteristic of it. Sometimes, too, it seems to encourage individualism.

The Church of England is sometimes said to be merely the consequences of political expediency in England in the sixteenth century, and not to be based on religious principles concerning which all its members agree; and there is very little about which they all do agree.

Compared with other Communions, the Anglican Communion has too often been lacking in missionary devotion, and, for example in England in the eighteenth century, it has been very insular in its outlook.

It is always possible for Anglicans, conscious of their strategic position as a link between Protestants and Rome and the Eastern Orthodox, to have a superior attitude; and Anglicanism has at times been Narcissist and in love with itself. Because of its appeal to those who want a faith which is not indifferent to beauty and reason, it has in some countries tended to be an upper-class religion; and the Church of England has been said to provide the maximum of social cachet with the minimum of demands on heart, mind, and conscience.

Not a few have thought that the mediating position of Anglicanism is not finally tenable. The Orthodox theologian Khomyakov, for example, wrote that the Church of England "is a narrow ledge of dubious *terra firma*, beaten by the waves of Romanism and Protestantism, and crumbling on both sides into the mighty waters". Another Orthodox[1] holds that if Anglicanism thinks it possible to have fellowship at the same time with the Orthodox Church and the Protestant Churches, this speaks clearly for the instability of its theological conceptions. In general, the Eastern Orthodox tend to think that Anglicanism does not sufficiently appreciate the importance of true doctrine, and that the Anglican doctrine of the Communion of Saints and its respect for our Lord's Mother are inadequate; they think that Anglicans do not attach enough weight to Church tradition, and make too many experiments.

Rome denies the Anglican claim to continuity with the medieval Church, and claims that the breach made at the Reformation was widened by heresy, such as the Lutheran doctrine of justification by faith alone, the rejection of five of the sacraments, and the denial of the Pope's jurisdiction in England.

Some Protestants regard Anglicanism as too rigid in maintaining traditional Church doctrine and in insisting on the retention of the ancient creeds, while others criticize it for the opposite reason, as being too vague and nebulous in doctrine. Many Free Churchmen think that Anglicans are too reluctant to experiment, and do not give enough scope to the laity or make enough use of lay people; nor, it is felt, do they sufficiently appreciate the importance of preaching.

Finally, it is an obvious criticism that even if the Anglican *via media* suits the British temperament, and it is on this ground that it is too often commended, numbers of English people do in fact prefer either one of the Free Churches, or the Roman Church. Moreover, and this is very important, so far as Anglicanism is specifically English it is obviously out of court in all other countries.

These criticisms contain far too much of substance for Anglicans simply to ignore them. They do indeed point to very real dangers in the Anglican standpoint, dangers which have not always been, and are not always,

[1] Bishop Hermogen, Rector of the Theological Academy in Moscow, in *Ecumenical Press Service*, 20 February 1948.

avoided; and they should be taken to heart by the most fervent and devoted of Anglicans, in the consciousness that there is much to be learnt from the other great Communions.

At the same time, a little consideration quickly shows that to a considerable extent these criticisms contradict each other and cancel each other out. It cannot, for example, be the case that Anglicans are both too hidebound and too lax in regard to doctrine.

The divergences between the various groups—the more Catholic, the more Evangelical, and the more Liberal—are not in fact as great as they seem to outsiders. There certainly is some tension between them, and the differences are real and far-reaching. It is an inevitable consequence that for Anglicans to come to a common mind on any subject takes time and may be difficult. But in our day the tendency is strongly centripetal, and only in appearance is there chaos in Anglicanism. J. H. Newman wrote that the Church of England, if not held together by the Establishment, would at once split into three separate bodies, for it had no internal consistency or individuality or soul, and others have held much the same opinion. History, however, has clearly disallowed this criticism; for in the United States, the English-speaking Dominions, India, and Ceylon, there are Churches of the Anglican Communion quite unrecognized by the State, which contain the same three tendencies as the Church of England, and which yet show no sign of impending dissolution.

Freedom, generosity, tolerance, a corporate spirit, all these things, so characteristic of Anglicanism, can only too easily be abused. The high ideals of Anglicanism are difficult to achieve, and are especially liable to abuse and degeneration: freedom may become individualism or laxity; balance and restraint may become cold and tame and formal, and lead to unprincipled compromise; gradualness may result in inertia and stagnation.

But a balance of freedom and authority, of experiment and tradition, of individual conscience and institutional continuity, is both right and what the world needs. Anglicanism is no vague and hesitating hotchpotch of conflicting private opinions, but a positive way of life which rejects equally the totalitarianism of Rome and the barren and unsatisfying negations characteristic of much Protestantism. It has perhaps to be admitted that Anglicanism has not yet achieved a complete synthesis of the various trends which she holds in tension. But in a very real sense the Anglican Communion stands for the wholeness of the Christian Faith and Tradition. It is, indeed, as Bishop Whipple of Minnesota, preaching before the Lambeth Conference of 1888, called it, "the Church of the Reconciliation". It does not need to change its fundamental principles. All that is necessary, and it is a task far from easy to achieve, is faithfully to carry them out, without abuse and without corruption. Anglican history may remind us that the best when corrupt becomes the worst, and that festering lilies smell far worse than weeds; but for all that it remains true that the best is to be sought and maintained, and that lilies are beautiful.

Bibliography

J. Mcleod Campbell, *Christian History in the Making*, Press and Publications Board of the Church Assembly.

H. P. Thompson, *Into All Lands*, S.P.C.K.

Stock, *History of the Church Missionary Society* (4 vols.), C.M.S.

Manross, *History of the American Episcopal Church*, Morehouse (U.S.A.).

C. J. Grimes, *Towards an Indian Church*, S.P.C.K.

J. W. C. Wand, ed., *The Anglican Communion, a Survey*, O.U.P.

The Lambeth Conferences, 1867–1948, S.P.C.K.

P. M. Dawley, ed., *Report of the Anglican Congress, 1954*, S.P.C.K.

C. M. Ady, *The English Church*, Faber and Faber.

P. E. More and F. L. Cross, ed., *Anglicanism*, S.P.C.K.

Report, *Doctrine in the Church of England*.

C. Dunlop, *Anglican Public Worship*, S.C.M.

H. P. Thompson, *Worship in Other Lands*, S.P.G.

G. K. A. Bell, *Christian Unity, the Anglican Position*, Religious Book Club (Foyle's).

Map, *The Churches of the Anglican Communion*, published by the Church Information Board.

Index

Abeokuta, 39
Abraham, C. J., 38
Accra, 70, 94 f
Adam, Karl, 103
Adelaide, 35 f, 92
Aglipayan Church, 154
Agra, 17, 49, 62
Ah Mya, Francis, 84
Alexander, M. S., 27
Alexandria, 44, 151
Alford, C. R., 34
Algeria, 98
Alopen, 67
Altar, 124
American Church Missionary Society, 24, 46, 53 f
American Prayer Book, 125 f, 128
Amoy, 31 f
Amritanand, J., 80
Amritsar, 50, 77, 80
Anderson, David, 24
Anglican and Eastern Churches Union (Association), 147, 152
Anhuei, 66
Anking (Wan-Kan), 53, 66
Antananarivo, 44
Antigua, 14, 23
Apocrypha, 106
Apostolicae Curae, 148
Apostolicity, 103, 114
Apostolic Succession, 134 ff, 151 ff
Aquinas, Thomas, 141
Arabs, 77 f
Archbishops, 137
Archdeacons, 137
Argentine and Eastern S. America, 61
Armenian Church, 47, 61, 78, 153
Arminianism, 112
Armstrong, John, 41
Articles of Religion, 101 f, 105, 107 ff, 111 ff, 117 f, 120, 131, 137, 140, 147, 152
Ascension, 42

Assam, 80
Association for Promoting the Unity of Christendom, 147
Assumption, doctrine of, 103, 111
Assyrian Church, 47 f, 61, 78, 106, 153
Atonement, doctrine of, 111, 118
Auckland, 36 ff, 93
Anking, 53
Augustine, 105, 117 f
Aung Hla, John, 84
Australia, 11, 17 ff, 25, 35 ff, 55, 69, 80, 92 f, 108, 126, 143, 158
Auxiliary Clergy, 138
Azariah, V. S., 62, 81

Badger, G. P., 27
Bahamas, 14, 23
Ballarat, 35, 69
Balya, A. K., 96
Bangkok, 63
Bangor, 2
Bannerjee, J. S. C., 80, 82
Baptism, 113 f, 139 ff, 149, 154
Baptists, 8, 24, 50, 76, 84, 157
Barbados, 3, 14, 23, 40, 45, 75
Basutoland, 57, 95
Batavia, 19, 30
Bathurst (W. Africa), 94
Baynes, A. Hamilton, 71
Bay of Islands, 20, 36
Bede, 99
Bell, G. K. A., 150
Bendigo, 69
Benediction, 128
Bengal, 16 f
Bermuda, 24
Bhagalpur, 80
Bible, The, Ch. 7, 102, 107 ff, 115, 130, 136, 145, 149, 151 f, 156, 159, 163 f
Bible Churchmen's Missionary Society, 78, 84, 86, 98
Bible Reading Fellowship, 106
Biblical Scholarship, 103

Bickersteth, Edward, 20
Bickersteth, Bishop Edward, 54, 68
Bishops, 134 ff, 141 f, 144, 149, 155 ff, 157
Biswas, N. K., 80
Blake, William, 166
Bloemfontein, 42, 57, 71 f, 95
Blyth, G. F. P., 47, 61
Bombay, 16 f, 32, 48, 80
Book of Common Prayer, 7, 54, 107 f, 118 ff, 130 ff, 147, 151, 160
Boone, William Jones, 30 ff, 51
Borneo, 30, 51, 63, 85, 93
Boston, 4
Bousfield, H. B., 57
Bowen, J., 39
Boxer Rebellion, 64 f
Brazil, 46, 61, 77
Brent, C. H., 60, 63, 85, 148
Breynton, John, 8
Brisbane, 19, 36
British Columbia, 26, 61
British Guiana, 14, 23
Brooke, James, 30
Brooks, Phillips, 60
Brooks, S. M. J., 65
Brotherhood of St Andrew, 68, 31
Brotherhood of the Epiphany, 48
Broughton, W. G., 19, 35 f
Brown, David, 10
Brown, W. Adams, 164
Bruce, Robert, 47
Buchanan, Claudius, 10, 16
Bucharest Conference, 159
Buddhism, 50, 62, 83 f
Bulawayo, 70 f, 95
Bulgakov, S., 100
Bunbury, 69
Burdon, J. S., 32 ff, 52, 132
Burma, 29, 49 f, 63, 79, 84, 108, 110, 126, 142, 153
Bush Brotherhoods, 93
Byrde, Louis, 64

Cairo, 21 f, 59, 73, 98
Calcutta, 10, 16 ff, 28, 30, 50 f, 80
Callaway, H., 57
Calvin, John, 101, 118
Calvinism, 110 ff
Cambridge Brotherhood, 48
Cambridge Mission to Delhi, 48, 80
Canada, 8 f, 15, 24 ff, 46, 60 f, 66, 68 f, 76 f, 80, 108 ff, 139, 143, 158

Canadian Church Missionary Society, 61
Canary Islands, 74, 98
Canon of Scripture, 104 ff, 134, 136
Canterbury Pilgrims, 37 f
Canton, 18, 52
Cape Town, 13, 21 f, 39 ff, 56 f, 72, 95
Carpentaria, 69
Carpenter-Garnier, M. B., 83
Carr, Thomas, 17
Carter, W. M., 72
Cassels, W. W., 53, 64
Catechism, 102, 113
Catholicity, 114
Cawnpore, 10, 17, 62
Cawnpore Brotherhood, 62
Central Africa, 43, 95 ff, 144
Central Tanganyika, 93, 96
Ceremonial, 128 f,
Ceylon, 17 f, 29, 50, 62, 79, 83, 108 ff, 126, 143, 153, 157, 168
Chambers, W., 51
Ch'angsha, 66
Chapman, James, 29, 43
Chase, Philander, 15, 23
Chefoo, 52 f
Chekiang, 31 f, 51 f, 64, 67
Ch'engtu, 64
Chillingworth, William, 102
China, 11, 18 f, 23, 30 ff, 51 ff, 61 ff, 77, 85 ff, 95, 108, 111, 127, 131 f, 137, 139, 143
China Inland Mission, 53
Chota Nagpur, 62, 80
Christchurch (N.Z.), 37
Christmas, Observance of, 4, 101, 123 f
Chung Hua Sheng Kung Huei, 65 (and see under China)
Ch'ungk'ing, 87
Church, doctrine of the, 114 f
Churches, Anglican, 143, 170 (and see under areas concerned)
Church Missions to Jews, 16, 27, 44, 78, 98
Church of England Doctrinal Commission, 116
Church of England in South Africa, 56, 71, 96
Church of England Zenana Missionary Society, 48, 62 f
Church of India, Pakistan, Burma, and Ceylon, see under areas concerned

Church Missionary Society, *passim*
Church of South India, 82 ff, 156 ff
Church of the East, 48, 106
Churchwardens, 141
Claggett, John, 7
Clarke, A. T., 10
Clergy, 134, 138, 140 f, 148
Clergy Reserves, 24
Clydesdale, 57
Cobbold, R. H., 32
Cochran, W., 15
Codrington, General, 3
Colenso, J. W., 41 f, 56, 71, 96, 144
Coleridge, W. H., 14
Collins, W. H., 32
Colombo, 29, 50, 83 f
Colonial Church Regulation Bill, 25
Commissaries, 4
Communion, 112 f, 123 ff, 152
Community of Nazareth, 91
Community of the Resurrection, 72, 85, 140
Community of St Mary the Virgin, 48, 140
Community of St Peter, Kilburn, 67
Confirmation, 114, 135, 139, 141, 154, 156 f, 159
Congregationalists, 3 f, 31, 44, 58, 82 ff, 130, 136, 156, 163
Connecticut, 4, 6 f
Consecration, 137
Consultative Body, 71, 145
Convocations, 107, 124, 142, 157
Cooper, Cecil, 89
Copleston, R. S., 50
Coptic Church, 22, 44, 59, 73, 98, 153
Corfe, C. J., 67 f
Cornish, R. K., 58, 73
Corrie, Daniel, 17
Cotterill, Henry, 41
Cotton, G. E. L., 29, 49
Councils, General, 107, 115
Coverdale, Miles, 100
Cranmer, Thomas, 107, 111 f, 121 ff
Creation, Doctrine of, 117
Creeds, 7, 102, 105, 107, 109 ff, 120, 125, 129, 134, 149, 160
Crowther, S. A., 1, 39 f, 55, 69
Cuba, 76, 126
Cutler, Timothy, 4
Cyprus, 78, 151

Daly, J. C. S., 94
Damaraland, 95
Danish Lutheran Mission, 10
Darling, T. Y., 28
Darwin, Charles, 46
David, Christian, 17 f
Deaconesses, 138 f
Deacons, 134 ff, 145, 157
Dead, prayer for the, 119, 124, 131 f
Delhi, 28, 48, 80
de Maistre, J., 161
de Noailles, Cardinal, 147
de Mel, Lakdasa, 83
Dera Ismail Khan, 28
Dioceses, 143
Doctrine, ch. 8, 142
Dodoma, 96
Domestic and Foreign Missionary Society (Canada), 46, 61; (U.S.A.), 15
Dominican Republic, 76
Dornakal, 28, 62, 80 ff
Dort, Synod of, 111
Dublin University Mission, 62, 64, 80
Duchesne, L., 148
Dunedin, 55
Dunlop, C., 133
Du Pin, L. E., 147
Durban, 41
Dwane, J. M., 72

East Africa, 42, 57, 73, 93, 96 f
Eastern Churches Association, 147
Eastern Diocese (U.S.A.), 14
Eastern Orthodox Churches, 16, 46 f, 78, 102 f, 110 ff, 114, 118, 120 ff, 126, 130, 135 ff, 140 ff, 151 ff, 160 ff, 166
East Equatorial Africa, 58, 73
East India Company, 10, 16, 29
East Pakistan, 82
East Szech'uan, 53, 86 f
Egypt, 22, 44, 47, 59, 61, 73, 78, 98
Elizabeth I, 123, 131
Emancipation Act, 23
Enabling Acts, 35
Ensor, George, 53
Episcopacy, 135 f, 144, 149, 155 ff
Eskimos, 15, 77
Establishment, 8, 24, 45, 50, 75, 166 ff
Ethiopia, 22, 27, 43 f, 98
Ethiopian Church (in South Africa), 72
Eucharist, 122 ff, 132, 136, 152 ff, 159 f
Eucharistic doctrine, 112 ff

Evangelical Revival, 10
Evensong, 122, 124, 127, 130, 132

Faith and Order Movement, 60, 110,
    149, 154
Falkland Islands, 46, 61
Fall, doctrine of the, 117 f
Fasting, 128
Ferguson, S. D., 70
Fiji, 55
Flew, R. N., 115, 136
Foochow, 31
Formosa, 54
Fourah Bay College, 21, 39, 56
Free Churches, 3, 5, 8, 51, 91, 98, 102,
    111, 120, 124, 133, 135, 140, 144,
    146 f, 149 f, 153 ff, 160 ff, 166 f
Freetown, 39, 95
French, T. V., 48 f
Fukien, 31 ff, 52 ff, 64 ff, 87 f
Fulford, F., 26
Funing, 52, 64
Furse, Michael, 72
Fusan, 53

Gambia (and the Rio Pongas), 94 f
Gelsthorpe, A. M., 98
George, 72
Georgia, 5
Gibraltar, 98
Gippsland, 69
Gladstone, W. E., 25, 35
Gobat, Samuel, 27, 47
Godley, J. R., 37
Gold Coast, 12, 20, 70, 94
Gore, Charles, 117 ff, 128
Goreh, Nehemiah, 50
Grace, doctrine of, 117
Graham-Campbell, A. R., 83
Grahamstown, 41, 72
Gran Chaco, 46
Gray, Robert, 40 ff, 56 f
Great Bible, 100
Greenstock, W., 70
Greenwood, M., 52
Grey, Sir George, 37
Griswold, A. V., 14
Gutzlaff, Charles, 18
Gwynne, L. H., 98

Hadfield, O., 38
Haiti, 76, 126

Hakodate, 54
Halifax (Nova Scotia), 8
Halifax, Lord, 148
Hamilton, Alexander, 6
Hamlyn, N. T., 79
Hangchow, 31 f, 51, 86
Hankow (Ngo-Hsiang), 51 ff, 66, 88
Hannington, James, 58
Hanson, F. R., 19, 31
Hanson, R. P. C., 104
Harper, H. J. C., 37, 55
Harris, D. W., 94
Harris, Townsend, 34
Harrison, J., 8
Hawkins, Edward, 102
Hawks-Pott, F. L., 52
Hazaribagh, 62
Heaven, 119
Heber, R., 17 f
Hebert, A. G., 105, 155
Hell, 119
Hermogen, Bishop, 167
"Higher Criticism", 102
Hill, J. S., 70
Hills, G., 26
Hobart, 14
Hobhouse, E., 38
Hodgson, L., 109 f, 115, 134, 136
Höhing, Augustus, 51
Hokkaido, 54, 68
Holt, Joseph, 3
Holy Communion, 112 f, 132, 139, 149
Holy Table, 124
Honan, 61, 66, 87
Honduras, 3, 14, 25, 45
Hong Kong (and South China), 31, 34,
    52, 54, 64 f, 87 f
Hooker, Richard, 101, 124, 130, 136,
    164
Hopkins, J. H., 144
Hornby, W. B., 73
Horsburgh, J. H., 64
Horsley, C. D., 83
Hort, F. J. A., 100
Huang, Quentin, 88
Hudson's Bay Company, 15, 26
Hunan, 64, 66
Hunt, Robert, 3
Huntington, W. R., 46, 148
Hupeh, 53
Hwong Kwong-ts'ai, 32
Hyderabad, 80
Hymns, 130

Ibadan, 95
Ich'ang, 66
Igorots, 63
Iliff, G. D., 66
Illinois, 15, 23
Imad-ud-Din, 49
Imai, John, 68
Incarnation, doctrine of, 112, 115 f
Inchon, 67
India, 9 f, 16 f, 28, 48 f, 62, 79 ff, 108 ff,
  126, 131, 143, 153, 157, 168
Indiana, 23
Indian Church Measure, 79
Indian Liturgy, 126
Indian Mission of Fellowship, 80
Indians (American), 3, 15, 24, 77
Indigenization, 48, 54, 66, 75, 81, 84 f,
  131 f
Indonesia, 63
Infallibility, 111, 154
Ingle, J. A., 66
Inglis, Charles, 9
Ing, Ong-Ting, 87
Inner Mongolia, 87
Inspiration, 105
Intercommunion, 148, 152 ff, 159 f
Intinction, 128
Invocation, of Holy Spirit, 125, 132; of
  Saints, 119
Iowa, 23
Iran, 9, 16, 27, 47, 61, 78 f, 157
Iraq, 78
Ireland, 2, 80, 106 ff, 125, 143, 152
Iremonger, F. A., 117, 160
Isfahan, 47, 61, 78 f
Islam, 27, 47 f, 63, 77, 105
Israel, 78

Jackson, R. D., 31
Jackson, W. H., 63
Jacob, C. K., 80
Jaffna, 18
Jamaica, 3, 14, 23, 45, 76
James, William, 165
Jamestown, 3
Japan, 23, 34, 53 f, 64 ff, 77, 81, 90 f,
  95, 108, 111, 127, 137, 143 f
Jefferson, Thomas, 6
Jermyn, H. W., 62
Jerome, 141
Jerusalem, 16, 26 f, 46 f, 61, 78, 98, 144,
  151
Jerusalem Bishopric Act, 27, 58

Jerusalem & the East Mission, 47
Jews, 26, 77 f, 105
Johannesburg, 57, 95
Johnson, James, 70
Johnson, Richard, 11
Johnson, Samuel, 6
Johnson, W. P., 58
Jones, W. W., 57, 71
Jordan, 78, 153
Judgement, 119
Julfa, 61
Jus liturgicum, 136
Justification, 118, 159, 167

K'aifeng, 66
Kalgoorlie, 69
Kampala, 72, 96
Kandy, 18, 29 f, 83 f
Karachi, 28
Karens, 50, 63
Karney, A. B. L., 95
Keith, G., 4
Kelly, H. H., 67
Kemper, Jackson, 23
Kenya, 73
Kerman, 61, 78
Key, B. L., 57
Khartoum, 74, 96, 98
Khomyakov, 167
Kiangsi, 66
Kienning, 52
Kienyang, 64
Kimberley and Kuruman, 72, 95
Kim, Mark, 68
King, G. L., 73
Kiukiang, 66
Klein, F. A., 59
Kneeling, 129
Knight-Bruce, G. W. H., 71
Kobe, 53, 68, 90, 92
Korea, 53, 67 f, 89 f, 110, 127
Korean Mission Brotherhood, 67
Kottayam, 16
Krapf, J. L., 42 f
Kristi Kunda, 94
Kuala Lumpur, 51
Kuching, 30, 85
Kudo, John, 89
Ku, Ho-ling, 87
Kumasi, 94
Kurunagala, 83
Kwaku, Philip, 1, 12, 20

Kwangsi-Hunan (Kwei-Hsiang), 64, 66, 86
Kweichow, 87 f
Kweilin, 64, 66
Kweiteh, 66
Kyoto, 68
Kyushu, 68

Labuan (& Sarawak), 30, 51, 85
Lagos, 39 f, 55, 70, 94 f
Lahore, 49, 80, 82
Laity, 134, 140 f, 145, 151, 163, 167
Lambeth Appeal for Church Unity, 104, 110, 149 f
Lambeth Conferences & Reports, *passim*
Lambeth Quadrilateral, 46, 104, 133, 144 ff, 148, 156, 160
Landis, E. B., 67
Lasbrey, B., 70, 94
Latin America, 26, 46, 61, 77
Laud, William, 5, 112, 124, 146
Lausanne Conference, 110, 149, 154
Lay Readers, 138, 141
Leacock, H. J., 40
Lebanon, 78
Lebombo, 71
Lectionaries, 99
Leeward Islands, 14
Leo XIII, 112, 119, 148
Liberia, 21, 23, 38, 70, 94 f
Libya, 78
Lieder, J. R. T., 22, 44
Liggins, J., 34
Lightfoot, J. B., 100, 115
Likoma Island, 73
Linton, J. H., 78
Lipscomb, C., 14
Litany, 121, 123
Liturgy, 121, 129, 133
Livingstone, David, 39, 43
Lockwood, Henry, 19, 31
Lollards, 100, 102
London Mission, 44, 71
London Society for Promoting Christianity among the Jews, 16, 21, 27
Long, W., 41
Lucas, W., 96
Lucknow, 62
Lutherans, 10, 12, 17, 27 f, 62, 76, 110 f, 118, 120, 148, 159 f
Luzon, 63

Machray, R., 46, 61
Mackay, Alexander, 58, 72
Mackenzie, C. F., 43
Mackenzie, K. D., 154
Macorie, W. K., 56
Madagascar, 44, 58 f, 73, 97
Madeira, 74
Madison, James, 7
Madras, 10, 16 f, 29, 49, 62, 81
Malabar, 28
Malagasy Episcopal Church, 97 (and see under Madagascar)
Malaya, 17 f, 29, 51, 63, 85
Malines Conversations, 150 f
Mandalay, 29
Manila, 63, 85
Maoris, 19 f, 36 ff, 55, 93
Marks, J. E., 29
Marriage, 114, 131, 141
Marsden, Samuel, 11, 19 f
Mar Thoma Church, 153
Martinson, E. D., 94
Martyn, Henry, 9 f
Maryland, 3, 6, 8
Masasi, 57, 96
Mashonaland, 71, 95 ff
Masih, Abdul, 1, 10, 17
Mass, 112 f, 123
Massachusetts, 4, 7, 14, 60
Masulipatam, 28
Matabeleland, 71, 95 ff
Matsui, P. Y., 90 f
Mattins, 124, 127, 130, 132
Mauritius, 22, 43 f, 97, 126
McClatchie, T., 31
McDougall, F. T., 30, 51
McKim, J., 68
Melanesia, 38, 55, 93
Melbourne, 35, 69
Melville-Jones, F., 70, 94
Mercier, Cardinal Archbishop, 150
Merriman, N. J., 41
Methodists, 8, 24, 72, 76, 82, 84 ff, 148, 156 f
Mid-China, 52
Middleton, T. F., 10, 16 ff
Mid-Japan, 61, 69, 91
Milman, R., 49, 62
Milton, John, 117
Mindanao, 63
Ministry, 134, 136, 138, 140, 149, 154
Minor Orders, 138
Miracles, 116 f

Missouri, 23
Mombasa, 43, 58, 73, 96 f
Monophysites, 106
Monrovia, 21, 70
Montreal, 9, 24, 26
Mooyart, 29
Moros, 63, 85
Mosher, G. F., 85
Mosul, 27
Motoda, J. S., 90
Moule, G. E., 52
Moulmein, 29
Mountain, Jacob, 9, 15
Multan, 28
Mukerjee, A. N., 80
Music, 123, 130

Nagasaki, 34, 53 f
Nagoya, 68
Nagpur, 62, 80
Naide, J. Y., 90 f
Namirembe, 72
Nanchang, 66
Nandyal, 82, 156
Nanking, 66, 86
Nanning, 86, 88
Nasik, 80
Nassau, 23, 76
Natal (& Maritzburg), 41 f, 56, 71
National Assembly of the Church of
  England, 124, 136, 142
Neale, J. M., 147
Negro Instruction Fund, 23
Neill, S. C., 121, 123
Nelson (N.Z.), 38
Nestorians, 27, 47, 106, 153
Newcastle (New South Wales), 35 f
New England, 3 f
Newfoundland, 24, 77
New Guinea, 55, 69, 93
New Hampshire, 14
Newman, J. H., 168
New South Wales, 11, 19, 35 f, 69
New Testament, 103 ff, 118 f, 165
New York, 3, 6 f, 9, 14 f, 76
New Zealand, 19 f, 35 ff, 55, 92 f, 108,
  126, 128, 143
Nicholas of Hereford, 99
Niebuhr, Reinhold, 130
Niger, 39 f, 70, 94 f
Niger Delta, 70, 95
Nigeria, 21, 39 f, 55, 69 f, 94, 157
Ningpo, 31 f, 51 f, 64

Nippon Sei Ko Kwai, 54 (and see
  under Japan)
Nixon, F. R., 35
North Africa, 74, 98
North China, 52 f, 64 ff, 87 f, 131
Northern Nigeria, 70, 95
Northern Rhodesia, 73, 97
North India, 77, 157
North-West Australia, 69
Nova Scotia, 8 f, 25
Nyasaland, 43, 57, 73, 96 f

Occasional Offices, 132
O'Ferrall, R. S. M., 97
Ogilvie, John, 9
Ohio, 15
Old Catholic Churches, 135, 154
Old Testament, 102 ff, 116
Oluwole, I., 70
Omdurman, 74
Ondo-Benin, 95
Onitsha, 94
Ontario, 9, 61
Orchard, W. E., 165
Order and Ordination, 134 f, ch. 10,
  148 ff, 152, 154, 160
Order of the Holy Cross, 94
Order of the Holy Paraclete, 94
Origen, 118 f
Original Sin, 117 f
Ornaments Rubric, 123
Osaka, 54, 68, 90 ff
Outcastes, 28
Oxford Mission to Calcutta, 48
Oxford Movement, 24, 40, 124, 147

Pakistan, 28, 48 f, 82 f, 108, 110, 126,
  143, 157
Palestine, 16, 26 f, 47, 59, 77
Panama Canal Zone, 76
Pan-Anglican Congress, 68
Parishes, 143
Parker, Matthew, 123, 163
Patagonia, 26, 46
Patna, 10
Patterson, C. J., 94
Patteson, J. C., 38, 55
Payne, J., 38
Peel, W. G., 73
Peking, 33 f, 52 f, 65 f
Pelagianism, 112, 130
Penang, 18, 51
Penhalonga, 71

Pennsylvania, 7
Penance, 114
Pentateuch, 104
Perak, 51
Perry, Charles, 35
Persia, 47, 61, 78 f
Perth (Australia), 35 f
Peshawar, 28
Pfander, 49
Philadelphia, 4, 7
Philippines, 63, 85
Philippine Independent Catholic Church, 86, 154 f
Phillips, S., 70
Pietermaritzburg, 41
Pilgrim Fathers, 3
Pilkington, George, 72
Polynesia, 55, 93
Poole, J., 54
Poona, 48
Portal, the Abbé, 148
Port Philip, 35
Portuguese East Africa, 71
Prayer, 119
Prayer Books, see under Book of, Common Prayer
Predestination, 118
Pretoria, 42, 57, 72, 95
Presbyterians, 3, 24, 47, 76, 79, 82 ff, 129 f, 136, 147, 156 ff, 162
Presiding Bishop, 137
Priests, 134 ff, 145
Primus, 137
Protestant Episcopal Church, 6 (and see under U.S.A.)
Province Wellesley, 51
Provincial Organization, 143
Provoost, S., 7
Psalter, 125
Puerto Rico, 76
Purgatory, 112, 118
Puritans, 3, 100 ff, 123 f, 136, 140, 146 f
Pusan, 89
Pyongyang, 89

Quebec, 9, 15, 25, 35 f
Queensland, 19, 36, 69, 93
Quicunque Vult, 110

Ranchi, 62
Rangoon, 29, 49 f, 84
Rashdall, H., 116
Rawal Pindi, 82

Rebman, John, 43
Red River Settlement, 15
Reformation, 101, 110, 127, 140, 163, 167
Religious Life, 140
Reservation of the Sacrament, 124, 127 f
Resurrection, doctrine of, 116, 119
Réunion, 97
Reunion Schemes, 147 ff, 158 ff
Reynolds, Edward, 124
Rhode Island, 14
Rio Pongas, 12 f, 40, 56, 94
Rockhampton, 69
Rodriguez, 97
Roman Catholicism, passim
Roots, L. H., 66
Rumanian Orthodox Church, 118, 151 f
Rupertsland, 24 f, 46, 60 f
Russell, W. A., 32, 52
Ryan, V., 43 f

Sacraments, 113 f, 128, 135, 140, 149, 151, 160
Saint Helena, 41 f
Saint John's, Kaffraria, 57
Salisbury (S.Rhodesia), 71, 95
Salvation, 118
Sandakan, 51
San Francisco, 3
Sarawak, 30, 51, 85
Sasaki, P. S., 91 f
Savage, T. S., 38
Savoy Hospital Conference, 124
Schereshevsky, S. J. J., 33 f, 52 f, 100
Schwartz, G. F., 17
Scotland, 2, 7, 57, 80, 108, 110, 125, 128, 137, 143
Scott, C. P., 52, 65 f
Scott, T. H., 19
Seabury, Samuel, 6 f
Selangor, 51
Selwyn, G. A., 35 ff, 55
Selwyn, J. R., 55
Seoul, 67, 89 f
Sermons, 127
Seychelles, 22, 43, 97
Shanghai (Kiangsu), 31 ff, 51 ff, 63 ff, 87
Shansi, 86 f
Shantung, 52, 65 f, 88
Shensi, 67, 87
Shen, T. K., 87 f
Shen Tsai-sen, 67

Shiomura, 34
Shiraz, 9, 61, 78
Short, Augustus, 35
Sian, 67
Sierra Leone, 12, 20 f, 39, 43, 56, 58, 74, 94 f
Simonstown, 13
Singapore, 18 f, 63, 84
Sino-Japanese War, 87 ff
Sisterhood of the Epiphany, 91
Sisterhood of the Holy Cross, 89
Sloane, Sir Hans, 11
Smith, George, 31, 34
Smith, William, 7
Smyth, W. E., 71
Smythies, C. A., 58
Society for Promoting Christian Knowledge, 2, 6, 10, 16 ff, 36
Society for Promoting Female Education in the East, 63
Society for the Propagation of the Gospel, passim
Society of the Sacred Mission, 67
Society of St Alban and St Sergius, 152
Society of St Francis, 140
Society of St Hilda, 68
Society of St John the Evangelist, 48, 50, 57, 91, 140
Solomon Islands, 53
Songpan, 64
Song, Ts'eng-Tsih, 87
Soochow, 31 ff, 66
Sophiatown, 95
South Africa, 13, 21, 40 f, 56 f, 70 f, 95 ff, 126, 144
South African Church Railway Mission, 71
South American Missionary Society, 46
South Australia, 35
Southern Rhodesia, 71, 95
Southgate, Horatio, 27
South India, 10, 16 f, 79, 82, 156 f
South India United Church, 84, 156
South Tokyo, 68
South-West Tanganyika, 96
Staines, R. J., 26
Stanley, A. P., 144
Stanley, H. M., 58
Steere, Edward, 57
Stileman, C., 61, 78
Strachan, J. M., 50
Strachan, John, 24 f
Straits Settlements, 51

Sudan, 22, 73, 78, 96, 98
Sugai, T., 92
Sundar Singh, 81
Swedish Church, 159
Sydney, 11, 19 f, 35, 37, 55, 69
Synods, 25, 35, 37 f, 41, 48, 54 ff, 60, 65, 69, 79 f, 88, 139 ff
Syria, 47, 78
Syrian Orthodox Church, 16 f, 28, 49, 153

T'aian, 52, 88
T'aiwan, 54
Talbot, J., 4
Talbot, Neville, 72
Tanganyika, 73, 96
Tarafdar, S. K., 80
Tasmania, 11, 19, 35, 92
Tat'ung, 86
Taylor, Jeremy, 103
Teheran, 78
Temple, William, 116 f, 128
Tertullian, 102
Thailand, 63
Thirty-nine Articles, 101, 107 f, 112
Thompson, H. P., 131
Thompson, Thomas, 12
Thompson, W. J., 78
Thomson, James M., 21
Tientsin, 64
Tillotson, John, 147
Tinnevelly, 28, 49, 81
Titcomb, J. H., 50
Tokyo, 34, 53 f, 68, 90, 92
Toronto, 24 f
Toungwoo, 50
Townsend, H., 39
Tozer, W. G., 43, 57
Tractarians, 147
Translations, Bible, 34, 37, 40, 52, 72, 77, 99 ff; B.C.P., 29, 32 ff, 51, 54, 59, 63, 77, 79, 97, 121 f f
Transubstantiation, 111 f
Transvaal, 42, 57, 72, 95
Travancore and Cochin, 49, 80 f
Trent, Council of, 103, 106
Trinidad, 3, 14, 45, 76
Trinity, doctrine of the, 112
Tristan da Cunha, 42
Trollope, M. N., 68, 89
Tsang Hai-song, Stephen, 88
Tsen Ho-p'u, Lindel, 87 f
Tsu, Y. Y., 87

Tucker, Alfred, 72 f
Tugwell, H., 70
Tunis, 98
Turkey, 47, 77
Turner, A., 67
Twells, E., 42
Tyndale, William, 100
Tyrrell, William, 35

Uganda, 58, 72 f, 96 f, 108
Umtali, 71
Umtata, 57
Unction, 114
United Church of Canada, 77
United States of America, 3 ff, 14 f,
  23 ff, 27, 45 f, 60, 63, 76, 80, 85,
  108 ff, 125 f, 128, 137 ff, 142 f, 147 f,
  152 f, 155, 157, 168
Unity, 114, ch. 11, 153, 160
Universities Mission to Central Africa,
  43, 57, 73, 96 f
Upper Nile, 96 f
Urmia, 27, 47, 61

Van, 61
Vann, Gerald, 109
Venkayya, 28
Vermont, 14
Vestments, 129
Victoria (Australia), 35, 69
Vidal, E. O., 39
Vining, L. G., 94 f
Virgin Birth, doctrine of, 115 f
Virginia, 3 ff, 15
Virgin Islands, 76
Visser 't Hooft, Dr, 146

Waiapu, 38, 93
Waikato, 93
Waimate, 36, 37
Wake, William, 147
Wales, 2, 108, 125, 143
Wand, J. W. C., 102, 113
Wangaratta, 69
Washington, George, 6
Weeks, J. W., 39
Wei Tso-min, Francis, 86
Wellington (N.Z.), 36, 38
Welton, W., 31
Wesley, Charles, 5, 130
Wesley, John, 5, 8, 112
West Africa, 12, 20, 30, 38, 55, 69 f,
  94 f, 144

West China, 53, 64, 87
Westcott, C. F., 48, 100
Western Australia, 19, 35 f, 69
Western Catholic Church, 122
Western Equatorial Africa, 70
West Indies, 2 f, 14, 23, 45, 56, 75 f, 94,
  144
West, John, 15
Weston, Frank, 73
West Pakistan, 64, 82
West Szech'uan, 87 f
Whipple, Bishop, 168
White, W. C., 66
White, William, 6 ff, 108
Whitley, J. C., 62
Wilberforce, William, 10
Wilkinson, C. R. H., 81
Wilkinson, T. E., 56
Williams, C. M., 33 f, 52 f, 68
Williams, Henry, 20
Williams, William, 20, 38
Willochra, 92
Wilson, Daniel, 17 f, 21, 28 ff
Windward Islands, 45, 75
Winnipeg, 15, 24
Wisconsin, 23
Witwatersrand, 57, 70
Wolff, Joseph, 16
Women, 143; ordination of, 138 ff
Wood, Thomas, 9
World Council of Churches, 146, 149
Worship, 121 f, 132
Wright, William, 21
Wuchang, 51, 86
Wuhan, 53, 64
Wuhu, 53, 66
Wusih, 33
Wycliffe, John, 99 f

Yale, 4
Yashiro, M. H., 92
Yen, Y. K., 1, 51, 64
Yezd, 61, 78
Yokohama, 34, 54
Yungts'ing, 65
Yun-Kwei, 88
Yunnan, 66, 87 f

Zambezi, 43, 71
Zamboanga, 63
Zanzibar, 39, 43, 57 f, 73, 96
Zululand, 21, 56 f